Talk About Beliefs

Talk About Beliefs

Mark Crimmins

A Bradford Book
The MIT Press
Cambridge, Massachusetts
London, England

© 1992 Massachusetts Institute of Technology

This book was set in Computer Modern by The MIT Press and printed and bound in the United States of America.

Library of Congress Cataloging-in-Publication Data

Crimmins, Mark D.
  Talk About Beliefs / Mark D. Crimmins
    p.   cm.
  "A Bradford book."
  Includes bibliographical references and index.
  ISBN 0-262-03185-X
  1. Belief and doubt. 2. Semantics (Philosophy). I. Title.
BD215.C825 1992
121'.6–dc20   91-31795
                                                                         CIP

For my parents, Elaine and James Crimmins

Contents

Preface

A problem that has exercised Frege, Russell, Carnap, Quine, Hintikka, Davidson, Kaplan, and Kripke, as well as many of their contemporaries in the philosophies of mind and language, is how to reconcile extremely reasonable assumptions about language with recalcitrant facts about how we ordinarily talk about what people believe. The difficulty in clearly understanding how this special type of language works has implications for foundational issues in the philosophy of mind, due to the connections between the question of what makes a statement of the form 'A believes that s' true, and the question of what it is to believe something. If we cannot square an account of what makes belief reports true with a sensible theory of believing, then we need to wonder what accounts for our failure. Can belief reports never be true? Is there really no such thing as believing? While some philosophers have taken to this sort of skepticism, most have hoped that it is our own fault, rather than the world's, that we lack a viable analysis of belief reporting. For surely our claims about what we and others believe are systematically meaningful and often true. People *do* believe things; we know it, and we say so.

My goal in this book is to present a unified approach to some of the troublesome questions about belief and belief reports. The approach starts from a fairly conventional theoretical foundation, in that I rely heavily on the following ideas: structured "Russellian" propositions are the contents of statements and of beliefs, structured representation is the internal basis of thought, and our referential practices are guided by conversational pragmatics. The centerpiece of the approach is the analysis of belief reports. In reporting what someone believes, I argue, we refer *explicitly* to the structured proposition that allegedly is the content of her belief and also *tacitly* to internal representations that allegedly are involved in the belief. In general, I argue that our ways of talking about thought are in one way extremely direct and in another shot through with pragmatic subtleties. When we say what someone thinks about or believes, the *objects* of thought or belief we attribute are determined by the referents of our words. But I think we very rarely say merely what someone thinks about or believes; almost always we add tacit provisos about *how* they think about the alleged objects of thought or belief. And the rules for adding and discerning these tacit provisos in particular statements are driven by all the subtleties of conversational pragmatics.

This book results from a project that began in discussions with John Perry at Stanford in 1985, which has led also to Crimmins and Perry 1989 and to my dissertation (1989b). This book includes a lot of material from the thesis, but it is different enough to make the coincidence in titles misleading. A part of chapter 3 appeared in Crimmins 1989a, and a much expanded version of section 2.3 has become Crimmins 1992c. I had wanted to fill in the most important gaps in the thesis and to provide detailed treatments of, among other topics, tacit belief, acquaintance, structured propositions, and referential pragmatics, as well as careful assessments of related approaches to these problems in the philosophy and linguistics literatures. But soon, instead of gaps, I had disproportionate outgrowths with gaps of their own, and finally it was clear that whatever value there would be in the book would not owe to closure under gap filling. So I have pared back the outgrowths, some of which nonetheless partially survive as significant portions of chapters 2, 3, and 6, as well as nearly the whole of chapter 4. Much of what was cut back I will pursue elsewhere. There are many recent proposals deserving critical attention and there are important issues bearing directly on my proposals that I have left untouched. (I start with a critical discussion of the "naive view" of propositional attitudes, in part because I think it is more plausible than it can initially appear, but primarily because the discussion allows me to set the stage for what will come.) What I hope to have done is to make available the essentials of an approach to these issues that is promising enough to attract the criticism and development of which, as things stand, it certainly is in need.

The strategy I develop has affinities of various kinds to recent proposals by Nicholas Asher (1986), Hans Kamp (1988, 1990), Graeme Forbes (1990), and Mark Richard (1990). Richard's account bears a particularly close relation to mine (as I argue in my 1992a). The similarities have resulted from convergent evolution, which I hope is some indication of the promise of features in common between our accounts.

I am of course greatly indebted to Perry, both for the discussions in which many of these ideas were born, and for his work on belief and language over the last fifteen years—his work comes up often in the text, but the explicit citations do not do justice to its value to me in thinking about these issues.

Thanks also to all those who have helped with comments, advice, and encouragement at various stages of the project, including Jon Barwise, John Bennett, Paddy Blanchette, Michael Bratman, David Braun, Mary Cain, John Etchemendy, Graeme Forbes, Carl Ginet, James Higginbotham, David Israel, Friederike Moltmann, Joe Moore, Julius Moravcsik, Stephen Neale, Michael O'Rourke, Mari Orser, Bob Pasnau, Sydney Shoemaker, Syun Tutiya, Leora Weitzman, Rob Wilson, Andrew Woodfield, Ed Zalta, participants in a seminar on propositional attitudes at Cornell, and some extremely helpful anonymous readers for publishers and journals.

Talk About Beliefs

1 Naïve Semantics

1.1 The Issue

Recently, some philosophers have been attracted to the view that belief reports report instances of a relation between agents and propositions. I say "recently" because until very recently a number of famous examples had conspired to make this quite natural position seem too naïve. These examples, from sources such as Frege 1952, Quine 1966a, Mates 1950, Castaneda 1966, 1968, and Kripke 1979, were taken by a number of philosophers to suggest that an account of the semantics of belief ascriptions would have to invoke more subtle relations, perhaps involving more than two argument places or being sensitive to something other than the proposition expressed by the report's embedded sentence. In the face of such apparently decisive counterevidence, the "naïve view" has been given new life with an ingenious pragmatic defense against the putative counterexamples. Scott Soames (1985, 1987a, 1987b, 1989) and Nathan Salmon (1986a, 1986b, 1989) are currently the most prominent exponents of this position. It has been championed by Barwise and Perry (1981, 1983), who have claimed that it satisfies the condition of "semantic innocence," and it has been incorporated in a number of other recent theories. Some useful discussions of the view can be found in Berg 1988, Richard 1983, 1987a, 1987b, and Schiffer 1987.

The recalcitrant examples exploit intuitions about the truth values of certain belief reports—intuitions that are directly contrary to the truth values predicted by the naïve view. Rather than modify the simple semantics for attitude constructions, naïve theorists have proposed to attack as spurious the intuitions about truth values that generally have been assumed to be unassailable data. These intuitions, they claim, are artifacts of confusing the two linguistic virtues of truth and appropriateness: the apparent counterexamples turn on a mistaken interpretation of intuitions about *insinuation* as being semantic intuitions about meaning and truth.

Current supporters of the naïve view champion also one or another version of the principle of *direct reference*. For them, the (true) proposition expressed with a use of the sentence 'Hesperus is an evening star' is the same as that expressed with 'Phosphorus is an evening star'; it is a proposition about the planet Venus, which goes under both names. The theorists maintain that this equivalence holds even within a belief report, which they take to report the holding of a relation between an agent and the proposition expressed by the embedded sentence. In particular, they hold that the following statements about the astronomer Caius (who, despite his name, lived prior to the discovery that a single celestial object is both Hesperus and Phosphorus) express the same claim, our intuitions that the former is true and the latter false notwithstanding:

Caius believed that Hesperus is an evening star.   (1)

Caius believed that Phosphorus is an evening star.   (2)

Both reports claim that Caius is related "in the belief way" to the proposition that Venus is an evening star. In fact, they say, both attributions are, *strictly speaking*, true.

However, they argue, in virtue of pragmatic mechanisms, a use of (2) to report a belief that Caius would express using the name 'Hesperus' would be misleading. It would license the hearer to infer, incorrectly, that Caius believed that the thing he called 'Phosphorus' is an evening star, thus violating an unspoken pragmatic rule to the effect that, when reporting a belief, one should stick as closely as possible to the words with which the agent would express the belief. Examples in the literature of the informativeness of identity claims, essential indexicality, and failures of substitutivity all have been met with explanations of the operative intuitions as "merely" pragmatic in this way—they are based on what the speaker insinuates, as opposed to what she says.

Now, many of those who at one time or another have advocated this simple analysis have at the same time recognized the following moral of these puzzling examples: propositions of the kind in question are of the wrong "grain" to serve as the objects of any binary relation behind the cognitive phenomenon of belief (as opposed to the linguistic phenomenon of belief reporting). The examples demonstrate the possibility that an agent can believe or fail to believe a proposition in importantly different *ways*. In the Hesperus-Phosphorus case, Caius believes and disbelieves a single proposition in different ways.

So instead of holding a simple, binary view, some of these theorists have suggested that a successful analysis of the phenomenon of belief will require the postulation of a more complex, ternary relation, involving not only an agent and a proposition, but also such things as "ways of believing" or "belief states" (Perry 1979, 1977). Soames (1987b) and Salmon (1986a) have agreed that there is some ternary relation at the base of the cognitive facts behind belief. Such a relation would hold among an agent, a proposition and, say, a way of believing, just in case the agent believed the proposition in that way. This is to abandon a naïve view of belief, though it does not require abandoning a naïve analysis of belief reports.

But it is not hard to see how a non-naïve view about belief might motivate a non-naïve analysis of belief reports—an analysis that invokes in a crucial way the third parameter in the supposed ternary relation behind belief. The ternary-relation view gives us a way of specifying a difference between what (1) and (2) report: they claim that Caius believes a certain proposition, in different *ways*. By adopting a non-naïve view of belief, one can leave room to respect the truth-intuitions generated by the counterexamples as genuinely semantic intuitions. We would not need to suppose that we are wrong about what seem to be obviously true (or false) statements.

The trouble with many non-naïve semantical theories is that their accounts of "ways of believing" and the mechanisms by which they might be specified in belief reports seem unmotivated, oversimplified, or simply false on psychological or semantical grounds. The naïve view is consonant with certain attractive semantical principles, and by its silence it involves no outlandish positions on psychological matters.

Since the analysis of belief reports that I will present in chapters 5 and 6 is a version of non-naïve semantics, I want to examine the reasons that have been advanced in favor of adopting the naïve analysis, and to expose the issues and arguments that divide the naïve theorists from myself.

The defenders of the naïve analysis focus on one version of the distinction between semantic and pragmatic facts about statements: Semantic facts include those about meaning, reference, content, truth and falsity. Pragmatic facts include those about the propriety, purposes, and intended effects (including insinuations, or "implicatures") of statements. Now, it is not controversial that it would be *wrong* to use (2) to describe Caius's belief. What is controversial is the classification of this fact: is the incorrectness a *semantic* fact about the use of (2), or is it a pragmatic one? Is the report false, or is it only misleading and inappropriate?

Certainly there is a strong intuition that the use of (2) is genuinely and unmistakably false. Suppose we were to ask someone familiar with Caius's astronomical beliefs, 'Does Caius believe that Phosphorus is an evening star?' Of course, the correct answer would be no. And such a person would correctly assent to 'Caius does *not* believe that Phosphorus is an evening star'.

But the question is perhaps not as simple as it seems. Our intuition that the assertion of (2) is incorrect cannot by itself decide the issue of its truth. For it is not always transparent to us as competent language users whether our intuitions of incorrectness are really intuitions about truth or about propriety. For instance, the strategy urged by Grice (1975, 1989) is to hold that 'Ann left her post before quitting time and she was fired' would be true even if Ann was fired before she left her post. It is, Grice would say, only an insinuation or pragmatic *implicature* of the statement that she was fired after she left her post.

Granting the possibility that some truth-intuitions are mistaken even when the facts are known, a debate over whether our hunches are wrong in the Hesperus-Phosphorus case might seem headed for deadlock. There clearly is misinformation *conveyed* in the statement of (2), but so far we have little reason to suppose that it is a statement *of* misinformation rather than simply an invitation for the hearer erroneously to *infer* misinformation. Our gut reactions to belief reports can provide evidence that our conversational conventions license or prohibit various inferences from statements made in various ways. But as long as the pragmatic-insinuation strategy is open our intuitions about truth values may offer little basis upon which to make a principled division between truly semantic and merely pragmatic facts about these cases.

Because of this, the issue between naïve and non-naïve semantics will not be decided by example and counterexample. Support for the naïve view can come only from arguments that lead us to question the indicated truth-intuitions—for surely we can legitimately demand a reason for rejecting them. I find in the writings of the advocates of this view four main sorts of argument:[1]

---

1. I ignore arguments that I consider non-starters. One such is that since belief reports assimilate naturally to expressions in formalized languages in which terms

1. *Support from Above:* The naïve view is claimed to follow directly from a small number of independently supported principles about the semantics of natural language, including principles about reference and "compositional" determination of the significance of a statement.

2. *Cancelability:* The alleged instances of mistaken intuitions exhibit many of the pragmatic features that an analysis-via-insinuation would predict; for one, the insinuations are "cancelable"—we can say things to counteract the usually licensed inference to non-naïve information.

3. *Translation:* Considerations about translation into a language with just one name for Venus support the claim that (1) and (2) express the same proposition—because they would receive the same correct translation in that language.

4. *The Steamroller:* Mark Richard (1983) has presented an explicit argument that purports to demonstrate, with respect to a case similar to that of (1) and (2), that the truth values assigned by the naïve view are correct, and that those assigned by our intuitions *must* be wrong.

I am going to explain and evaluate these sources of support for the naïve view in turn; not surprisingly, I will reject them. In the end, I will suggest, the support that has been offered in favor of the naïve view is misconceived, and the arguments against that view are clear and strong. The only remaining consideration in favor of the naïve analysis is its status as "the best game in town": no non-naïve, well-detailed strategy for analyzing belief reports has been given that has so *few* unacceptable consequences. This evidence supports the inductive conclusion that non-naïve semantics is doomed to failure. This, surely, is the reason that so many philosophers have been willing to adopt a view with the obvious embarrassments of the naïve semantics. The only truly persuasive argument against such a view is not an argument at all—what is needed is a better analysis of belief reporting. And I am

---

function merely as devices of reference, and sentences merely as expressors of propositions, they must do so as well in English. This argument forgets that the way we *understand* a formal expression like '$Bel(a, t, Tall(Cicero))$', unless we are carefully warned not to, is simply to assimilate it to English.

confident that there is a better analysis. Some crucial features of the account I envision—the one I will offer in chapters 5 and 6—will become apparent as my consideration of the arguments for the naïve analysis progresses. These arguments systematically and indefensibly presuppose the impossibility of what I see as the only kind of semantics that can make honest sense of our practices of reporting beliefs: a semantics that is sophisticated enough to treat the phenomenon of tacit reference.

1.2   Support from Above

The supporters of the naïve view are quick to point out that their analysis is supported by general semantical principles of compositionality and direct reference. To a certain extent, this is correct. But the principle of compositionality giving this support can only be one that satisfies the constraint of *full articulation* at least with respect to the particular case of belief reports, as I will explain. And the implausibility in general of a principle of compositionality meeting this constraint (*articulated compositionality*), I will claim, vitiates the supposed support for the naïve view. Articulated compositionality fails to apply in a fully general way to English. This would be no problem—if we had reason to think that belief reports were not among the exceptions. But I will argue that we have no such reason; to the contrary, certain quite ordinary cases in which this principle fails—cases involving what John Perry calls "unarticulated constituents"—manifest important parallels to belief reports.

Semantics is concerned with the meanings of expressions in a language and with the truth values and literal significance of the uses of such expressions. According to the strains of philosophical semantics in which the naïve view has arisen, a statement—one kind of assertive use of a sentence—*expresses* a proposition. Propositions are determinate, abstract claims, which are the ultimate bearers of truth or falsity and which are identical with, or essentially tied to, their truth conditions. In a typical statement, there is a single distinguished proposition that is *the* proposition expressed by the statement, though there may be, and often are, other propositions conveyed in the statement. A statement has a truth value derivatively: it is that of the proposition it expresses. The central enterprise of semantics, on this picture, is to explain in a systematic way which propositions are expressed by which statements.

Given the infinite variety of possible statements in a natural language, the task of specifying the propositions expressed by statements can be manageable only if there is a systematic way in which features of statements contribute to the determination of the propositions they express. Many philosophers and linguists have held something like this also to be a condition on the learnability of a natural language. To suppose that semantics is possible is to suppose that this condition, of *systematicity*, holds.

1.2.1   Compositionality

One way in which systematicity may hold is reflected in various principles that go under the name of "compositionality." To explain what a principle of compositionality is, it is necessary to describe the project of *valuation semantics*.

Valuation semantics involves assigning semantic values to expressions as they occur in statements. Some expressions have, in a statement, meanings and/or referents; these are examples of semantic values of which a theory might make use. The proposition that is expressed in a statement is a kind of semantic value of the statement, or of the sentence as used in that statement. Following current usage, I will call the proposition expressed by a statement, the *content* of the sentence, relative to that statement, or, sometimes, of the statement itself.[2]

It is obvious that the expressions that are parts of a sentence typically play very important roles in determining the content of the sentence in a given statement. A statement of 'Rex bit the neighbors' daughter' has as its content a proposition about Rex, because the name 'Rex' is used to refer to Rex. The content is about biting because that is the

---

2. The content of a sentence (relative to the statement, or to the context of the statement) is usually not distinguished from the content of the statement in which it is used. The reason for this is that in valuation semantics, we are concerned with how the content of a statement arises from the contents and meanings of the (utterances of the) expressions within the sentence. The sentence itself is what is used to make the whole claim—so this claim is its content. It is not obvious that one should tie the semantic totality (the content of the statement) to the syntactic totality (the sentence), given that a statement involves more than just a sentence. It may well be the conception of the semantic enterprise as seeking the contents of sentences, rather than of utterances, that leads to the uncritical assumption of principles of compositionality that satisfy the constraint of full articulation, which I describe below.

relation the word 'bit' expresses. The expressions that occur as parts of this sentence make specifiable, systematic contributions to the content of the sentence as a whole. The name 'Rex' provides Rex, the verb 'bit' provides the relation of biting, and so on. Thus it is natural to talk of the contents of subsentential expressions, and to ask how the contents of such expressions, in a given statement, help to fix the content of the sentence of which they are parts. Principles of compositionality are answers to this question.[3]

A composition rule describes how the content of a complex expression used in a statement depends on the contents of its component expressions. To apply such a rule we need to know, for each expression to which it applies, the component-structure of that expression. Theories that employ principles of compositionality nearly always exploit a recursive model of syntax for the expressions considered. Any complex expression, including a sentence, is composed from simpler expressions—its immediate constituents—by a formation rule. Here is an example of such a rule:

Formation Rule for Unary Predications: If τ is a (simple or complex) singular term and ψ is a (simple or complex) unary predicate, then the expression obtained by adjoining τ and ψ is a sentence.

Given that we know that 'the transcendental deduction of the categories' is a singular term, and that 'is extremely confusing' is a unary predicate, this rule tells us that 'The transcendental deduction of the categories is extremely confusing' is a sentence.

To each such formation rule (or sometimes just to a subclass of the expressions formed by the rule) there corresponds a composition rule describing how the content of the composite expression depends on·the content of the component expressions. A simple example is:

Composition for Unary Predications: If ϕ is a unary predication obtained from τ and ψ by the formation rule for unary predications, such that in statement s of ϕ the content of ψ is the property P, then:

---

3. There also are principles of compositionality that advert not to content but to meaning (construed as a partial determiner of content in context). What such principles come to, of course, depends enormously on one's account of meaning. The principles of compositionality I discuss are not principles of meaning-compositionality, but of content-compositionality (since it is these that offer the alleged support for the naïve view).

1. if the content of τ, in s, is an object a, then the content of ϕ in s is the proposition that a has the property P.

2. if τ is a definite description that, in s, has as its content the condition C on objects, then the content of ϕ in s is the proposition that the object meeting the condition C has the property P.

3. if τ is an indefinite description that, in s, has as its content the condition C on objects, then the content of ϕ in s is the proposition that at least one object meeting the condition C has the property P.

This principle tells us that the content of 'The transcendental deduction of the categories is extremely confusing' is, yes, the proposition that the transcendental deduction of the categories is extremely confusing.

If this composition rule is correct, then the following principle of compositionality is a fact about unary predications: The content of a unary predication, as used in a statement, depends *only* on the contents of its immediate component expressions, in the same statement. This is to say, the composition rule needs only these contents as "inputs." In general a principle of compositionality states, of a class of complex expressions, that the content of any such expression in a statement depends only on certain other things, usually including the contents of its component expressions.

Since the contents of complex expressions presumably are determined *somehow* and depend systematically on *some* features of the uses of the expressions, then some principle of compositionality must be correct. To have any real bite, a principle of compositionality must put some significant limits on what goes into determining the content of the relevant complex expressions. It very often is assumed that a principle of compositionality worthy of the name must satisfy the constraint of full articulation; such a principle will be called a principle of articulated compositionality.

1.2.2 Full Articulation

Precisely what full articulation amounts to depends on the theory of propositions adopted. A semantics assumes that a statement is fully articulated, when each item that it uses to generate the content of the sentence (each "input" to the composition rule for sentences of that kind) is itself the content of some expression within the sentence. For example, it is plausible that a use of the sentence 'Rex is now scratching' is fully articulated. The proposition expressed is generated from Rex, the property of scratching, and the time of the statement. And for each of these "building blocks" of the proposition, there is an expression in the sentence with that building block as its content ('Rex', 'scratching', and 'now'). A principle of compositionality satisfies the constraint of full articulation if it entails that every statement it concerns is fully articulated.

For theories in which propositions are structured entities containing individuals and properties as constituents, the constraint full articulation places on principles of compositionality is easy to state: each constituent of the proposition expressed in a statement must be the content of some expression in the sentence. Of course, some accounts of propositions, including most versions of possible-worlds theory, need not employ anything answering to the notion of a propositional "constituent." But even in these theories, the semantics of statements assigns contents to subsentential expressions in the inductive process of generating the content of the sentence. In the case of 'Rex is now scratching', these intermediate contents correspond to Rex, the property of scratching, and the time of the statement.

What counts as a "component expression" in a sentence is not uncontroversial. We can buy increases in simplicity and power of syntactic theory at the price, for instance, of claiming that a sentence can contain covert "expressions" that are not uttered or written down when the sentence is used. This is one of the ways in which there may be more syntactic structure to a statement than the sequence of expressions uttered or written in it. This renders sentences less observable than we might pretheoretically have supposed; our intuitive knowledge about our sentences as ordered sequences of overt expressions reflects only their projections into the concrete world of inscriptions and utterances. For now, I will require that the component expressions mentioned in principles of articulation and compositionality be entirely overt; I will explain the purpose this requirement when I look critically at full articulation below.

This, then, is the principle of articulated (universal) compositionality: The content, in a statement, of any complex expression depends only on the contents, in the statement, of its component expressions.

1.2.3   Direct Reference

Semanticists recently have favored some version of the following very compelling idea: statements made with simple predications of the form '$P(a_1, \ldots, a_n)$' express the proposition that a certain property (the one contributed by the predicate 'P') holds among certain objects (the ones contributed by the names 'a_1',...,'a_n'). The content of a use of a name is an object. In contributing their contents to the composition rules determining the proposition expressed by the simple statement, the names donate only what they denote (in the statement), and the predicate donates only the property or relation it denotes. In particular, no Fregean senses, modes of presentation, descriptions, or concepts are contributed by these terms to the propositions expressed in statements of the simple predications.

It does not follow directly that the contents of uses of names must be their referents in uses of more complex expressions. However, many semanticists, the naïve theorists among them, have been sufficiently impressed with the Millian idea of names as simple labels to espouse a strong principle of *direct reference* to the effect that the content of the use of a name is *always* simply its referent.

It will be valuable to distinguish between the following general principles of reference:

1. The content of a use of a name in any statement is the object it denotes (call this simply *direct reference*).

2. The contribution *traceable to* the use of a name to the content of the containing statement is simply the object it denotes (call this *direct contribution*).

The principles are by no means equivalent. For instance, if full articulation is false, a name might contribute more than its content to the content of a statement. Even if a statement is fully articulated, it is possible that a use of a specific name (rather than another with the same content) can influence the contents of other (overt and covert) expressions used in the statement. While I will not challenge the principle of direct reference here, I will give reasons below for rejecting the principle of direct contribution.

1.2.4   Deriving the Naive Analysis

I will detail two ways in which the naïve analysis can be defended with the semantic principles we have seen. First, if the principle of articulated compositionality applies to belief reports, then the semantics for belief sentences is constrained to an enormous degree by the semantics for simpler expressions. To show why, I will sketch an argument from this principle, together with direct reference in simple predications, for the conclusion that statements of (1) and (2) have the same content. Second, I will present a simpler argument from just the principle of direct contribution for the conclusion that the two reports have the same content.

Assume that Caius's astronomical beliefs are being discussed, and consider again the statements of (1) and (2). By direct reference, 'Phosphorus' contributes as its content only the object Phosphorus (that is, Venus) to the use of that simple predication in the statement of (2). By parallel reasoning, the use of 'Hesperus' in 'Hesperus is an evening star' makes exactly the same semantic contribution. Thus, the two simple predications 'Phosphorus is an evening star' and 'Hesperus is an evening star' are expressions with the same structure composed of parts with the same contents. By the principle of full articulation, these simple predications themselves have the same content in the statements of (1) and (2) (presumably, the proposition that Venus is an evening star). The principle of full articulation tells us that all the materials used to determine the contents of (1) and (2) must themselves be the contents of expressions in those sentences. Since it is implausible to suppose that the content of 'believed that' or of 'Caius' changes between the two claims, it follows that the contents of the two reports are cobbled from the same materials. Our hand is forced: there is no difference between the two statements that a composition rule for determining their contents can use. Therefore, (1) and (2) have the same content—they express the same proposition.

More formally, the argument is as follows:

1. 'Hesperus' in 'Hesperus is an evening star' and 'Phosphorus' in 'Phosphorus is an evening star' have the same content in the respective statements (by direct reference).

2. 'Hesperus is an evening star' has the same content in (1) as 'Phosphorus is an evening star' in (2) (by full articulation).

3. Thus, the reports (1) and (2) are statements of sentences composed in the same way of parts with the same contents.

4. And therefore, the two reports have the same content (by full articulation).

Notice that we have shown that (1) and (2) make the same claim without appealing to any principles specifically about belief. The principles that have gotten us here are those of articulated compositionality and direct reference. Neither of these principles is needed in its full strength—we could simply assume a version of each principle restricted to the example under consideration, or to belief reports. But of course that would be to vitiate the alleged support from *general* and independently supported semantical principles.

Depending on one's theory of relations the conclusion of this argument may not quite be the naïve account of belief reports. What does follow is that the proposition expressed by a belief report is a function of (and only of) the agent, the time, and the propositional content of the embedded sentence. In particular, we have seen that on these principles statements of (1) and (2) express the same proposition and so are either both true or both false, which demonstrates the primary counterintuitive consequence of the naïve view. The result derives from the guarantee given by full articulation that the propositions expressed by the statements of (1) and (2) must be the *same* function of the referent of 'Caius' and the proposition expressed equally by 'Hesperus is an evening star' and 'Phosphorus is an evening star'. This result is strong motivation for adopting an analysis of belief reports that is sensitive only to the agent referred to and the proposition invoked in the report. The naïve analysis obviously fits this bill; so to whatever extent the principles cited are plausible (as they apply to belief reports), we have an argument in favor of the naïve analysis.

This argument is closely related to many given in a series of recent articles by Soames. In these papers, however, Soames supports moves paralleling the step from 3 to 4 by citing various principles that are specific to attitude reports, such as: "Propositional attitude sentences report relations to the semantic values of their complements—an individual i satisfies 'x v's that S' iff i bears R to the semantic value of S"

(Soames 1985; cf. Soames 1987a, 1987b, 1989). Since he does not support this principle with any more general semantic principles (like our general principle of naïve compositionality), Soames actually assumes what is one of the most controversial features of the naïve analysis of belief reports. The arguments he gives explicitly in favor of this principle mainly consist in the consideration of some implausible alternatives (1987a, 63–64). Soames considers belief relations that are sensitive to the Kaplanian *character* of the embedded sentence and/or to the properties that "fix the reference" of terms "as a matter of linguistic convention." He rightly rejects these alternatives. He suggests elsewhere that to reject the naïve view is to cut support out from under the principle of direct reference, but he does not elaborate on this claim (1987b, 106). I should note that Soames's aim in these papers is more to push a particular conception of proposition and to defend the naïve view against certain objections than to argue directly for it. Soames, by the way, endorses Richard's steamroller argument (to be considered below), which depends on a tacit assumption of full articulation.

Salmon, in arguing for the naïve view, cites a principle that sounds much like articulated compositionality (but with hedges like "typical compound expression" and "are semantically correlated systematically" that make it hard to be sure). This is his principle: "The information value, with respect to a given context and time, of a typical compound expression, if any, is a complex, ordered entity (e.g. a sequence) whose constituents are semantically correlated systematically with expressions making up the compound expression, typically the simple (noncompound) component expressions. Exceptions arise in connection with quotation marks and similar devices, and may arise also in connection with compound predicates" (Salmon 1986, 42). That he takes the constituents of this ordered entity to be the contents of their syntactic correlates is clear from the following passage: "... a piece of information is a complex abstract entity whose components are the information values of the components of a sentence that contains the information [modulo certain qualifications that do not concern us]" (Salmon 1986, 55).

Now to the quicker argument from the principle of direct contribution alone. Direct contribution licenses the principle that substitution of names with the same referent, like 'Hesperus' and 'Phosphorus', preserves the proposition expressed by a statement. The reason is that if all the name contributes to the content of the statement is its referent, then names with the same referent make the same contribution—so we should be able to swap them at will. Thus, we conclude again that (1) and (2) must express the same proposition and, hence, have the same truth value.

Salmon clearly adopts the principle of direct contribution: "The information value (contribution to information content), with respect to a given context c and time t, of any simple singular term is its referent with respect to c and t (and the world of c)" (Salmon 1986, 41).

1.2.5   How the Theoretical Support Goes Wrong

The naïve semantics for belief reports is strongly motivated by general principles of articulated compositionality and direct reference—or by the principle of direct contribution by itself. If there is good reason to think that these principles are true in general, then there is good reason to think that they apply to belief reports, and hence, by the above arguments, there is good reason to accept the naïve analysis of belief reports. But I will show that articulated compositionality does not hold in general—that there are counterexamples to full articulation. So its role in an argument about belief reports is suspect—it is not a true, general principle about English, and we have no specific reason to think that it holds for belief reports. And I will present counterexamples to direct contribution that also are clearly relevant to the case of belief reporting. I suspect that even direct reference is not true in a fully general form. But the principles that fail in ways most pertinent to the arguments for naïve semantics are full articulation and direct contribution. The examples I give in which these principles fail exemplify kinds of context sensitivity that, I think, are exhibited also by belief reports like (1) and (2). The arguments for the naïve analysis are incorrect precisely because they rely on denying the very possibility of these kinds of context sensitivity.

Full articulation must be taken as a contingent claim about the semantics for a language or group of languages. It is easy to concoct artificial languages with entirely systematic semantics in which it is clear that the proposition expressed with a sentence depends on more than its structure and the contents of its overt parts (consider a language in which any statement S made after one of 'Lincoln was tall' expresses a claim that is the conjunction of the one that S normally would express in English, and the claim that Washington was a sloppy eater). But we do not need to get hypothetical; English has many underarticulated constructions.

Cases in which full articulation fails involve what John Perry (1986) calls "unarticulated constituents" of a statement's propositional content. An unarticulated constituent of the content of a statement is an item that is used by the semantics as a building block of the statement's content but is such that there is no (overt) expression in the sentence that supplies the object as its content. In a semantics that takes propositions to be structures containing objects and properties, an unarticulated constituent is simply a propositional constituent that is not explicitly mentioned—it is not the content of any expression in the sentence.

In many but not all of the examples we will consider, it is natural to speak of the unarticulated constituents as objects of *tacit reference*. Propositional constituents that are not articulated nonetheless are *provided* by some mechanism or other as propositional constituents. Some mechanisms that provide unarticulated constituents might deserve to be classed as kinds of tacit reference.

Now, as I mentioned above, it is always possible to hold that there is a covert syntactic expression that has as its content any propositional constituent whatever (including the proposition about Washington in our hypothetical language). Such a move will be more plausible in some cases than others (some plausible cases of this might involve "deletion" or ellipsis: 'Did you eat?' 'I did'). But the distinction between plausible and implausible posits of covert expressions is not one that can be made pretheoretically; it will be drawn in one way if all we want from syntactic structures is an explanation of grammaticality intuitions, but in another if we want also a tight relation to semantic structures. In most of the counterexamples to full articulation, a posit of covert expressions will seem natural only on a way of drawing the distinction that is tied to semantic intuitions—intuitions that there is more to the truth conditions of uses of the expression in question than is overtly expressed. I have no particular objection to positing covert expressions for such reasons, but I want to emphasize two points. First, if we allow semantically motivated posits of covert expressions, then our pretheoretic intuitions about what are the syntactic constituents of a given sentence are no sure guide. And second, if our intuitions suggest that the claims made with a single belief sentence can vary across different statements (in which the contents of its overt components do not appear to change), then belief reports are certainly prime candidates for semantically motivated posits of covert expressions.

I choose to frame the definition of full articulation in terms of overt constituent expressions because the possibility of covert expressions in belief reports is just as damaging to the first argument for the naïve theory as that of propositional constituents that are neither overtly nor covertly articulated. The version of full articulation needed to support this argument must be strong enough to prohibit constituents provided tacitly by any means whatever (and thus must be at least as strong as the principle I have given).

On, then, to examples of underarticulation. 'It's raining' invokes the relation of raining. What we know about rain makes it obvious that this relation must have as arguments at least a time and a place. The present tense construction in 'It's raining' points indexically to the time of the statement. But if a determinate proposition is to be expressed, *some* feature of the statement must determine the place at which it is claimed to be raining. A rain claim *can* be made in which there is a component of the sentence used that contributes the place described, as in 'It's raining in New York' or 'It's raining outside'. But in the simple 'It's raining', the place is left unarticulated—there is no component of the sentence to contribute the needed constituent of the proposition expressed. Note that the place described with 'It's raining' is not determined *indexically*, on the model of the expressions 'I' and 'here'. For, first, there is no expression in 'It's raining' to serve as the indexical. Second, 'It's raining' is not in general "elliptical" for 'It's raining here' (not that it would be a problem for my account if it were). It need not be the location of the statement that is described; consider the forecaster in California who says, "Now we turn to the weather in New York. It's raining." She has described New York, not California, as having rain. In cases like this, the very subject matter of a statement is left unmentioned in the statement. Knowing what is being talked about is crucial to knowing what is said, but in cases of underarticulation this information is not signaled by an expression that stands for the subject matter.

In short, the verb 'to rain' picks out a relation that has more parameters in it than we sometimes explicitly label when we use it. Rain *reports* are "of the form" $Rain(t)$, but the propositions those reports express are of the form $Rain(t, l)$ (where 'l' stands for a location). So in

Table 1.1
Underarticulated expressions

Expression	Unarticulated Parameter
three o'clock	the location or time zone
John's book	the relation John is supposed to bear to the book (authorship, ownership)
forward	the perspective from which direction is judged (similarly with 'under', 'to the left of', 'moving')
relevant	the issue or discussion relevance to which is in question (as in 'her height was not relevant')
normal	the relevant comparison class and dimension(s) (as in 'this is a normal deck of cards')

these cases we cannot read "logical form" (the form of the proposition expressed) directly from the overt sytactic form of a sentence. Perry (1986) has claimed that our minds may work in such a way that we need not always represent even *cognitively* the parameter of location.

Other plausible cases of expressions that often are used to express relations with some parameter only tacitly specified are given in table 1.1. I will not argue that each of these expressions introduces unarticulated constituents. Enough if the reader agrees that some of them might.

Other cases in which full articulation fails involve implicit restrictions of general claims. From a physics textbook: "The motion of a free body in an up and down direction will be uniformly accelerated motion; the acceleration is approximately $9.8 m/s^2$." This claim, given the author's knowledge about gravitation, and the surrounding text, cannot be interpreted as a fully general claim; there is an implicit restriction to situations near sea level on Earth. The claim is not false, even strictly speaking. Rather, it is clear in context that sea-level situations are those being discussed, and the statement makes a true claim about such situations. There is nothing in the sentence that serves to provide the restriction *explicitly*; thus the true claim made in the statement, the semantic content of the sentence, is not a function of the contents, in context, of the components of the sentence. Again, the needed component of the proposition *could* be supplied explicitly, either with 'in the situations we're discussing' or with a fuller characterization of those situations. Also, the same sentence could be used to make a fully general, false claim.

More commonplace examples of this sort are typical uses of these sentences:

Cars start when the key is turned in the ignition.

A match will light when struck.

He can't get the dart in the bull's-eye.

In each case, there is an implicit restriction to normal or relevant or understood circumstances, which accounts for the truth of such claims, when they are true. These restrictions must be reflected in the contents of the statements, since it is only *because* of the restrictions that the statements are true. Thus, a semantics appropriate to these claims must violate full articulation.

The examples of underarticulation are relevant to the first argument for the naïve theory because we cannot ignore the possibility that belief reports exploit mechanisms of underarticulation. To assume that the principle of articulated compositionality applies to belief reports is to assume that belief reports are not underarticulated; and we have no reason to make this assumption. The claims made in belief reports may well be sensitive to parameters that are fixed in context, yet are not contributed semantically by any overt expressions. Though I will argue that this is more than an idle possibility, the very possibility is enough to defeat the first argument for the naïve analysis of belief reports. That it is a live possibility is suggested by a look at our intuitions about the puzzles. We form conflicting truth-value intuitions about uses of sentences of the same overt form, composed of parts with the same meanings and referents. If there are no differences in what the expressions provide, where can the difference in propositional content come from? Only from what no expression provides.

The second argument for the naïve analysis relies only on the principle of direct contribution—that as a contributor to the proposition expressed by a statement, the use of a name donates only what it denotes. An example from Quine 1953 is, I believe, enough to defeat this principle, and the connection to the case of belief reports is clear:

Giorgione was so-called because of his size.   (3)

Quine wrote that 'Giorgione' in (3) plays a "role" in addition to the
typical, referential role that it plays, for example, in

Giorgione played chess.   (4)

The sentence (4) is a simple predication; so, by direct contribution, the
use of 'Giorgione' (in the obvious sort of context) supplies as its semantic
contribution simply the artist, Giorgio Barbarelli, as seems right. But
this cannot be true of the occurrence of 'Giorgione' in (3). There, the
name is used to supply not only the man being discussed, but also *itself*
as the name that Barbarelli is said to have been called because of his size.

Is this a failure of direct reference? Not at all. Direct reference
does not entail that the semantic contribution of the use of a name is
simply its content—that is, its referent. But of course that is precisely
what direct contribution does entail, and so the Giorgione case is a clear
counterexample. Note that the example does *not* show that the *content*
of the use of a name can change. For one can hold consistently and,
I think, correctly, that the content of 'Giorgione' is simply its referent,
Barbarelli, in both (3) and (4). That is, one can hold that the second
role played by the use of 'Giorgione' is its *pragmatic* function of raising
the name itself to contextual salience, so that it can become the referent
of the 'so' in 'so-called'. So the name 'Giorgione' gets into the content of
(3) *because of* its use in that statement, but it is no part of the content
of its own use. I agree with Quine that this dual-role phenomenon is at
the bottom of many of the puzzles about substitutivity in belief reports
as well. But understood correctly, this phenomenon should not lead us
to complicate our semantics for names. All we have to do is notice that,
as in the Giorgione example, although names stand simply for things,
they do more than just stand—they contribute to context in ways that
can be exploited by constructions like 'so-called' and, as I will suggest
in chapters 5 and 6, 'believes'.

The principles needed to support the arguments for the naïve theory "from above" are not all true, fully general principles governing
the semantics of English. I have not shown that they do not apply
in the troublesome cases about belief reports, including the Hesperus-
Phosphorus example. But the principles can support the naïve view of
belief reports only if we have special reason to think they apply in these
cases or we have independent reasons to hold them as general principles.
We have neither. The assumption that they do apply to belief reports

yields a semantics that conflicts with our intuitions about truth values, and we have independent reasons to believe that the principles are not true in general.

1.3   Implicature and Cancelability

Next I want to look at the claim that the presence in belief reports of a certain symptom of pragmatic implicature, namely cancelability of "extra" information, counts as a feather in the cap of the naïve analysis. To do this, I need first to sketch the theoretical framework in which the notion of cancelability figures.

Communication involves a speaker intentionally bringing about changes in the hearer's beliefs. Much of our interest in semantics is grounded in the assumption that a central sort of communication involves statements in which *what is expressed* is a big part of what is communicated. In a typical statement, however, there are many propositions "conveyed" apart from what is literally said. Austin, Grice, Searle, and others have looked at some of the systematic ways in which statements convey information that they do not strictly speaking express.

Assertive uses of sentences can for systematic, intentional, even conventional reasons, convey nonexpressively the information whose communication is the primary goal of the statement. A simple example of this is irony, in which a statement is intended to convey the proposition that is directly contrary to the one expressed. Other such devices, perhaps, are metaphor, hyperbole, sarcasm and expressions of sympathy ('you're hurt!'), surprise ('you brought a gift!'), and knowledge ('you're dating Wendy'). Many have claimed that there are other, more subtle cases of this sort. A statement of the form '*a* is *b*', where *a* and *b* are names, for example, can be taken as serving primarily to convey the information that the thing *called* '*a*' is the thing *called* '*b*'. After Grice, (some) propositions that are conveyed nonexpressively in a statement are called pragmatic "implicata" (or "implicatures"); these are conveyed by mechanisms of "implicature."

These cases show the inadequacy of possible simple characterizations of what proposition is *expressed* by a statement: that it is what the statement is primarily intended to convey; that it is what statements of that sentence (or sort of sentence) typically convey; that it is what such statements are conventionally understood to convey. In compensation for this difficulty, we are given a technique for explaining some semantically stubborn expressions: we can claim that our troubles in finding truth-conditional analyses of certain locutions stem from a bad assumption that what these locutions are typically used to convey must be what they are used to say. This "assertion fallacy" (Searle 1969) or "fallacy of misplaced information" (Barwise and Perry 1983) can throw illusory monkey wrenches into the systematic machinery of semantics. A careful pragmatic analyst can restore functional harmony to semantics by pointing out instances of the fallacy.

And this is exactly the goal of the defenders of the naïve theory of the attitudes. Consider these sentences:

Caius believed that Hesperus is Hesperus.   (5)

Caius believed that Hesperus is Phosphorus.   (6)

Statements of sentences like (5) and (6) typically convey very different propositions; that much is clear. In fact, in the obvious kind of context, (5) would be used to convey something true, whereas (6) would convey something false. But we cannot, on pain of fallacy, thereby conclude that two such statements express different propositions. In fact, the argument goes, we have some reason not so to conclude. The antecedently plausible principles of articulated compositionality and direct reference, as we have seen, imply that uses of (5) and (6) express identical propositions. We have, it seems, many of the symptoms of a subtle case of pragmatic implicature.

Our naïve (or super-naïve) intuitions tell us that a statement of (5) is true, while one of (6) is false. What evidence might ground this hunch? Our intuition is based largely on the knowledge that the ancients (including Caius) wrote and talked extensively of Venus under the names 'Hesperus' and 'Phosphorus', without anywhere suggesting that the "two" heavenly bodies are identical. Their situation was of the common sort in which one has two names for, or notions of, a single thing, without linking the names in the way one normally does with alternative names for a single thing (call this "identity-linking"). In addition, they did not believe that the thing they called 'Hesperus' was the thing they called 'Phosphorus'. Something like this is what we convey with a statement of the denial of (6). A statement of (6), it seems, conveys the proposition that Caius *did* identity-link the two names and the two notions in the way we do today.

So the path of the naïve analysis is clear: (6), but not (5), conveys the proposition that Caius identity-linked his notions of 'Hesperus' and 'Phosphorus'. This proposition is conveyed, though not expressed, by a statement of (6). A statement of (5) conveys no such proposition, though perhaps it implies that Caius had a notion of a thing to which he attached the name 'Hesperus'—tame stuff, compared to the implicatures of (6).

Grice wrote that we should expect of implicatures that they can be "canceled": that we have devices by which we can use the sentence to express its semantic content without conveying the usually implied information. We can, in this case, say "Caius believed that Hesperus is Hesperus. So, though he would not say 'Hesperus is Phosphorus', he really did believe that *Hesperus* is *Phosphorus*." The wording of this suggests that, in virtue of its *literal meaning*, what a statement of (6) says is true. The information usually conveyed, that Caius identity-linked his 'Hesperus' and 'Phosphorus' notions, can be left out in a use of (6) without rendering the statement figurative, ironic, or anything less than literal. The observation that the "extra" information is cancelable provides an instance of the predictive success of the hypothesis that this information, when conveyed, is conveyed through pragmatic implicature.

But it turns out that on any useful, natural construal of the notion of cancelability, it is not a property exclusively of pragmatic implicatures. We thus cannot assume that cancelable information is merely implied, and not expressed, in a statement. The general problem is that surrounding, 'canceling' statements can disambiguate what is said with a sentence whose content can vary with context. In particular, I will argue, cancelability cannot distinguish implicature from underarticulation.

Here is a tentative definition of cancelability:[4] A proposition p con-

---

4. Grice himself tried more than one definition of cancelability; the first one given here is very much in the spirit of some of these. Grice regarded cancelability as one among several symptoms of implicature, no group of which he counted as necessary and sufficient conditions.

Richard holds the following: "Loosely formulated, the principle is that the information conveyed by a number of conversational contributions instead of a single contribution, is a matter of pragmatic implicature, not truth conditions" (1987, 261).

veyed with a statement of sentence s in context c_s is *cancelable* if, for
some c_s' that differs from c_s only in that the speaker of s in c_s' makes
additional statements before and/or after the statement of s, p is not
conveyed by the use of s in c_s'. Call the use of s in c_s the "original"
use, and that in c_s' the "canceled" use. By this definition, the information that Caius would have *said* 'Hesperus is Phosphorus'—information
that is conveyed in a typical use of (6)—is cancelable. This is because
the speaker can stipulate that she does not mean to describe how Caius
would express his belief.

However, the proposed definition allows many propositions to be
deemed cancelable that are clear cases of directly *expressed* propositions.
A typical use of 'It's raining', for example, expresses the information
that it is raining at l, where l is a location at or near the location of the
statement. But, by saying first, 'Now we turn to the weather in New
York', the forecaster in California has on our definition canceled that
information. An isolated use of 'Professor X's book is very interesting'
would express a different proposition (one about a book X wrote) from
a use of the same sentence followed by ' — not, of course, the book he
wrote, but the one he lent me'. So in the second use, the proposition
expressed about the book X wrote is canceled.

A would-be Lothario who says, 'I'm hungry. I don't mean for food'
has canceled the information that otherwise would be expressed with
'I'm hungry'. But this case is a bit different: the use of 'hungry' takes
on a different *meaning* from its usual one of 'craving food', namely, that
of 'eagerly desirous'. In the cases of rain and books, the meanings of the
words in the canceled use are the same as those used in the original. The
statement 'I don't mean for food' has given a nondefault resolution to a
lexical ambiguity, about which one of the several meanings of 'hungry'
is invoked. This case is akin to 'I'm going fishing down at the bank. I
sure hope I get a loan'. Just as default meaning can be overridden, so
can default reference. In a conversation about Shakespeare, 'He wrote
many tragedies' would by default be about Shakespeare. But preceding
it with 'Ibsen's career was remarkably similar' would alter the reference
in the use of 'he'.

The meaning- and reference-shifting cases of "cancelability" must
be excluded, if cancelability is to be any indication of nonexpressed
information. It should not be enough, to show that information is merely
implicated, simply to provide a case in which the same *words* are used,

but which have different contents because of surrounding statements. And it is easy to patch the definition of cancelability to disallow these cases. We require, amending the above definition, that the canceled use of s be such that the meanings and references of expressions in s are identical to those in the original use of s. I am not sure how to spell this out in a non-question-begging way (ambiguity is notoriously difficult to distinguish from implicature), but perhaps we can trust our intuitions to tell us when apparent cancelability is of this bogus kind.

In any event, it seems to me that the cancelability of the propositions expressed with 'Professor X's book is very interesting' and 'It's raining' is not of this sort. Different propositions are expressed in the original and canceled uses, to be sure, but this is not in virtue of different meanings or references of the overt parts of the sentence used.[5]

I have not seen, and cannot concoct, a non-question-begging criterion of cancelability that will count as cancelable only propositions that are "merely conveyed." This is no proof that one cannot be devised, but I remain skeptical. For lack of such a criterion, the apparent cancelability of the information that the naïve theorists claim to be merely conveyed in belief reports cannot provide support for that claim.

Merely conveyed propositions comprise one important class of cancelable propositions. Our examples suggest that propositions expressed by statements that exploit unarticulated constituents form another class of cancelable propositions. Indeed, this should be expected: if a constituent of the expressed proposition is not overtly mentioned in a statement, but comes in as something like a default value, it is quite useful to have context-shaping devices to override the default. So, it appears likely that a criterion of cancelability will never be able to distinguish the merely expressed from the underarticulated. Cancelability of a proposition is just as good evidence for its being expressed and underarticulated, as for its being merely conveyed. The cancelable "extra" information

---

5. Of course, here again it is important to distinguish between overt and covert expressions. For reasons similar to those discussed in the last section, a requirement of meaning and reference preservation is useful in a test for cancelability only if we can agree on the constituents of a sentence. And as before, the possibility of covert expressions in belief reports is consistent with the observations about cancelability, and this is sufficient to defuse the evidence for the naïve analysis. So a suggestion that there is a covert expression with varying reference in 'It's raining' is fine by me.

conveyed in belief reports, then, may well be part—an unarticulated part—of what the reports literally express.

1.4   Translation

Another source of support for the naïve view comes from considerations about how (5) and (6) might be translated into other languages, real and invented. Translation is a subtle business, no doubt, but, the argument goes, surely our common practices of translation preserve the truth values of translated statements. Consider a language almost exactly like English, but with just one name, 'Venus', for Venus. How would we translate 'Hesperus is an evening star' into that language? Obviously, with 'Venus is an evening star'. In general, when we have a proper name for something, we use it to translate a coreferential proper name in another language. 'L'Allemagne est au nord' becomes 'Germany is to the north', for example. Since the hypothetical language has just one name for Venus, this must serve as the translation of both 'Hesperus' and 'Phosphorus'. So (5) is rendered 'Caius believed that Venus is an evening star', as also is (6). Since the two reports receive the same translation, they surely must have the same truth value.

The argument from equivalence of sentences under translation has its source in Church's 1954 criticism of Carnap. Such an argument, slightly modified, underlies the much-discussed puzzle due to Saul Kripke (1979). In the version just sketched, the most obvious flaw is the overly simple account of our standard practices of translation. But this flaw is not the only one. A more basic problem with the argument is the assumption that *sentences*, instead of statements or propositions, are the bearers of truth values. The crucial step involves comparing the translations of two sentences, noticing that they are the same, and inferring that the sentences must have the same truth value.

The inference is not valid, even if the conclusion is interpreted as the claim that *statements* of the sentences must have the same truth values. The same reasoning would show that any two uses of 'it's four o'clock', say, one at three o'clock and one at four, must have the same truth value. The simple version of the argument from translation assumes that any possible difference between what the reports of (5) and (6) express stems from a difference in what the words used in the reports *refer to*, and *mean*. Translation preserves the meanings and referents of the words used in belief reports, we can suppose. But, as cases of underarticulation clearly demonstrate, the meanings and referents of words do not always determine the proposition expressed in a statement.

Taking sentences as the bearers of truth seems less obviously troublesome in the case of belief ascriptions. For this reason, it will be worthwhile to consider a version of Kripke's argument from translation that respects as carefully as possible the distinction between statements and sentences:

The Frenchman Pierre lived and was raised in France, where he heard tales of 'Londres' and sincerely affirmed 'Londres est jolie', which we normally translate as 'London is pretty'. He moved to London, not realizing that it is the city he called 'Londres', and found the city ugly. Having learned English, he now sincerely affirms 'London is not pretty'.

For someone who heard Pierre's statement in France, it clearly would have been true to say 'Pierre croit que Londres est jolie', which we would normally translate as 'Pierre believes that London is pretty'. But this report attributes, in a perfectly ordinary way, a belief that Pierre had and has been given no reason to abandon. In fact he still affirms 'Londres est jolie' in conversation (say, over the phone to France). So, it is still true for us, now, in describing Pierre's beliefs, to say,

Pierre believes that London is pretty.   (7)

But Pierre *says* 'London is not pretty', and is sincere about it. He also dissents whenever anyone says 'London is pretty'. This is as good a reason as we ever get to say, now, in describing his beliefs, that 'Pierre believes that London is not pretty', and even,

Pierre does not believe that London is pretty.   (8)

It seems clear that these claims as made by us, now, are true.

But surely it is impossible that we, now, would speak truly by saying *either* 'Pierre believes that London is pretty' *or* 'Pierre does not believe that London is pretty'. This is the puzzle.

And here is the resolution: From the fact that a Frenchman, in her circumstances, makes a true claim with 'Pierre croit que Londres est jolie', it does not follow that *we*, in *our* circumstances, make a true claim by using even an unexceptionable translation. Nor does it follow from (i) that it was true for us at one time, describing Pierre's beliefs,

to say 'Pierre believes that London is pretty', and (ii) that Pierre still
has the belief we so attributed to him, that (iii) we would make a true
statement in our present circumstances by using the same sentence.

What might make us think that such inferences are valid in this
case? The needed extra premise is something like this: the expression
'believes that London is pretty', in its ordinary use, denotes a *property*—
always the same one—in the same way that 'is over six feet tall' or 'is
made of tin' does. There is *the* belief that London is pretty. Pierre,
puzzlingly, seems both to have it and not to have it. If 'believes that
London is pretty' works like that, then the inferences just mentioned are
sound. So it will be worth considering why one might think it works like
that.

It is not unreasonable to think that 'believes that London is pretty'
contributes a property to the content of a sentence in which it is the
major verb phrase. All that is left for the subject-expression to provide
is the agent to whom the property is attributed. Such an ascription,
then, makes it quite explicit just what sort of belief is attributed, and
just to whom it is claimed to belong. There are no indexicals or other
types of varying overt reference in the attributions considered in the
example. So there is a natural assumption that the *claims* made in the
uses of the sentence 'Pierre believes that London is pretty' cannot vary
(ignoring time differences).

But, as I have been suggesting, there is no reason to presuppose that
belief reports are fully overt, articulated statements. The absence within
a sentence of indexicals and other overt terms with varying content does
not guarantee that the claims made in different uses of the sentence will
be the same. We cannot look only to contents of the overt components of
an expression for evidence of sensitivity to context. The reason that we
can feel strongly that the statements of (7) and (8) are both true *must*
involve differences between the contexts of those statements, since, as
Kripke discovers, there is no single context in which they both seem
true.

Here is a caricature of the puzzle to reinforce my point: Pierre, in
Paris, is on the phone to New York, is told of a storm in New York, and
sincerely affirms, to a friend at his side, 'It's raining.' Clearly, what he
says is true: it *is* raining. After his phone conversation, he looks out
the window, sees a clear day, and sincerely affirms 'It's not raining'. Of
course, he is right: it is *not* raining. But the fact that made it true to

say 'It's raining' on the phone still holds true (it is still raining in New York); thus, it *is* raining. So *is it raining or not?* The moral, of course, is that the truth value of a use of 'it's raining' depends (at least) on the location, to be supplied in context, that the statement is about. If a context does not supply, even by default, such a location, there can no more be a determinate claim made with that sentence than there can be with an "assertion" of 'Pierre is the father of'.

The arguments from translation do not support the naïve view. But the puzzling examples they depend on are of great use in studying the subtle effects of contextual features on the use and contents of belief reports. And none is better at that than the case to be discussed next.

1.5   Richard's Steamroller

An argument by Mark Richard (1983) purports to demonstrate that in a case somewhat similar to the Hesperus-Phosphorus case, our intuitions about truth values are faulty. *A* is talking on the telephone to *B*. *A* sees, out his window, a steamroller about to crush a phone booth, at obvious peril to its occupant. Unbeknown to *A*, *B* is in that phone booth. Explaining the situation to *B*, *A* affirms:

I believe that she is in danger.   (9)

But *A* would *not* sincerely affirm and would in fact deny:

I believe that you are in danger.   (10)

Richard argues that (9) and (10), in the described context, are both true, *A*'s intuitions notwithstanding. Suppose *B* is watching *A*'s panicked behavior and says:

The man watching me believes that I'm in danger.   (11)

Since, as we suppose, (9) is true, (11) is true also. *A* now echoes (11) from his perspective:

The man watching you believes that you are in danger.   (12)

(12) is true, since (11) is, and *A* is agreeing. Consider now, as words put in *A*'s mouth:

I am the man watching you.   (13)

This is clearly true in the described circumstances. According to Richard, it follows that (10) is true as well. A defense of this step might cite the fact that (12) and (10), considered as spoken in the same context, attribute to the same agent a belief, using precisely the same words in the embedded clause—words that are understood in precisely the same way. Thus they must make the same claim, and hence our truth-intuitions are mistaken. Though this case is significantly different from the Hesperus-Phosphorus case, and it is not clear that the argument could be adapted to that example, Richard's argument calls into question intuitions that seem of the same basic sort as those operating in Caius's case.

Richard's argument provides a sophisticated puzzle that is "context sensitive" in ways that the translation arguments are not. However, Richard makes what is a more sophisticated version of the mistake committed in the translation arguments: he assumes that the features of context that determine the contents of the *parts* of a sentence are sufficient to determine content, and hence the truth value, of the statement as a whole. Like Kripke, he ignores the possibility of unarticulated constituents in the contents of belief reports.

Richard claims that it is inconsistent to maintain that (12) and (13) are true and (10) is false, considered as asserted by A in the circumstances described above. It seems to me clear that it is correct, and a fortiori consistent, to maintain that the uses of (12) and (13) are true and (10) is false. The story told in the argument makes these facts plain. For now, I will argue only that the ordinary intuitions about the case are consistent, by showing that Richard's argument fails to demonstrate that they are inconsistent. As I see it, Richard describes his example quite clearly, evokes solid intuitions about the truth values of these claims, and then makes a mistaken logical move to show the inconsistency of these intuitions.

Richard claims that since in A's present context (12) and (13) are true, so must (10) be true. Why? Richard clearly thinks that the reports made with (12) and (10) attribute the same belief to the same person. There is no denying that the agent whose beliefs are being characterized is the same in the two reports. But why suppose that the beliefs being attributed are identical? Why suppose that the reports claim the same thing about A?

The needed principle is full articulation. Assuming full articulation, the inference from (12) and (13) to (10) goes through, because of the following: in virtue of the true identity (13), the uses of (12) and (10) are about the same agent; since the object clauses of (12) and (10) are identical, and are composed of words with the same contents, they have the same content; and, finally, the uses of (12) and (10) must have the same content, since they are composed in the same way out of parts with the same contents.

But the principle of full articulation is an unwarranted assumption about the semantics of belief reports—an assumption placing an undefended restriction on the ways constituents of the propositions expressed in belief reports may be provided. It ignores, for one thing, the possible relevance of the expression used to refer to the agent in helping to provide unarticulated constituents.

To give a hint of what I think is going on in Richard's example (a hint I will expand on in chapter 5): with (12), A is attributing to himself (though he does not recognize that) a belief of a specific sort that would have certain relations to his perceptual situation and likely actions. With (10), he is (knowingly) attributing to himself a belief of a sort that would have quite different relations to his perceptual situation and likely actions. He really does have the belief he unknowingly attributes to himself with (12), but lacks the belief that he (hypothetically) attributes to himself with (10). And the difference in what the reports claim is traced to a difference in the effect on context made by the different terms for the agent A. The terms make salient different notions that A has of himself, in one case his self-notion, and in the other a notion connected with his beliefs about the scene B is describing. Because of the salience of the different notions, the two belief reports express claims that are *about*, in an unarticulated way, different things—the different notions are tacitly referred to in the reports.

The notions of "substitutivity *salva veritate*" and "referential opacity" were originally defined in terms of the truth values of sentences. There is more than one way to adapt these notions to apply to statements. Here is one likely candidate: For sentences $\phi(t_1)$ and $\phi(t_2)$ with singular terms t_1 and t_2 in the same position, if there is a context c such that a use of $\phi(t_1)$ in c would be true and a use of $\phi(t_2)$ in c would be false, but in which the uses of the terms would co-refer, then we say that this constitutes a *failure of substitutivity salva veritate* and that the position of the singular terms in ϕ is *referentially opaque*. Frege and Quine held that substitutivity does not hold in general for singular terms to the right of 'believes that' in belief reports. The Hesperus-Phosphorus case is Frege's example of such a failure of substitutivity. The position of the term 'Hesperus' in 'Caius believed that Hesperus is Phosphorus' is, for Quine, opaque.

If my claim is correct, then Richard's steamroller case shows that the *subject* position in a belief ascription is opaque! The sentences (12) and (10) differ *only* in that they contain in the subject position different terms that denote the same individual. Yet their uses, in the same circumstances, have different truth values. The right account of how this happens, which must wait until chapter 5, makes this seem a good deal less surprising: the expression used in the subject clause is just one of the many features of a belief report that can help pragmatically to supply information about just what sort of belief is being attributed, by disambiguating tacit reference. In Richard's example, it is a crucial feature.

1.6   Persisting Beliefs and Platitudes

I will close this chapter with two reasons, beyond the lack of convincing support for it, to doubt the naïve account.

1. Reports that someone has believed something for a year, or for over a week, or all his life, cannot be given a plausible straightforward naïve analysis. Suppose in January Caius comes to believe that Hesperus is pretty, then in June comes to believe that Phosphorus is pretty, and then in August gives up his belief about Hesperus and in December his belief about Phosphorus. All along, Caius has had one or another belief with the content that Venus is pretty. But it would clearly be false to say that Caius has believed all year that Hesperus is pretty.

Persisting beliefs are not just persisting relations to propositions. When we talk about persisting beliefs, discussing when they were formed, how long they lasted, and when they were abandoned, the truth of what we say cannot be explained with reference to only our having or not having *at least one* belief with a certain content. Naive semantics does not explain what this means: Caius believed from January to August, and not thereafter, that Hesperus was pretty, and he believed only from June to December that Phosphorus was pretty.

2. The naïve view is committed to denying even the approximate

truth of commonsense "platitudes" that have been discussed under the name "folk psychology." For example: If an agent believes that a person is in danger, and the agent wants to yell a warning to her, and believes that he can yell a warning to her over the phone, then, in the absence of competing claims on his actions, he is likely to try to yell a warning over the phone. But this principle comes out as false on the naïve analysis for the Richard case we just discussed. For these statements all come out as true:

A believes *B* is in danger.

A wants to yell a warning to *B*.

A believes he can yell a warning to *B* over the phone.

And the conclusion of our platitude comes out false: *A* is not likely to try to yell a warning over the phone. The reason the naïve analysis makes the principle come out false is clear: the platitude is not naïve; it is understood that the agent must "think about" the relevant person in the same way in the reported beliefs and in the desire for it to be a true general claim. Is this platitude—a general claim about how people behave—strictly speaking false, but somehow appropriate to describing behavior?

I think each of the following statements (in the natural contexts) makes a true claim; and each comes out false under the naïve view, for reasons similar to those just given for the Richard case:

If an agent believes that there is a bee on his back, he will likely be worried.

If an agent wants food and believes that there is food in the bag in front of him, he will likely eat that food.

If an agent believes that she is talking to a person, and she wants to congratulate that person, she will likely congratulate him.

Of course it would be nice to be able to hold that these principles are not just *getting at* truths (a strategy urged in Richard 1987) but in fact express truths.

In order to explain why these principles *seem* true, and why in the puzzle cases our ordinary intuitions are mistaken, the naïve theorists are committed to a program (which they will call a strictly pragmatic enterprise) of explaining what belief reports are meant to convey, what they are used to get at. Now, suppose that the naïve theorists come up with an account of what is conveyed in belief reports that is much like the account of what they *express* in an analysis in terms of unarticulated constituents. What would count as a reason to choose between the analyses? Not simplicity, since the different accounts would be of equal complexity when the semantic and pragmatic packages are weighed together. Not independently supported general principles of semantics, since these do not support one over the other. Not arguments from cancelability, translation, or phone booths, since these are equally ineffective in distinguishing between the accounts. What remains? Only a simple criterion of reasonableness: where you can adopt an account that is consonant with intuitions, and there is no reason not to, do so.

2 Instances of Believing

In this chapter I will press some views about the cognitive facts that belief reports are used to describe. After a critical discussion of an account of belief as fundamentally grounded in shareable cognitive states, I will argue that implicit in our ordinary understanding of the phenomenon of belief is a conception of believing as grounded in unshareable concrete particulars. Finally, I will reconcile this view with a treatment of the phenomenon of *tacit* belief, which I hope to show is no obstacle for a theory of believing couched in terms of concrete particular representations.

2.1 Belief States

I will claim that certain difficulties about the individuation of the facts behind believing are best handled not by positing abstract, shareable belief states, ways of believing, intensions, characters, or senses, but by explaining instances of believing in terms of concrete particulars, while allowing that they might be classified, for various purposes, by such abstract entities. In abstracting away from all but one feature of the cognitive particulars that are (or are involved in) beliefs, I will suggest, some philosophers have discarded what is essential for getting straight the basic facts behind believing. The cure is to retain the abstract entities to whatever extent they are useful for other reasons, but to let particulars, with all the features arising from their place in the world of the concrete, handle the difficult aspects of individuating instances of believing.

In this chapter I will let a system of shareable abstract *belief states* serve as the representative candidate for a scheme of individuating beliefs by abstract entities. Several sorts of things have gone under the name of "belief states," including truly statelike attributes of minds, properties of being "belief-related" to various sorts of abstract object, and rather less statelike entities like shareable belief-types. I will argue that we cannot individuate beliefs correctly and completely with criteria that are appropriate (on a reading of "appropriate" that I will detail) to such universal, shareable, typelike entities. I will claim that an adequate account of belief should instead explain belief in terms of agent-bound, unshareable concrete cognitive particulars. In this I side with those who take seriously the existence of *token* mental entities, although I have some reservations about that label, as I explain below (even particular, or token, mental entities have misleadingly been labeled "states" in the literature).

There is a good deal in common between what I will claim here and what a number of other writers recently have argued. Stephen Stich (1983), for instance, has argued that there is no such thing as *the property* of 'believing that *s*'. And Hilary Putnam (1988) has argued that two organisms, each of which counts as having the belief that there are cats in the neighborhood, need not be in the same internal state in any important sense. Stich's reasons for his conclusion focus on the judgments of similarity that, he says, underlie our intuitions about belief reports. Putnam's arguments depend on his view of belief reporting as relying crucially on the woolliness of "interpretative practice" with respect to different kinds of possible organisms. Both are interested in the analysis of belief *predicates*—expressions of the form 'believes that *s*'. Both assume that, if we are to make sense of belief, then we will have to make sense of these predicates. Having demonstrated important ways in which these predicates are "ill-behaved," these writers draw dire conclusions about the very notion of belief.

My reasons for thinking that belief predicates do not in general express shareable features of the internal states of believers do not sanction any such verdict about our ordinary notion of belief. A great deal of the trouble with belief predicates, I think, comes from some systematic, if poorly understood, contextual features of our uses of these predicates in belief reports. And it seems to me likely that we can—and ordinarily do—make systematic sense of the phenomenon of belief without appeal to a system of shareable mental states picked out by these predicates.

My reasons for being suspicious of attempts to analyze belief in terms of shareable belief states have to do with concerns about individuation. Specifically, I think that a theory of belief in terms of such states will not be able to individuate instances of believing in the right way, because of a certain tension between the complexity and interconnectedness of actual mental representation on the one hand, and the supposed simplicity and independence of the posited belief states on the other. To argue for this claim, I need first to explain the kind of philosophical task that the posit of belief states is meant to accomplish. This will yield some adequacy conditions for an analysis of belief in terms of belief states—conditions that I will argue cannot be accommodated in any acceptable account of belief states.

The first step is to realize that belief states are posited as *central individuating parameters* in the relation that is supposed to be at the bottom of the phenomenon of believing.

When we wind up our analysis of a phenomenon, say, of *scratching*, by introducing a term for a relation, '*Scratches*(a, x, t)', we aim at specifying a relation on one or more parameters as what is at the bottom of the phenomenon. The choice of a relation and its accompanying list of parameters is not always either obvious (as it may be in the case of *FatherOf*) or arbitrary. There are some clear requirements that need to be met by the correct relation in a relational analysis. For one, we need our relation to individuate co-possible *instances* of the phenomenon, as I will now explain.

Suppose we are to ask, what is the phenomenon of eating? A first step toward an answer would be to point out that, whenever there is a case of eating going on, there is an eater and a thing being eaten. In addition, any case of eating must take place over a period of time, though there can be stops and starts. This information about the phenomenon of eating gives us principled ways of individuating instances of eating— of deciding when we are considering two different cases of eating, or really just one. If we are clever enough in searching for parameters that individuate instances of eating, we may end with a *complete* set of individuating parameters—one that yields a set of necessary and sufficient conditions for the identity of co-possible instances of eating (instances that can happen in the same possible world).[1] For any complete set of individuating parameters, co-possible cases of eating are identical if and only if they are alike with respect to every parameter in the set.

---

1. I say "co-possible" rather than possible instances (each of which can happen in *some* world) because I do not require individuating parameters to adjudicate "trans-world" questions like 'If I had eaten the cake just ten minutes earlier, would it have been the same case of eating?' We do not ask our *relations* to decide questions about the modal properties of their *instances*, but only that (ignoring problems about vagueness) they determinately hold-or-not-hold in each world with respect to an appropriate specification of their parameters. Note that any set of parameters provides us with a necessary condition for the identity of two cases of eating, since the function from an instance to a parameter (say, to the agent in that instance) is just that, a function. What completeness guarantees us is a sufficient condition for identity.

A relational analysis aims at explaining a phenomenon by positing a relation on a complete set of individuating parameters. This condition on the adequacy of a relational analysis suggests two simple tests. First, if a relation we tentatively have posited as being at the bottom of some phenomenon seems both to hold and not to hold under one specification of its argument roles, then we have not found a complete set of individuating parameters for the phenomenon, and so the supposed relation on those parameters is not a relation at all. Second, if we notice that the relation can hold *twice over* under one such specification, in that two instances of the phenomenon can exist (or occur), with these parameters fixed in the same way, then again we have not found a complete set of individuating parameters—the relation we have posited is in this case too *coarse-grained* to distinguish between some co-possible instances of the phenomenon. The first test rests upon Aristotle's (*Metaphysics* 1011b18) version of the principle of noncontradiction: a relation cannot both hold and fail to hold of the same things in the same respect. The second test relies upon not a logical principle, but a metaphysical one: for any relation posited as underlying a phenomenon, if there can be two co-possible instances of the phenomenon that share all the parameters to which the relation is sensitive, then the relation does not give an adequate analysis of the phenomenon (as it is based on an incomplete set of individuating parameters). These tests are useful only in cases where intuitions about instances of the phenomenon in question are easy to come by.

In general, not just any relation over a complete individuating set of parameters will constitute an acceptable relational analysis of a phenomenon. The reason is that we can in some cases find uninteresting sets of parameters that completely individuate a phenomenon—we might find, for example, that just the thing eaten can serve to identify cases of eating (if we decide that the same thing cannot be eaten twice). A relation on an uninteresting set of individuating parameters will not allow us to say much of what we want about the phenomenon, and so cannot constitute an analysis. If we were to choose just the food item to play a role in the *Eating* relation, we could not use that relation to talk about who ate a thing, or when it was eaten. The usual practice, for this reason, is to posit a relation whose argument roles reflect a complete set of individuating parameters that includes all those parameters *central* to the phenomenon, for the purposes of the investigation. The notion of a central parameter of a phenomenon will be left unanalyzed; the relational strategy works best when the central parameters of a phenomenon are relatively obvious, as in the examples of *being greater than*, *being the father of*, and *loving*.

The belief puzzle cases reveal insufficiencies in initially plausible identification criteria for instances of believing. They do this by showing the inadequacy of the relations, which are *based* on those criteria, that have been posited as being at the bottom of believing. Belief states—of the sort I will discuss here—have been postulated for just such a reason: they are meant to fill the need revealed by the puzzles for additional individuating parameters in "the belief relation." But, as I hope to show, we can concoct the same kinds of puzzles to demonstrate that belief states are not up to this individuative task.

When we make a true belief report, it is true because there is an instance of believing that the report gets at. An instance of believing is always a case of *someone* believing *something* at some *time*.[2] Does this suggest a complete set of individuating parameters for instances of believing—a set that provides us with a criterion of identification for co-possible cases? If so, then any instances of believing that share agents, times and things believed are identical. To test this, we look for a counterexample: *two* instances of believing that share each of the three parameters. This would be an example in which an agent, at a single time, believed the same thing *twice over*.

Looking for a counterexample, we soon meet trouble: we need to clarify what we mean by believing the same thing. To see this, consider a simple dilemma generated by a case due to John Perry (1979). Hume sincerely utters, "I wrote the *Treatise*." The madman Heimson sincerely utters the same sentence, "I wrote the *Treatise*." Each has *expressed* a belief: each has said something he believes. Each believes himself to be Hume, so the two believe the same thing. But what Hume says and believes is true, while what Heimson says and believes is false; also, what Hume believes is about *Hume*, while what Heimson believes is about *Heimson*. So what they believe must be different—they believe different things.

---

2. Perhaps a time period would be more appropriate than a specific time, if continued belief is to be seen as the persistence of an instance of believing. The decision here may be arbitrary and anyhow it does not affect the argument in this chapter, which turns on different instances that exist at some one time.

Perry's response to this dilemma is a natural one: Hume and Heimson believe different *propositions* in virtue of being in the same cognitive belief state. We should carefully distinguish propositions from belief states, both of which apparently sometimes are labeled the "things believed" in instances of believing. On the one hand, we have the proposition on which the truth or falsity of the belief hangs, that is, the proposition that having the belief commits one to. This is the proposition believed, or the content of the belief. On the other hand, we have the sort of thing that Hume and Heimson share; Perry calls this a "belief state."[3] A belief state is, more or less, the partial state of an agent's mind that underlies the agent's believing a proposition. Hume and Heimson are each in a belief state such that, whenever an agent is in that state, he believes that *he* wrote the *Treatise*. Such an agent believes this proposition *in virtue of* at least two things: being in that belief state, and being the person he is. The notion of a belief state as distinct from a proposition believed has proved popular among philosophers, in part because it is compatible with the general notion of a mental state familiar from the philosophy of mind, and in part because it suggests very natural explanations to a great number of belief puzzles, including the indexical puzzles like that about Heimson.

Consider also Quine's Tom, who appears to believe of Cicero that he was a famous Roman orator and that he was not a famous Roman orator. Tom agrees to 'Cicero was a famous Roman orator', but dissents from 'Tully was a famous Roman orator' ('Tully' is a name for Cicero). Tom's beliefs are puzzling in part because they are not at all bizarre; Tom simply does not realize that 'Cicero' and 'Tully' are names for the same person. But what does Tom believe about that person: that he

---

3. The notion of a belief state has since evolved in Perry's work. See Perry 1980a and 1980b for some thoughts relevant to the dialectic in this chapter. In the latter paper, Perry's considerations about "internal identity" among sentences accepted show that his belief "states" were losing much of their statelike character. "Internal identity" itself should not be construed as a relation among abstracta—*sentences* an agent accepts—as Perry has it in that article, but a relation among concreta: either utterances, *acts* of assenting to sentences, or particular token beliefs (which I discuss below). Perry's notion of an internal "file" in that paper seems to reflect this point, since files are surely particular things in agents' minds, rather than statelike, shareable things. In Barwise and Perry 1983, beliefs are explicitly countenanced as particular cognitive structures, but the theoretical apparatus used to classify beliefs does not take advantage of this insight; beliefs are classified with abstract "schemas," which cannot individuate them.

was a famous Roman orator? that he was not? both? neither? The state/object distinction gives us a natural answer to these questions. Tom is in two states. One of these states leads him to agree to 'Cicero was a famous Roman orator'; he believes the proposition that Cicero was a famous Roman orator in virtue of being in this state. The other state causes Tom to dissent from 'Tully was a famous Roman orator'; he believes the proposition that Cicero was not a famous Roman orator in virtue of being in this belief state.

Above, we had tentatively recognized a single "object" as a parameter in instances of believing. These puzzles show that "thing believed" has at least two readings; we might mean a proposition believed, and we might mean something like a belief state that the agent is in.

The simplest way to salvage the proposed set of individuating parameters for instances of believing (agent, time, object) would be to specify either the proposition believed or the belief state as the thing we mean to fill the "object" slot.

Suppose, first, that we take the proposition believed to fill the "object" slot, yielding an agent-time-proposition set of individuating parameters. It is straightforward to show that this is not a *complete* individuating set. There are two *ways* that Tom might believe the proposition, call it p, about Cicero, corresponding to two belief states that he might be in: one of which he would express using the name 'Cicero', the other with 'Tully'. In fact, we can consider a slightly modified "two-belief" version of the example in which Tom believes p in *both* ways. In the new version, Tom still does not recognize that 'Cicero' and 'Tully' name the same person, but he assents to both 'Cicero was a famous Roman orator' and 'Tully was a famous Roman orator'. So our set of individuating parameters, containing the agent, the time, and the proposition believed, is not complete. There must be at least one individuating parameter that we are missing.

There is of course something different about the two instances of believing in the two-belief Cicero-Tully case. But it is something that does not result in different propositions being believed. This more internal kind of difference is exactly what we have been offered the notion of a "belief state" for; belief states are candidates for the missing individuating parameters in instances of believing.

So we divide the "object" slot in the belief relation into two: one for the proposition believed, and one for the belief state involved. We now ask, must any two instances of believing that share agents, times, propositions believed, and belief states really be just a single instance? To decide this, we need to say more about what belief states are and about how they are to be individuated.

The concept of a belief state is the natural sum of two ideas. First, there is an internal dimension to instances of believing. An agent believes something partly in virtue of goings on inside her head. To be sure, some of the puzzle cases show that factors external to the mind are crucial to determining which propositions an agent believes, but this fact can only stress the need for an account of the *agent's contribution* to an instance of believing: the features of the agent's mind that underlie her belief.

The second idea is that believing something really involves being in a mental *state*, having one's mind arranged in a certain way. There surely can be nothing to the internal facts underlying a belief beyond facts about how things are in the agent's head. States are universals; they belong to objects (or, objects are *in* them) at times. So the agent's contribution to an instance of believing must be a state that the agent is in (not, of course, a total state, but a partial state). In addition, belief states, being universals, can help to account for intuitions about internal similarities and differences among agents' beliefs—internally different beliefs involve agents in different belief states. Hume's and Heimson's beliefs are internally similar, and these beliefs differ in an obvious (if not easy to explain) way from my belief that it is threatening to rain.

The resultant concept of a belief state, then, has both these features. Belief states are *shareable universals* that classify agents' *internal contributions* to instances of believing: they are shareable states that agents are in, which underlie the beliefs that the agents have.

I want to argue that, for any natural way of individuating belief states so construed, they cannot, along with agents, times, and propositions, serve to individuate instances of believing. There thus can be no way of classifying instances of believing that preserves all the ideas about what belief states are. These are the important features belief states are assumed to have:

1. *Individuation:* Belief states *internally individuate* instances of believing: there cannot be two instances of believing involving the same agent, the same time, the same proposition believed, and the same belief state.

2. *Locality:* Belief states are largely separable and independent. Given all the belief states an agent is in, it is conceivable that the agent be in some of those, and not in others.

3. *Publicity:* Belief states are shareable: different agents can be in the same belief state.

4. *Explanation:* We have intuitions that can be explained as being about agents being in the same or different belief states.

The first requirement is just what we mean by saying that belief states are the internal, mental underpinnings of belief. The second gets at the strong intuition that beliefs, though they may be to a large degree interdependent, must also be to a large degree *independent*. For instance, one can give up one belief about a thing without abandoning all one's other beliefs about the thing. I can give up my belief that there is a pen in the desk without abandoning my belief that the desk is black; being in the state that underlies the second belief cannot require being in the state underlying the first. Instances of believing are to this extent partial and separable. If belief states are to classify instances of believing internally, they should respect this separability and independence—they must themselves be individuated by their more or less *local* features. A vague enough requirement, but I will rely on very plausible applications of it. The third requirement is that belief states are *public* states that different agents can be in. The fourth requirement embodies the point that belief states are meant to explain a kind of internal dimension of similarity we recognize among instances of believing. For instance, I will assume that the description given above of the Hume-Heimson case is sufficient to ensure that the two agents share a belief state—that *that's* what our intuitions of internal similarity amount to in this case. This assumption, which we will reconsider in a moment, is simply that the case that motivated our countenancing belief states in the first place really is one in which belief states are shared. Even if Hume and Heimson do not share a belief state, belief states must be not only shareable in principle, but must also be such that we can have some idea of what it would mean for two agents to share or not share a belief state. Otherwise we may as well talk about "parameter X" and give up the pretense at explanation.

I believe that many theories of mind either explicitly or implicitly exploit belief states, as they are loosely construed here. Many theories that hold the internal facts about believing to be simply relations to abstract objects like senses, intensions, sets of ("notional") possible worlds, or natural language sentence-types are in this category, as are many that more explicitly countenance dispositional or functional states. These views are committed to there being a system of states meeting the four requirements.

My argument will be that on any plausible criteria for individuating the belief states involved in certain instances of believing, belief states must fail to satisfy one or more of these requirements. The requirement of *individuation* demands a very *fine-grained* criterion for telling belief states apart. The reason is that we must rule out the possibility of two instances of believing, or one of believing and one of not believing, involving the same agent, time, and belief state. If this can happen, belief states are inadequate to the task of individuating instances of believing—and not because they "only" individuate such instances internally, but precisely because they *cannot* individuate them internally. The trouble with a criterion that is of fine enough grain to satisfy *individuation*, is that it will thereby be *too* fine-grained and holistic to satisfy *locality* and *publicity*. These requirements insist that, as ways of classifying instances of believing, belief states have to be individuated coarsely enough to allow us to identify the belief states of different agents, and in a way that respects their independence and separability. If we make belief states coarse enough to share and to pull apart, we enable a single agent to be in one state twice over.

The argument has little to do with specific ways of identifying and individuating belief states, but it will be helpful to start with one natural candidate. A suggestion by Perry (1980a), and others, is that we can individuate belief states by certain associated sentences—sentences an agent *accepts*. An agent, at some time, accepts a sentence if she understands it, and thinks that it is true, considered as put in her mouth at that time. The idea is that *by* being in a belief state picked out by the acceptance of sentence S, an agent at a time believes the propositional content of her hypothetical utterance of S at that time. This no doubt is too simple, but we will have occasion below to consider modifications, and, again, many of the specifics of this method of individuation will be irrelevant to the main argument. I will use it simply in showing that the criterion of *individuation* demands finer grain.

Consider the Hume-Heimson case. Each believes that he wrote the

Treatise, as each accepts 'I wrote the *Treatise*'. So, on the proposed criterion, Hume and Heimson are in the same belief state, but believe different propositions, corresponding to the different things they would say if each were to utter 'I wrote the *Treatise*'. But now let's create a "belief-disbelief" version of the example. As before, Heimson knows that Hume's masterpiece is a book called 'the *Treatise*', and he takes this to be his own book. But Heimson also has heard of an unpopular book promoting the worst kind of skepticism, called '*A Treatise on Human Nature*', and has heard this book, too, referred to as 'the *Treatise*'. He does not realize that the "two" books are really identical, and he sincerely denies writing the skeptical book.

We had identified a belief state as what is in common between two agents who assent to 'I wrote the *Treatise*'. In the belief-disbelief case, Heimson still assents to that, as long as he thinks it is the "correct" book being discussed, but dissents if he thinks it is the skeptical book. Does he in this case have a belief involving the belief state we identified before as the one shared with Hume? It seems he must, since, by assumption, he has the same beliefs as before, together with a further disbelief that he wrote what he takes to be a different book.

But it is not at all clear that, on the proposed definition, he still *accepts* the sentence 'I wrote the *Treatise*', since his judgments about the sentence vary across different contexts. First, we might detail a context in which it is clear to Heimson that it is *Hume's* book being discussed. In that case, Heimson would accept the sentence. Second, we might make it clear that the book he had heard criticized for its skepticism was under discussion; now, he would not accept the sentence. Third, we might provide no clue to enable Heimson to decide which of the "two" books was being discussed. In this case too, Heimson does not accept the sentence. For, in this third case, how will he consider the sentence as spoken by himself? Which of the "two" *Treatises* would the hypothetical statement be about? Heimson thinks there are different propositions that he might use that sentence to express, one of which he believes, one he does not. Though the same instances of believing (involving Heimson at a single time) are present in the three contexts, his acceptance of the sentence 'I wrote the *Treatise*' is not constant. So acceptance cannot be an adequate test for individuating the instances of believing of an agent at a single time. It follows that belief states, *if* they are to be individuated by sentences accepted, cannot themselves individuate instances of believing.

It should not be very surprising that accepted sentences will not serve to completely individuate instances of believing, because it is not even plausible that they completely individuate belief states. Surely we want to be able to distinguish belief states on the basis of the different ways Heimson understands the name 'the *Treatise*'; so perhaps we should try sentences under a reading, or sentence meanings, or something similar.

Rather than canvass moves of this kind, I will argue that distinguishing between Heimson's belief states on the basis of the different ways in which Heimson understands the name 'the *Treatise*' will lead to a notion of belief state that divides up instances of believing more finely than we are allowed by the requirements of *locality* and *publicity*, together with the assumption that Hume and Heimson must, in the original example, share a belief state (though this last assumption will eventually prove unnecessary). And the argument has nothing to do with our using acceptance or sentence meanings to individuate belief states.

We want belief states to individuate instances of believing finely enough so that, for an agent at a time, there can be at most one instance of believing involving any one belief state. But we want more from belief states; for one thing, we want belief states to be what different agents share when their beliefs are internally alike. We posited belief states initially as what Hume and Heimson have in common when each believes what he would express by saying 'I wrote the *Treatise*'. But we have concocted a case in which, for Heimson, there are *two* possible instances of believing that might underlie his saying 'I wrote the *Treatise*'. And it is easy to imagine the "two-belief" case (Heimson believes that he wrote "both" *Treatise*s), in which *both* instances of believing are real. We must suppose that these co-possible instances of believing are classified by different belief states, if belief states are to do the individuative job they are meant for. If so, just which of these belief states is the one that Heimson shares with Hume? In setting up the original case for identifying Hume's and Heimson's belief states, it now seems, we were too quick; we specified nothing about Heimson's belief that could not be true of *two* different instances of Heimson's believing that he wrote the *Treatise*. We have no basis on which to identify either of Heimson's belief states with Hume's belief state, since there is nothing we know that decides between the two.

At this point, we have seen that the list of desired characteristics of belief states, together with the assumption about Hume and Heimson, cannot be met. Whatever basis we have to identify Hume's and Heimson's belief states in the original example, we also have to identify Heimson's two belief states in the modified example (in which Heimson believes himself to have written two *Treatises*). Note that though we had assumed belief states to be individuated by accepted sentences, this assumption did not prove to be necessary in the argument about Heimson. The argument rests on the fact that there was nothing we provided in the original example as a basis for identifying Hume's and Heimson's states that is not equally a basis in the two-belief example for identifying two of Heimson's states.

All hope is not lost, of course. Though it is important to require that belief states are shareable, we need not assume that they are so easy to share. That is, we need not assume that the little we have said about Hume and Heimson guarantees that they share a belief state. Certainly, part of our motivation at first for positing belief states was to account for the sense of "believing the same thing" in which Hume and Heimson believe the same thing. But perhaps we can retreat from the claim that this requires them to be in *identical* belief states, holding instead that they are in states that are *similar* in some yet-to-be-specified way. We must retreat from the identity claim, if we are to retain the condition on belief states of *individuation*; for the sense in which Hume and Heimson believe the same thing in the original example is the same as the sense in which Heimson believes the same thing twice in our most recent version of the case.

So belief states must be more finely individuated than the "same things" agents like Hume and Heimson believe. It remains to give this finer principle of individuation. There are a number of moves the belief state theorist can make. The usual one (for good reason, I will argue) is to differentiate belief states, at least in the case of beliefs about objects, by the ways the agents think about the objects.

We must, at any rate, differentiate belief states at least finely enough so that beliefs that differ only in the way the agent thinks about a thing are assigned different belief states. For, first, where an agent can think about the same thing in two different ways (without recognizing that she is doing so), she can have two distinct beliefs about the thing, which we must, because of the criterion of *individuation*, assign different states. Heimson thinks about the *Treatise* in two ways. Correspondingly, there are two ways he can believe that he wrote the *Treatise*. Hume thinks about the book in just one way. There is a corresponding way he can, and does, believe that he wrote it. And, second, it is a central part of the intuitions motivating the positing of belief states that Heimson's two belief states differ *in that* they involve different ways of thinking about the *Treatise*. There is not some other, more subtle difference between the two public belief states Heimson is in that is *evidenced* by the different ways of thinking; the difference between the states *consists in* the difference between the two ways Heimson thinks about the *Treatise*. Ways of thinking are posited as explaining this difference. Agents in identical belief states must think about the relevant things in the same way. If we can equate the way Hume thinks about the book with one or the other of Heimson's ways of thinking about it, we would have our answer as to which belief state, if any, the two share.

The problem here is obvious: how are "ways of thinking" about a thing to be individuated? How can we decide if Hume's way of thinking about the *Treatise* is numerically identical to one of Heimson's? Since a difference in ways of thinking implies a difference in belief states, ways of thinking inherit requirements of publicity and locality: publicity, because if two agents can be in the same belief state, they must share ways of thinking; and locality, because if an agent's abandoning one belief can result in a change in her way of thinking about a thing, we cannot allow this change in turn to require that the agent abandons a host of other beliefs in a way that violates belief state locality. The trick, again, is to divide up the ways agents think about things in a way that keeps them public and locally individuable, while still making it impossible for an agent to count as thinking about a thing in a certain way twice over. For instance, it should be conceivable to identify Hume's way of thinking about the *Treatise* with one of Heimson's, but it must turn out impossible that the two ways Heimson thinks about the book are identical.

So we need to fill in the idea of a way of thinking about a thing. To start, we can observe that our intuitions about sameness and difference in the ways people think about things are driven to a great degree by comparisons of ascribed properties. Agents ascribe properties to the things they think about—they believe the individuals to have certain properties. Though it may be hard to say just what counts as the *same* way of thinking, there is a solid intuition that vast difference in ascribed properties is incompatible with identity in ways of thinking. Perhaps, then, we can individuate ways of thinking about things in terms of some or all of the properties agents associate with the thing.[4]

One move along these lines, related to Frege's theory of sense, is to suppose that to every way of thinking about a thing there corresponds a property, perhaps a complex one, that the agent believes to hold uniquely of that thing. Hume, for example, might associate the property of 'being my first major publication' with the *Treatise*—this corresponds to his single way of thinking about that book. Some of the problems with this view are familiar from the critical literature on Frege. For instance, it has been questioned whether agents must really have in mind a uniquely identifying property for a thing in order to be able to think about it.

But the decisive problem with individuating ways of thinking in terms of associated properties, I think, has nothing to do with uniqueness. The real trouble is that individuating a way of thinking about a thing in terms of properties the agent associates with *it* only manages to take the first step on the path to a fatally holistic regress. In order to individuate the way of thinking, we must first individuate the agent's ways of thinking about those associated properties, some of which surely will be *relational*—involving other individuals; to accomplish this feat of individuation, we need first to individuate the ways the agent thinks about these related individuals, and so on. This simple regress is the Achilles' heel of views that individuate ways of thinking in terms of ascribed properties.

To see the problem, consider the example from Frege's footnote in "On Sense and Reference." The property I associate with Aristotle may well be that of being Plato's best student. Suppose you also associate with Aristotle the property of being Plato's best student. Do we, then, think about Aristotle in the same way? That depends on how

---

4. Other candidates for accounts of ways of thinking are canvassed and condemned by Schiffer (1987). Those who part company with me at this stage of the dialectic should consult Schiffer's book. Schiffer takes his attack on ways of thinking (or really "modes of presentation") to argue against even the sort of view about belief that I take to be correct. But I think this is only because he mistakenly assumes that he has considered all plausible views in a certain class.

we think about Plato. Suppose I associate with Plato the property of being Socrates' best student, and you associate with Plato the property of being the author of *The Republic*. Might we nonetheless think about Aristotle in the same way? We cannot. For suppose I think there are two "Platos," and associate with 'the other Plato' the property of being the author of *The Republic*. Suppose also that I think there are two "Aristotles," to the second of which I attach the property of being (the second) Plato's most famous student. This generates a case in which I have *two* ways of thinking about Aristotle, which cannot *both* be identical to your way of thinking about him.

Surely, my second way of thinking about him—as the student of the author of *The Republic*—is more similar to yours. Can we go ahead and count it as identical to your way of thinking? The next move is predictable—we will have to ensure that we think about *The Republic* in the same way, if we are to prevent another case in which we mistakenly identify similar, but distinct, ways of thinking about Aristotle. And surely a notion of a "way of thinking" about things is of little use for individuating belief states if identifying such ways across agents requires precise agreement in the agents' beliefs about matters so far removed from the things in question. For this results in the impossibility of *publicity* except in cases of near global cognitive similarity.

Locality goes by the board as well. For clearly I can abandon my belief that Plato wrote *The Republic* without abandoning my belief that Aristotle wrote the *Metaphysics*. These beliefs of mine are indirectly connected, but they do not depend on each other for their very *identity*. We cannot allow my remaining in the belief state underlying my belief about Aristotle to *require* that I remain also in the belief state underlying my belief about Plato. (If these beliefs seem closely enough related to make this questionable, the reader need only imagine the regress carried two or three more stages.)

Note that this trouble confronts equally the view that a way of thinking about a thing is simply the entire conjunction of the properties the agent believes the object to have. Our beliefs about objects are so intertwined that this view would take a small change in my beliefs about a single thing to effect changes in the ways I think about a huge class of (what we would normally take to be) entirely unrelated things—and this entails that I lose all the belief states in which these ways of thinking figure. All that is needed are beliefs that relate a thing to a second thing, the second to a third, the third to a fourth, and so on. Views of way-of-thinking identity that require significant overlap in associated properties are in the same boat. It is not the number of properties required to be in common that causes trouble; the difficulty is in spelling out what it is for two ways of thinking about a thing to have any ascribed property in common. We cannot get the overlap view off the ground if we cannot explain just what it is about the two ways of thinking that must overlap.

Now, it is not unreasonable to suggest that the regress about individuating some ways of thinking in terms of others will stop at certain ways of thinking that may not be dependent on others in the way assumed by the argument, and so will eventually hit bedrock of some kind. Some possibilities for bedrock ways of thinking include indexical ways of thinking about oneself, the current time, and one's present location. We might suppose that, eventually, the regress about my way of thinking about Aristotle will "bottom out" when we come to relations to myself, or to the present time. Does this call the regress argument into question? I think not. Either the bottoming out will be quick or it will be far down the tree of regress. If far down the tree, the failures of locality and publicity will still occur. If quick (e.g., my way of thinking about Aristotle is as the person *I now* am remembering being referred to as 'Aristotle'), then the particular ways in which my two ways of thinking about Aristotle bottom out can be identical, giving us no way to distinguish these ways of thinking. The intuitions here *do* suggest that there may be some important kinds of belief that can usefully be thought of as involving repeatable, public states, as perhaps a belief that one is alone, or that it is dark now. But this fact will not save the view that there is a system of belief states that meet all the requirements we have placed on them.

The argument is worth a recap. If belief states are to individuate instances of believing in the way we want, we have to distinguish among belief states in which agents think about things in different ways. For the same reason, we have to distinguish among ways of thinking about a thing finely enough so that a difference in properties ascribed even to things quite removed from the thing in question can imply a difference in ways of thinking about the thing. But if we distinguish between belief states *this* finely, then we have violated *locality*, since we make one belief (that is, being in one belief state) contingent on other far-removed beliefs (being in other belief states)—we deny the obvious independence and separability of beliefs.

The argument depends on assuming each of the four adequacy criteria for an account of belief states. The criterion that plays the least obvious role is that of *explanation*, which imposes standards of intuitive similarity among identical belief states, or ways of thinking. For a view that violates *explanation*, consider the following theory of belief states: a belief state is, for some n, the state of retaining one's n-th belief, that is, of perpetuating the nth instance of believing one has become involved in. It is easy to verify that such "belief states" satisfy the other three requirements (if we grant that instances of believing can be temporally ordered). The obvious problem is that such states do not do the explanatory job that we want belief states for in the first place—not only do they not underlie the internal *facts* behind instances of believing, but they also do not explain our intuitions about an internal dimension of similarity among beliefs.

These arguments tell against the view that instances of believing can be internally individuated with a system of shareable belief states. It does not follow—and it is not true—that there are *no* instances of believing that usefully can be thought of as involving repeatable states. It is no doubt conceivable that there is, or might have been, a certain neural state such that, when any person is in that state, the person believes that it is raining then and there. It is conceivable even that there are complex systems of such states. And certainly there are important internal properties that are shared across different instances of believing. But as I have argued, it is not possible to classify and individuate all instances of believing with a system of independent and shareable belief *states*.

In order to retain the required individuative features of belief states, we must use identity criteria that are extremely holistic or *global*. Whether two instances of believing involve the same belief state, it turns out, must depend on whether, in those instances, the agents think about things in the same way. And satisfactory identity criteria for ways of thinking must reach far across an agent's belief corpus. But belief states are intended to have much more local individuating properties. They are supposed to be separable and independent from one another in a way that, given the above arguments, now seems to be impossible.

The local/global metaphor is apt. If we try to individuate beliefs

with criteria that compare only local features, we run the risk that there
may be "twin beliefs"—beliefs of a single agent at a single time that share
these local properties. In the same way, we can try to identify a city
or a drop of water using only its local features; but of course there can
be two cities, or two drops of waters, with all such features in common
(this is a point Kant makes in crticism of Leibniz). Ontologically, it is
obvious that cities and water drops are best looked at as nonrepeatable
concrete particulars, rather than as types or states. These arguments
about individuation suggest that the agent's internal contribution to
an instance of believing also should be taken to involve nonrepeatable
particulars, rather than simply shareable belief states.

In searching for a characterization of the notion of a belief state, I
suggest, we really have been conflating two projects. The first project
is to find a way to *individuate* instances of believing based on what is
in an agent's mind. The second project is to find a way of *classifying*
these internal contributions that accounts for our intuitions about internal similarities and differences between the beliefs of different agents.
That is, we wanted belief states to be, or to yield, types or properties of
what agents contribute—types or properties that are sufficiently fine for
individuating instances of believing. We had hoped that we could find
a way to classify these contributions that satisfied certain constraints—
for example, that no agent can have two "internal contributions" to
instances of believing that are classified by the same belief state. This
hope now seems unlikely to be realized; we cannot individuate and classify instances of believing in a way that satisfies all the requirements
for a plausible account of belief states. However, we have no reason to
hold in suspicion the idea of an internal contribution to an instance of
believing.

2.2   Cognitive Particulars

It is obvious that the agent's internal contribution to an instance of believing must depend on some aspects of the agent's cognitive situation.
But we have seen reason to doubt that there is a single typing of internal contributions fit to serve individuative and explanatory purposes.
This suggests that we should separate the task of internally individuating instances of believing from that of explaining internal dimensions

of similarity among the beliefs of different agents. If we do this, then internal contributions can be individuated in an *idiosyncratic* way— an agent's contribution to an instance of believing can be ontologically peculiar to the agent, or *agent-bound*, something that cannot even in principle literally be shared. If we do this, we can explain internal similarities among instances of believing simply by looking for similarities among the agents' idiosyncratic internal contributions.

One straightforward suggestion along these lines is to hold that what the agent contributes is a persisting concrete particular *belief*. While I doubt that this proposal is adequate to explain all instances of believing (because of the phenomenon of tacit believing), I will hold that in some cases, namely cases of *explicit* believing, an agent has a concrete particular belief and thereby believes a proposition. Beliefs of different agents, like those of Hume and Heimson, may be quite similar, but still they are *distinct* beliefs; one is Hume's, one is Heimson's. I will hold that beliefs, the internal contributions to instances of explicit believing, are *concrete particulars*. They are not shared, because they are not shareable. They can no more occur twice in an agent's belief corpus than a particular coin can occur twice in one's pocket.

I think that not only beliefs, but also "ways of thinking" should be explained as concrete cognitive particulars, namely as persisting *representations*. Heimson has two representations of the *Treatise*; neither is numerically identical to Hume's single representation of it, since representations are agent-bound particulars. If representations are agent-bound, then there can be states *involving* representations that are agent-bound as well—states such that there is only one agent who can be in them. In the next section, I will hold that tacitly believing a proposition is (at least in paradigmatic cases) a matter of being in such an agent-bound state, characterizable dispositionally in terms of actually existing representations.

To say that beliefs and representations are concrete particulars is just to say that they are neither abstract nor universal. It is of course not to say that they are chunks of grey matter or anything of the kind. There are plenty of kinds of causally robust entities—knots, ocean waves, utterances, epidemics and traditions, for instance—that are not simply masses of stuff, and just as certainly are neither abstract nor universal.[5]

---

5. I rely on philosophical common sense about the abstract/concrete and univer-

Concrete particularity in itself puts little constraint on what might, for all I have said, be a belief. Since I think beliefs might be, or might have been in a suitably designed system, kinds of particulars similar to many of those I have mentioned, this is the highest degree of constraint I so far see reason to accept as a starting point.

Of course there are cognitive particulars that are not beliefs, and so adopting the strategy of taking beliefs to be particulars opens the question of just which particulars they are (which is not answered by pointing out that they might have been many very different kinds of particular). The sort of answer I envision is the familiar functionalist schema (which, just as familiarly, I will not fill out in any detail): what is special to beliefs is a matter of their causal powers amid other cognitive particulars, states, faculties, and events. Beliefs are the things that have belief-ish causal powers, no doubt including characteristic effects on theoretical and practical reasoning. I will not here pursue questions about the correct form of a causal/functionalist explanation of beliefs.

Despite the strange sound of the slogan "beliefs are particulars," the idea is relatively common, at least as one side of a standard equivocation about the notion of a "mental state." Pain, for example, is often explained as a mental state, and yet we distinguish Jones's pain from Smith's pain. If pain is a state, and Jones and Smith are both in it, how can this distinction arise? Is Jones's pain something like the fact that Jones is in the state of pain (for this is different from the similar fact about Smith)? Clearly not, since Jones's pain can be stronger than Smith's—a comparison we cannot make between two facts. Nor is it plausible to hold that Jones's pain is the case of the property 'being-in-pain' holding of Jones, since, again, cases of a property holding, unlike pains, cannot be strong, throbbing, and so on. There are two distinct particular *events*, one in Jones and one in Smith, which are pains, one a stronger pain than the other. In virtue of the existence of those distinct events, Jones and Smith are at a certain time in the state of being in pain.

Some philosophers talk of mental state *tokens*, to be distinguished from mental state *types* (which, often, really are *states* that agents can be in). Mental state tokens are taken to be particulars: unrepeatable, un-

---

sal/particular distinctions, of which I do not want to assume any specific account, since I hope that my points will not rest on a specific account.

shareable things that belong to individuals. These are labeled "tokens" in analogy to sentence tokens, which are inscriptions or utterances of sentences. I have various reservations about this label, but of course I think the distinctions between mental states, types of mental particulars, and mental particulars is crucial.[6] The term "token" carries with it the unfortunate connotation that the thing is of some distinguished type, as an utterance is a token of some single sentence-type. It may be that there is some single, public type-classification of beliefs as natural and useful as syntactic typings of utterances, but I can see very little reason to suspect that there is.[7] Also, there can be a confusion between two notions of a token state: Jones's *being in pain*, and Jones's *pain*. For these reasons I prefer to speak of beliefs, representations, pains, and such as *cognitive particulars*.

Perhaps the notion of a cognitive particular can bear some explanation by analogy. Call a rope "overhanded" if it has an overhand knot on it. Then "being overhanded" is a state in the usual sense: many ropes can be overhanded, a rope can be overhanded at one time and not overhanded at another. Could we say all we want about knotted ropes using the language of overhandedness and similar terms for other kinds of knottedness? One thing that we could not do is get at the claim that a rope has *two* overhand knots on it. Nor could we express the claim that a rope has retained an overhand knot that was on it before. Imagine a rope with an overhand knot; a second knot is tied and then the first is untied. Throughout, the rope is overhanded, but it has not retained any particular overhand knot. The wording of the last sentence demonstrates the usefulness of the notion of a particular overhand knot. There is a sense in which an overhand knot is nothing more than a state

---

6. Field (1978) makes the distinctions between attributes of organisms at times, inner "occurrences," and types of these occurrences, each of which, he says, is often meant by the term "state." States, in my terminology, are attributes of the things in those states. And particular beliefs are "internal" entities, like Field's inner occurrences. None of my arguments about belief-states depends on their being states rather than just "types of inner occurrences," "modes of presentation," or "ways of believing." The arguments demonstrate that no system of such types, modes, or ways would be able to individuate beliefs completely, correctly, publicly, and locally, in the ways required of belief states.

7. I think there probably is a natural useful structural typing of the "ideational" (conceptually articulated) beliefs of any one individual (which I discuss in chapter 4), but not of beliefs in general.

of the rope; given the rope and its total state over time, there is nothing "more" to the existence of the knot. But, still, a knot is a particular. It is not repeatable, it is created and can perish, and there can be many knots on a rope. A belief, a representation, a pain, or any concrete cognitive particular is like a knot.

I will leave for the next chapter issues about the structure and constituents of explicit beliefs. There, I will hold that (at least many) beliefs are structured entities that have as constituents concrete particular representations of things and relations.

If we hold that beliefs are concrete particulars (and presuppose an account of their individuation), the solution to the problem of individuating instances of *explicit* believing is simple. A case of explicit believing is one in which an agent has a belief and thereby believes a proposition. We can accept the distinction between the agent's contribution to an instance of believing and the content of the belief, and claim that the internal contribution in these cases is simply the agent's concrete, particular belief. As a set of individuating parameters for instances of explicit believing, we can take the agent, a time, the agent's belief, and the content of that belief (at that time). Thus, we are committed to the claim that there are not two co-possible instances of believing involving the same agent, time, belief and content. Certainly, none of the puzzling examples in the literature on belief puts this claim in jeopardy. And, if there *are* such things as particular beliefs, this would seem to be a pretty safe claim.

We can posit the relation $Believes_E(a, t, p, b)$. This relation holds if there is an instance of explicit believing involving agent a at time t, and a belief b of a, with the content p at t. Wherever there is an agent with a belief that has content, there is an instance of explicit believing. So we have the following equivalence:

$$Believes_E(a, t, p, b) \Leftrightarrow BeliefOf(b, a, t) \ \& \ ContentOf(p, b, t).$$

It is an equivalence, because, where there is not a belief, there is not a case of explicit believing, and where there is a belief without any content, where there is nothing believed, there also is no instance of explicit believing (a decision on this last point seems somewhat arbitrary; I return to this in chapter 6).

I do not mean to claim that $Believes_E$ is *the* belief relation, or the relation at the bottom of the phenomenon of belief, or anything of the sort. I suggest only that it is a relation and that instances of its holding correspond one-to-one to instances of explicit believing.

2.3   Tacit Belief

It sometimes is supposed that the fact of tacit belief must be a stumbling block for any theory of beliefs that takes them to be concrete cognitive particulars. Indeed, there is reason for concern about tacit belief. However, I think that the phenomenon can be adequately handled in a representationalist account of belief (and some aspects of it can, I think, be handled *only* in a representationalist account). I will argue for this point in presenting a view on which there are instances of tacit believing, but on which these do not involve particular beliefs.

Do you, or did you before I raised the question, believe that station wagons are inedible? This example (John Searle's) is a typical case in which there is a proposition—call it a *tacit commitment*—such that it would at least be extremely odd to claim that the agent in question does not believe it, but is also such that it is implausible to suppose that the agent has an internal entity with causal powers appropriate to an explicit belief in it.

The problem of tacit belief arises out of the conflict among the following three principles:

1.   Belief reports of the form '*A* believes that *s*', where *s* expresses one of *A*'s tacit commitments, are *true*.

2.   The truth of a belief report of that form requires that the agent have a particular, concrete belief with content p, where p is the proposition expressed by *s*.

3.   Agents do not have particular, concrete *beliefs* with tacit commitments as their contents.

I will hold that belief reports do not have the simple analysis required by the second principle—that the truth of a report does not always require an agent to have a concrete, particular belief with the specified content. Nonetheless, I will also hold, all believing is definitionally dependent on explicit believing, in that all belief reports are to be analyzed as claims indirectly about explicit believing. This idea is not in the least unusual in treating tacit belief; it is standard to explain tacit belief in terms of hypothetical explicit beliefs. But I hope my specific version of the strategy avoids some difficulties encountered by the two accounts most frequently offered in the literature, which I will discuss soon.

A key move in the two accounts I will consider—the *formation-dispositional* and *simple-consequence* accounts—as well as in my alternative, is to distinguish believing from having beliefs, in the sense of 'beliefs' on which they are mental entities rather than propositional contents of belief. True belief reports, on these views, do not always require an agent to have a belief with the specified propositional content. There are at least two reasons to think this distinction is plausible apart from any particular theory of tacit belief.

First, we can draw support from ordinary usage. Even if we think it is not odd to claim that you believe that station wagons are inedible, it clearly is odd to claim that you have *a belief*, or a *firm* belief, or that you have long had a belief, to the effect that station wagons are inedible. All the uses of 'belief' that plausibly attach to mental entities—including claims about their formation, their intensity, and what they cause one to do—seem out of place in talking about tacitly believed propositions. If we can make sense of them, it is only by roundabout readings on which they are claims about what is believed.

Second, a plausible view of cases of absentmindedness treats them as involving agents who have certain explicit beliefs, but who do not at the time believe their propositional contents. When I put my wristwatch in my coat pocket, I may form an explicit belief that the watch is there, but minutes later neglect that belief in my reasoning. While I am searching for the watch, it seems true to say of me that I do not believe the watch is in my coat pocket, despite my having retained an explicit belief in the proposition. (Actually, there are yes-and-no intuitions about such reports; I will return to this.) In contrast, it seems clearly true to say that, in this example, I have all along had a belief that the watch is in my coat pocket, and that I have neglected my belief during the search. Cases of unconscious belief may also give yes-and-no intuitions about whether the agent believes something, along with firmer intuitions that the agent has a belief.

Apparently, then, we often do distinguish between possessing a cognitive entity properly called a belief and simply believing something. If so, the semantics of 'A believes that s' ought not to require for its truth that A have a *belief* with the specified content.

An important attraction of explaining tacit believing in terms of hypothetical explicit beliefs stems from the fact that treating tacit belief simply by speaking of believing *propositions* is really too simple. For surely one can tacitly believe a proposition in one *way* but not in another. For instance, Quine's Tom tacitly believes that Cicero wore togas but not that Tully wore togas. Thus it is plausible that instances of believing— cases of at least tacitly believing a proposition—will be individuated by not merely an agent, a time, and a proposition, but also a "way of believing." Different way of believing, different case of tacit belief.

I have argued that the right way to discriminate among ways of believing a proposition is in terms of the ways the agent thinks about the individuals, properties and relations it is about, and that the right way to explain ways of thinking of individuals, properties and relations is not in terms of shareable, abstract objects like intensions or descriptive senses, but in terms of unshareable particulars: persisting representations. If this is right, then a case of tacit believing can be underspecified unless we indicate not only the agent, time and proposition believed, but also which of the agent's representations must represent which constituents of the proposition. In the example, the two ways in which Tom might believe that Cicero wore togas differ exactly in which of Tom's *actual* representations of Cicero are involved in them. Here, the individuation of instances of tacit believing is driven in part by the explicit concrete cognitive structures to which they are tied. So, if I am right about how ways of believing are individuated, then even though tacit beliefs are not directly encoded in concrete structures themselves, they can be individuated by such things—such things are internally involved in them. We need a theory of concrete representations to individuate tacit beliefs, as well explicit ones.

Now, it is possible to honor this observation in an account that does not focus on explicit beliefs. One way of individuating tacit beliefs by the representations involved in them would be to posit abstract structured entities that contain an agent's real representations, and treat believing as involving a relation to these abstract things (as in Richard 1990). If Tom's two representations of Cicero are ρ_C and ρ_T, and his representation of the relation of being more famous than is ρ_F, then we can classify Tom's tacit belief that Cicero is more famous than Tully with an abstract structured object that we might depict as follows:

$(\rho_F; \rho_C, \rho_T)$.

(I call such abstract structures *thought maps*; I will discuss them in more detail in chapter 4). If he is belief-related to this thought map, Tom believes that Cicero is more famous than Cicero, in the way he would express by saying 'Cicero is more famous than Tully'.

But of course to note that instances of at-least-tacitly believing can be individuated by such structured abstract objects is not to explain why. Why should believing be explicable as a relation to arbitrarily complex, abstract entities containing an agent's representations? The hypothetical-belief proponent has an answer: an instance of believing can be viewed as a relation to an abstract structure containing representations because believing is to be explained in terms of a hypothetical *concrete* entity of the same structure, with the same constituents. The abstract structures are structural types of explicit beliefs—they map out the structure and constituents of a hypothetical explicit belief.

To a way of believing, then, there corresponds a thought map, which determines the property that an explicit belief must have to qualify the agent as believing something in that way. The thought map that "maps" a particular belief specifies the logical arrangement within it of the agent's representations of individuals and relations. We can therefore extend the relation,

$Believes_E(a, t, p, \tau)$,

to hold of an agent, a time, a proposition p and a thought map τ, just in case at that time the agent has an explicit belief with content p, that is mapped by τ.

The strategy of individuating an instance of tacit belief (in some cases) by a structural feature (a map) of a hypothetical explicit belief allows for a clear connection between tacit and explicit believing, and gives the individuative role of thought maps an obvious source.

How, then, do belief reports work, given that they can be satisfied either by cases of explicit believing (having an explicit belief) or by cases of tacit believing? To put off until later the difficult questions about how and to what extent ways of believing (thought maps) are specified or constrained in belief reports, assume for now that we are concerned with claims to the effect that an agent believes a proposition in a specified way (according to a specified map).

Formation-dispositional accounts explain tacit believing in terms of hypothetical explicit beliefs in the following way: A believes p (in way τ) iff, if it were the case that such-and-such, then A would have an explicit belief that p (of type τ). Despite the attractions of such accounts, they have not met with much success. As Audi, Stalnaker, Lycan, and others have pointed out, the most natural ways of filling in the "such-and-such" clause lead to analyses that are vulnerable to clear counterexamples. One popular candidate for that clause is 'A considers whether p (in way τ)'. But the resulting account gives neither necessary nor sufficient conditions for believing, as can be seen from the following kinds of examples:

- *Obvious discoveries:* You probably did not believe that the question 'Do geese see God?' is a palindrome, but you have been disposed to believe it explicitly on consideration. Similarly, consider Audi's 1982 case of an excited speaker's attitude toward the proposition that he is talking too loudly. Such examples can easily be multiplied.

- *Obvious refutations:* I tacitly believe that it is still possible to get to the plane before it leaves (I am blithely packing); but, on consideration, I am disposed to form very quickly a belief that it is *not* still possible to get there (I "put together" some beliefs about the current time and the takeoff time).

- *The opinionated man:* (Lycan 1986) This man forms firm opinions, when considering a proposition that he antecedently neither believes nor disbelieves, on the basis of irrelevant features of his cognitive state. For example, if he is hungry, he comes to believe it, otherwise he disbelieves it.

I will make no attempt to canvass possible emendations of the formation-dispositional account. Possible approaches include constraining the circumstances in which the agent considers the proposition (see Dummett 1973, 285–288), moving to some kind of circumstance other than considering, and constraining the "categorical basis" of the disposition (see Lycan 1986 for a critical examination of such a move). While these avenues are worth pursuing, the examples seem to me to point to a clear distinction between tacitly believing—which is *actually* believing something—and merely being disposed to believe it.

Certainly there are muddy intuitions in some cases about whether we have believed something all along or merely have been disposed to believe it when asked. Some of these intuitions are forcefully pushed by Audi (1982), who takes them to suggest that, strictly speaking, we do not believe what many philosophers claim we believe merely tacitly. This skeptical view has been defended as a commonsense principle by Stich (1982, 158) and with realism about beliefs in mind by Sterelny (1990, 163). While I think this line is to some extent defensible (the analogy to indirect speech reports is useful in its defense), in the end it is implausible if tacit belief may for all we know be the normal case of what we usually report as believing. In any event, we need a theory of our reporting practices, and the skeptical view leaves that task undone, since the things we are comfortable in reporting as believed seem to go beyond what we believe explicitly and appear not to be adequately characterized as the things we are disposed to believe.

The second popular account requires that an at-least-tacit belief be a *simple consequence* of the agent's explicit beliefs:[8] *A* believes p (in way τ) iff p (as thought of in way τ) is a simple consequence of *A*'s explicit beliefs.

A distinctive problem with the account (similar to one pointed out in Lycan 1986) involves one reason that some tacit commitments, like mine that I have never eaten a bicycle (well, it was tacit a moment ago), are not likely to be standardly *logical* consequences of explicit beliefs: it seems likely that all my explicit beliefs could have been true while the proposition that I have never eaten a bicycle was false. When I consider this proposition, I come explicitly to believe it in large part because of my *lack* of a belief to the contrary, and the belief (whether tacit or

---

8. See Field 1978 (83), Dennett 1987a (216) and, less seriously, Dennett 1987b (45). Actually, both Dennett and Field mix in a little of the formation-dispositional account. In the earlier paper, as Lycan notes, Dennett can be seen as proposing (if only for the sake of argument) a formation-dispositional account, with a constrained categorical basis: he focuses on the consequences of explicit belief drawn by a supposed "extrapolator-deducer mechanism" in the mind. In the later paper he distinguishes "implicit" beliefs, which are consequences of explicit ones, and "potentially explicit" ones, which are consequences that may actually be drawn.

explicit) that I would remember such an achievement. Lacks of belief
do not standardly show up in logical derivations from beliefs.[9]

Now, the specific problem about lacks of belief may be met with an
only slightly nonstandard notion of consequence, since after all lacks of
explicit belief supervene on what explicit beliefs one has. But there is a
deeper problem about taking tacit believing to supervene on explicit believing, as would be required by familiar notions of consequence. It seems
quite possible that many tacit beliefs depend on cognitive states and
structures other than explicit beliefs (on what are called "subdoxastic
states" in Stich 1978); straightforward versions of the simple-consequence
view are committed to denying this, and so may undergenerate tacit beliefs. There may be some agent-relative notion of consequence on which
the simple consequences of one's explicit beliefs do not supervene on
them, but the only plausible candidates I know of treat consequences
in the formation-dispositional way—as explicit beliefs that would be
formed in such-and-such circumstances. We have seen that this leads to
an unsatisfactory account of tacit belief.

If we adopt an intuitive understanding of "simple consequence," as
well of what explicit beliefs one has, then it seems the simple-consequence
account is also bothered by many cases of obvious discovery and refutation; in these cases there are trivial consequences of our explicit beliefs
that we clearly do not believe in advance of *drawing* the consequences.
In this way, the view also overgenerates beliefs. All told, this view, like
the formation-dispositional account, seems to get wrong the sense in
which tacit beliefs are there all along.

A final problem with taking tacit belief to amount to simple consequence or potential belief is that the tacit/explicit distinction is applica-
ble not only to belief but to other attitudes as well. Nonexplicit desires,
suspicions, doubts, hopes and statements are not plausibly treated as
attitudes that are simple consequences of explicit attitudes, nor as dis-

9. This example is clearly handled better by the formation-dispositional account.
But Lycan takes a similar case—a belief that Omaha was not nuked in 1979—to
count *against* a formation-dispositional account, since it seems likely that we do not
store premises that would entail this proposition. But all one needs is a disposition
to believe that one does not believe the contrary, plus the obvious belief that one
would know it if it were true, or at least a belief-forming mechanism sensitive to these
facts.

positions to form attitudes (since there seems to be no situation related to, say, explicit hopes, in the way consideration is related to beliefs).

My proposal is this:

A believes p (in way τ) just in case   (1)

   it is as if A has an explicit belief in p (mapped by τ).

Tacit beliefs, on this view, are explicit beliefs present not potentially or by implication, but *virtually*, or *in effect*. I will refer to this as the *virtual-belief* account.[10] This is only the beginning of an analysis, since it involves a phrase ('it is as if') whose interpretation ordinarily depends heavily on contextual cues, including facts about what is relevant to the purposes of the surrounding statement. In general, a statement that it is as if such-and-such, expresses a claim to the effect that a relevant actual situation is relevantly like relevant hypothetical situations in which such-and-such is the case. So the correctness of (1) as a first step turns on both (i) whether the claims that ordinary belief reports express can correctly be analyzed as comparisons of actual and hypothetical situations, and (ii) whether the determination of just which situations and respects of comparison are invoked in these claims exhibits the patterns of context sensitivity that are characteristic of as-if claims.

As a start toward filling in (1), I suggest that the relevant comparisons in paradigmatic belief reports have to do with cognitive dispositions, by which I mean dispositions to have particular attitudes and emotions in various circumstances. I limit this claim to paradigmatic belief reports because I think it is an important advantage of the virtual-belief account that it can explain examples of "looser" belief reports in which there are no dispositions relating to explicit attitudes to be found. By "looser" belief reports I mean a class of reports that can be quite natural, but which we hesitate to take fully seriously. These include

---

10. I suspect this idea has been on the tip of many tongues. For instance, Dennett occasionally uses 'virtual belief' when talking about nonexplicit beliefs (1987a, 56), but when he carefully explores ways of making such a contrast, he finds only dispositional and simple-consequence accounts (Dennett 1978, 45–46; Dennett 1987b, 216–217). Field (1978), as well, writes as though he has something like this in mind, while giving his simple-consequence account. I have not seen the account explicitly offered or considered in the literature (though it has tacitly been dismissed countless times!).

reports about the beliefs of lower animals and artifacts, as well as our own "tacit knowledge" of principles of biophysics and English syntax.

Cognitive dispositions include what we may call reasoning dispositions—dispositions to form beliefs and intentions and to attempt actions (in various circumstances)—and also dispositions to emotions such as boredom and surprise.[11] It should not seem outlandish to propose that typically when we claim that it is as if A has an explicit belief that p, we mean that A's cognitive dispositions are relevantly as they would be if she had such a belief. After all, it is clear that on any plausible account of explicit beliefs there will be especially tight connections between having a certain explicit belief and having certain cognitive dispositions. It is clear as well that our interest in what people believe typically involves an interest in what they are disposed to conclude, decide, feel and do. So I propose that in paradigmatic cases the following is a contextually appropriate paraphrase of 'it is as if A has an explicit belief that p' (and hence of 'A at-least tacitly believes that p'):

A's cognitive dispositions are relevantly as if A has an   (2)

   explicit belief in p (mapped by τ).

This leaves open questions about which actual and hypothetical cognitive dispositions we are to compare, and in what respects we are to compare them, since (2) is itself a context-sensitive as-if statement. I will not be able to answer these questions in any detail here, but I want to show that even a broadly drawn virtual-belief account of the kind suggested by (1) and (2) is genuinely different from the formation-dispositional and simple-consequence accounts, and to suggest that as a general approach to tacit believing it is prima facie more plausible than the others, and so is particularly worth developing carefully. It will be useful to look at a few examples, including some that are troublesome for the other accounts, while taking (2) simply at face value.

You believed, before I brought it up, that station wagons are inedible, because having an explicit belief to that effect (as you perhaps have now) would have made (and will make) no relevant difference to your

---

11. John Bennett pointed out to me that since dispositions to have emotions like surprise are especially relevant to questions about belief, there is no good reason to think we normally focus only on reasoning dispositions in deciding questions about at-least-tacit belief.

dispositions to believe, decide, feel and do things. The same holds for my tacit belief that I have never eaten a bicycle. I may have an explicit belief to that effect now, but aside from (irrelevant) reasonings about what explicit beliefs I have, the cognitive difference explicitness makes will be nil. You do not tacitly believe that Shakespeare had eleven toes, since having an explicit belief to that effect would alter your reasoning in a (clearly relevant) situation in which you are asked for the number of his toes.

In the case of an obvious discovery, there is a difference to one's reasoning dispositions before and after the discovery. For instance, not before, but only after considering the proposition that he is talking too loudly, the speaker will reach relevant decisions (say, to quiet down) to which he would be disposed by an explicit belief that he is talking too loudly. And the speaker's disposition to be surprised at the claim that he has been talking too loudly vanishes after he considers the proposition. So a virtual-belief account does not entail that he tacitly believes that he is talking too loudly. Instead, since before the discovery he has only cognitive dispositions of the kind to which he would be disposed by an explicit belief that he is *not* talking too loudly, the account entails that he believes he is not talking too loudly.[12] If I relate the episode to someone who was not present, saying, "He believed that he was not talking too loudly; so he was surprised to see our hands over our ears," I speak the truth.

These examples demonstrate the broad plausibility of a virtual-belief account, and also reveal some details that need attention. Certainly we cannot assess whether the account may ultimately be satisfactory until it is made more precise than in (2). This would mean at least spelling out more carefully what "cognitive dispositions" come to, and how it is determined which circumstances and which respects of similarity are relevant to the truth of the comparison of actual and counterfactual cognitive dispositions. A satisfactory account of cognitive dispositions may require a fuller explanation of the characteristic

---

12. Of course, to *report* that he believes that he is not talking too loudly might in certain circumstances be misleading, but that is nothing unusual. Owing to the conversational presumption of relevance, the speaker of an obviously true belief report can implicate that the alleged belief is a *considered* belief: "Smith believes that the Earth has existed for more than 130 years." To cancel this implication we use 'takes for granted' or 'presupposes' instead of 'believes' (cf. Stalnaker 1984, 68).

cognitive role of an explicit belief. But in explaining typical cases of tacit belief, the level of detail I have already given about what cognitive dispositions come to seems sufficient: the virtual-belief account requires for tacit believing at least that (in the relevant situations) the agent has similar dispositions toward decisions, emotions, conclusions, and actions as those he would have given an explicit belief.

What cannot be left at the present level of detail, however, are the considerations about relevance. For while (2) is plausible when the interpretation of 'relevantly' is left to untutored intuition, there is the question whether too much of the plausibility comes from unexplained concepts that drive our judgments of relevance. More specifically, a virtual-belief account needs to overcome objections of this sort: for all we have said (2) may be a trivially correct analysis, because the relevant respect of similarity (between actual dispositions and dispositions given the explicit belief) can simply be this: in both cases A has dispositions that suffice for believing that p. And since understanding *that* respect of similarity requires a prior understanding of what cognitive dispositions suffice for believing, we have not explained what believing is, but have merely said that it depends on cognitive dispositions (which is perhaps less than ambitious).

Now, while it is possible to understand (2) in the unhelpful way the hypothetical objector fears, I doubt that this understanding of it explains even its initial plausibility as an analysis of tacit believing. But the objection does point to the need for explanations—that do not "viciously" presuppose the concept of tacit belief—of how the parameters relevant to relevance are determined in typical belief reports. My hope, of course, is that such explanations can be given for all aspects of relevance in all belief reports; I think I can show that they can be given for many. My strategy will be to propose some guidelines about relevance, and to motivate them from considerations *not* about what is needed for believing, but about what kinds of similarities (between actual dispositions and dispositions given an explicit belief) we typically have reason to allege.

Let's start with an example of what must be a nearly universal restriction on relevance. If explicit beliefs are salient players in cognitive processes, then it is obvious that in any situation in which a hypothetical explicit belief would come into play, its presence or absence will make *some* differences to cognitive processes. And so it is obvious that we would rarely or never have reason to claim that, while lacking a certain explicit belief, the agent's cognitive processes in situations in which such a belief would come into play are in all respects exactly as they would be if the agent had such a belief. So clearly in claiming that the agent's cognitive dispositions are as they would be if she had an explicit belief, we normally would not mean to allege detailed similarities of cognitive processes, but more rough and ready similarities—such as similarities in decisions and conclusions reached, in emotions had, in the broad *upshots* of cognitive processes.

Consider another plausibly universal guideline: we cannot typically require that reasoning dispositions be just as they would be, given an explicit belief, in situations in which the object of reasoning concerns such things as explicitness of beliefs and facts about which propositions the agent has considered. For naturally a tacit believer that p can be disposed to reason differently from an explicit believer that p when considering questions about whether she has considered or has explicitly believed that p. I suggest that this restriction on relevance arises from the fact that we are never interested in claiming that an agent's cognitive dispositions are so amazingly similar to how they would be given an explicit belief, that, for example, the agent herself is disposed to believe on consideration that she *has* all along had such an explicit belief. In general, it seems, we do not require similarities of cognitive dispositions that involve *second-order* attitudes that are about the hypothetical explicit belief.

A disposition is a disposition for something to be the case (call this the outcome) in some kind of situation (call this the trigger situation). What kinds of trigger situation would we typically be concerned with in comparing cognitive dispositions with and without a hypothetical belief? Since it is clear that an agent's cognitive dispositions depend on her explicit attitudes and on other "internal" aspects of her cognitive situation, we must consider only situations in which the internals of the agent's cognitive situation—including the agent's actual explicit beliefs—are relevantly similar to the actual situation. It is actually as if I explicitly believe that I have never eaten a bicycle, and this fact surely does not hinge on what would be the case if I were to lose many of my memories about what I have done and about what is edible, nor does it hinge on what would happen if screws came loose. The source of this kind of restriction is familiar: the dispositions we mean to characterize in a belief report have their grounding (or "categorical basis") in the internals of the agent's cognitive situation, so of course the trigger situations for the dispositions must be compatible with the *existence* of their categorical basis. The same thing goes on when we say that a piece of wood is fragile—we mean that it is disposed to break in situations in which it is hit, but we exclude from relevance situations in which the wood has been reinforced with steel bars. Why? Because that would obviously threaten the categorical basis of the disposition we mean to describe. No doubt there are subtle questions about just how, in attributing a disposition, we manage to restrict attention to trigger situations compatible with the categorical basis of the disposition we mean to ascribe, especially in cases in which we cannot (as perhaps we can in the wood case) simply insist that in all relevant trigger situations the subject be internally just as it in fact is. The difficulty, if it is one, affects lots of ordinary talk about dispositions; I see no reason to think that it presents a special problem for the virtual-belief account.

So much for trigger situations we must exclude in considering whether the agent is disposed to reason as if he has an explicit belief. We need to include a variety of situations in which an explicit belief of the kind in question normally would come into play—even if such situations are not likely to arise. So for one thing we do not consider only situations in which the agent is unconscious. Also, in assessing whether you believe that Shakespeare had eleven toes, it will not do to point out that, since no situation is likely to arise in which an explicit belief in that proposition would come into play, you are disposed to reason just as if you had such a belief. This puts some importance on the notion of a reasoning situation in which an explicit belief normally would come into play. Certainly, these include ones in which the agent considers the proposition—this surely is behind the initial plausibility of formation-dispositional accounts. But situations of considering are not *always* relevant trigger situations, since they may be eliminated from relevance by the restriction to situations compatible with the categorical basis of the dispositions in question. In cases of obvious refutation, it is clear that the dispositions that make for the fact of believing hinge on the agent's *not* considering the proposition. Their categorical basis is incompatible with the agent considering the proposition. Luckily, situations of considering are not the only relevant trigger situations. Which other situations are such that in them the explicit belief normally would come into play depends on the agent's other attitudes. Perhaps a plausible generalization is that a situation is one in which an explicit belief normally would come into play, if for at least one of the alternative decisions or conclusions open to the agent in that situation, the belief would have to be neglected or suspended if the agent were to take that option. A more careful statement of this would require a fuller account than I am able to offer of explicit beliefs and their role in cognition.

I will stop here with general considerations about relevance; as I said, I expect that there is a lot of interesting complexity below the surface that we have been grazing. But we now have some reasonable preliminary guidelines for what normally counts as relevant in assessing whether someone is cognitively disposed as if he has an explicit belief. Certainly, a given context may provide further restrictions on relevant situations, or on relevant aspects of comparison. The point is that reasonable guidelines seem to follow from the right sorts of consideration— about what kinds of similarity we typically have reason to allege. If the virtual-belief account is on the right track, then the task of explaining what believing is becomes the project of giving a systematic characterization of the mechanisms that determine relevant dimensions of comparison.

We can define, in detailing a virtual-belief account of paradigmatic belief reports, a technical concept $Believes(a, t, p, \tau)$ (read, a agent at least tacitly believes a proposition p at t in the way characterized by thought map τ) as follows:

$Believes(a, t, p, \tau)$ iff a is disposed cognitively as if

$Believes_E(a, t, p, \tau)$.

Like ordinary "as-if" claims, this definition of $Believes$ is vague and context sensitive in various ways (this is why I have said say that the definition is not of a relation but of a technical concept). There is vagueness traceable to at least two origins: vagueness about whether an agent would or would not reason in a certain way when faced with a given kind of situation, and vagueness about which situations are relevant in assessing whether having an explicit belief would make a difference. To show that these kinds of vagueness are appropriate in the definition, it suffices to point to examples of belief claims with unclear or indeterminate truth values, where the indeterminacy is traceable to the two sources I have described. It has often been noted that, while we are comfortable saying that an agent tacitly believes many simple consequences of his explicit beliefs, we get less comfortable as the consequences get more remote, and this results in indeterminate statements halfway down the slippery slope.[13] My explanation for this is that (i) it is sometimes not determinate whether an agent, when confronted with a situation of some kind where such a consequence would clearly be relevant, would deduce that consequence (in part because this can depend on minute differences in fatigue, emotional state, and so on)—or is otherwise disposed appropriately to a belief in it, and (ii) in delimiting the situations we must consider in comparing the agent's reasoning with and without an explicit belief, we make a vague allowance of *some* time for inference-like processes (perhaps on the order of magnitude of the time needed to "retrieve" an explicit belief), but not too much.

The vagueness, then, is appropriate; but so also is the interest sensitivity brought in by the restriction to relevant situations. Cases of absentmindedness make this clear.

Suppose I have consciously formed an explicit belief that I have put my watch in my pocket, and suppose that a few minutes later I neglect that belief while searching for the watch. I take it that there are divided pre-theoretic intuitions on the question whether, when searching elsewhere, I believe that the watch is in my pocket. The presence of the neglected explicit belief may appear decisive on the virtual-belief account—if there *is* a belief, then of course it is *as if* there is a belief. This does show that the account explains one side of the divided intuition, which is strongest in a report such as 'Although it did not come to me at the time, I knew that the watch was in my pocket'. Here, a situation relevant to assessing my cognitive dispositions must be like the actual one with respect to my neglecting various beliefs at the time the situation arises.[14]

---

13. The vagueness is pointed out in Dummett 1973 (285–288) and defended as appropriate in Field 1978.

14. In this example, I have also a "tacit neglected belief" that the watch is on my person, since I am disposed to reason as I would if I had an explicit neglected belief to that effect—a belief that would cease to be neglected if I were to consider seriously whether the watch is on my person. I am indebted to discussions of such cases with Richard Feldman and Bob Pasnau, who pointed out difficulties in the way I had been explaining them.

But if the explicit belief is not functioning in reasoning like a normal explicit belief, then there is a clear sense in which, despite having it, I am *not* disposed to reason as if I have an explicit belief. In searching for my watch, I am not disposed to reason as I would if I had an explicit belief in a situation in which it functions normally. The intuition that I do not believe that it is in my pocket is strongest in a report explaining my actions, such as 'While searching for my watch, I believed it was in my pocket', which seems false. In taking the report to be false, we consider situations in which the hypothetical explicit belief functions normally, and notice that in such situations I would not search for the watch. Which situations are relevant in a given context depends on our interests—in particular, on whether we are concerned with the explanation of my search or with what information is within reach of relevant prompting. Despite the explicit belief, the relevance restriction allows the virtual-belief account to capture the yes-and-no intuition. I have made and "stored" an explicit judgment that the watch is in my pocket, so *of course* I believe it; but I am looking around to find the watch, so *of course* I do not believe it.

Though this approach to at-least-tacitly-believing certainly needs further development, it seems promising enough that it is reasonable for us to proceed on the assumption that tacit belief is not inexplicable for accounts that explain believing primarily in terms of concrete cognitive particulars.[15] But I want to emphasize that much about the virtual-belief account is not crucial to the central task of this book. If the reader rejects the particular account, but agrees that instances of tacit believing must in paradigmatic cases be individuated by reference to hypothetical explicit beliefs (which themselves can be characterized by the concrete representations they involve), or indeed by reference merely to thought maps, then she will want to replace my definition of *Believes* with a relation sensitive to the same parameters. The use of this relation in what follows will not, I suspect, turn on the details that separate this reader's view from my own.

Since representations have been implicated as central individuating parameters of instances of believing, just what they are, and how they are "involved" in beliefs, certainly needs clarifying. That is the task of the next two chapters.

---

15. I expand the ideas of this section in Crimmins 1992c.

3 Ideational Belief

My belief that Ockham was a metaphysician is a belief about an individual and, in a sense, about a property. If I were asked to list facts about Ockham, I would include his being a metaphysician. If I were asked to list metaphysicians, I would include Ockham. Though there may be other sorts of belief that are in other ways about things and properties, my belief about Ockham is of the common sort that involves *persisting representations*. The belief involves two representations: my representation of Ockham, and my representation of the property of being a metaphysician. Beliefs that involve representations of things, properties and relations—beliefs that are "conceptually articulated"—I call *ideational beliefs*. Among the representations that figure in ideational beliefs, I will call the representations of things *notions*, and the representations of properties and relations, *ideas*.

The considered philosophical view that thought involves representations of things and relations is as old as Plato's *Theatetus* and has in one version or another been held by more philosophers than almost any other position. However, even though evidence from cognitive science has lent the view a new scientific respectability, philosophical support for "representationalism" is not universal. Many philosophers have doubts that the simple, commonsensical picture of the mind could really cut at the joints what must after all be complex, neural phenomena. I have no intention of presenting this debate here, much less of entering into it (a good introduction to recent discussion of representationalism is Sterelny 1990). Instead, I will assume that it is prima facie plausible that many of our beliefs contain representations of individuals and relations. In this chapter, I will discuss a number of issues about ideational beliefs that I see as particularly relevant to belief reports. I intend many of the simpler points I make about ideational belief to be aspects of common sense that are supported foundationally by recent work in the philosophy of intentionality, and empirically by work in cognitive psychology. Those who question this foundational and empirical support can nonetheless agree that what I say is grounded in common sense—and on that basis alone they might be able to stomach the use of the account in the semantics for belief reports (we need not be realists about ghosts or holes or debts to agree that ordinary folk sometimes quantify over them).

After sketching the essentials of a plausible account of notions and ideas, I will enter into controversial terrain. First, I will explain how I take the considerations of the last chapter to support the non-shareability of notions and ideas as well as beliefs. Second, I will address the question of a notion's content: how is it settled just which individual a notion is *of*? Third, I will distinguish two sorts of questions: on the one hand, questions of cognitive access, about what things and relations given notions and ideas are *of*; and on the other, questions of cognitive grasp, about what it takes to have a concept, or to know who or what an individual is. These are of course central issues for any representational account of cognition, but their special relevance for my project owes to their connection to a version of the problem of other minds: to what extent can we have cognitive access to other agents' representations? I will hold that on a plausible account of what it takes to think about something, we are typically in a very good position to think (and to talk) about each other's representations.

3.1 Ideas and Notions

I will start with a brief credo concerning basic features of ideas and notions that can plausibly be attributed to our commonsense picture of thought.

The representations that are involved in ideational beliefs are cognitive tools; they enable agents to form multiple beliefs, desires and intentions that are *about* the same things and relations. Beliefs that involve representations are about things and relations because they involve notions and ideas that are notions and ideas *of* those things and relations. Different beliefs can be about the same thing or relation in virtue of sharing the same representation. Representations are cognitively mobile— they are involved in some beliefs (as well as thoughts, desires, and so on), and they are available for incorporation in others. The cognitive mobility of our notions and ideas is a large part of the explanation of the "combinatorial proliferation" of our potential beliefs. Our notions and ideas give us the conceptual resources to form any of an almost arbitrarily large number of beliefs about the things and relations they represent. Though it is unlikely that you will ever form these beliefs, you have the resources to believe that Cicero was the inventor of the cotton gin, that your mother descended from a childhood friend of Saint Augustine, and so on.

Notions explain an internal sense in which some beliefs can be about the same thing. Quine's Tom has two beliefs, one of which he would express by saying 'Cicero was a Roman orator', the other of which he would express with 'Tully denounced Catiline'. These are beliefs about the same thing, a certain Roman, but nothing about the internal, cognitive properties of Tom's beliefs determines this. Instead, it is a relational, circumstantial fact that the notions involved in these beliefs are both notions of Cicero. But the belief that Tom would express with 'Cicero wrote *De Oratore*', involves the same notion as his belief that Cicero was a Roman orator. It is in virtue of the cognitive property of sharing the same notion that these two beliefs are about the same thing (though it is for circumstantial reasons that this thing is Cicero). In the same way, beliefs can be about the same property or relation in virtue of sharing an idea.

Representations also explain one kind of systematicity in pure and practical reasoning. Suppose Tom has a belief that either Cicero or Boethius wrote *De Oratore*, and comes to believe that Boethius did not write that work. Then, *if* both these beliefs involve the same notion of Boethius, Tom will come to believe that Cicero wrote *De Oratore*. Similarly, if I want to be friendly to Tom, and I believe that it is Tom I see in front of me, I will greet him, *if* the same notion of Tom is involved in my belief and in my desire. Identity of ideas and notions is in this way crucial to typical explanations of actions in terms of reasons.

When an agent expresses a belief by making a statement, there often are close relations between words used in the statement and notions and ideas involved in the belief. In a simple case, like a statement of 'Rick is loud', it is clear that the agent attaches the name 'Rick' to one of his notions and attaches the words 'is loud' to one of his ideas. This kind of attachment normally makes the name a name not of the representation, but of what the representation itself is *of*. In expressing his belief, the agent expects that his use of 'Rick' will succeed in referring to the individual his notion is about, and that 'is loud' will succeed in picking out the property that his idea is about. The agent may well have multiple names, or other terms, with which he can refer to the object of his notion, as well as multiple predicate phrases he can use to express the content of his idea. There may then be several sentences the agent can use to express a belief. In addition, the agent may attach the same name to two notions (as in the *Treatise* example in section 2.1), and may attach the same predicate phrase to two ideas ('wrote the *Treatise*' in the same example). Of course, there also may be no public language words attached to an agent's notion or idea.

An action that is directed *toward* an individual is motivated and guided by beliefs, desires, and intentions involving a notion of the individual. For example, when a child shouts "Dad!" on a crowded beach, she intends for her father to come to her in virtue of his recognizing the name 'Dad' as attaching to him. The child has a notion of her father involved in these attitudes, and her action is directed toward the person that her father-notion is *of*.

When an agent perceives an individual and forms beliefs about the object of perception, she may or may not recognize the individual. If she recognizes it, she will connect the perception with a pre-existing notion. Then, some of the beliefs about the thing that arise through the perceptual situation will involve the notion she links to her perception, and her beliefs, desires, and intentions that involve the notion can do their part in helping further her goals.

Failure of recognition involves having multiple notions of a single individual. When I do not recognize you at a distance, I do not connect the notion I form in perception with my stable notion of you. Many of the belief puzzle cases turn on just this phenomenon: an agent has two unconnected notions (often, both stable notions) that happen to be of the same individual.

3.2 Representations as Particulars

Notions and ideas, like beliefs, are concrete particulars, belonging only to single agents. Agents can have similar representations—perhaps even "type-identical" in some way (though that way would need explanation!)—but cannot share them. The strategy of focusing on representations as particulars is supported by the arguments in chapter 2 *for* individuating instances of believing by means of how agents think about objects and properties, and *against* treating such ways of thinking as shareable entities. In the present account, representations take the explanatory place of ways of thinking or modes of presentation, but they are really neither ways nor modes, but particulars. (My uses of the terms 'idea' and 'notion' are technical. I do think that we sometimes use these words to mean what I intend by them, but nothing depends on this. Certainly the words also have ordinary senses on which it makes good sense to ask if your notion or idea is the same as mine.)

I do not assume that a notion has internal logical complexity in the way a description, a bundle of predicates, a cluster of beliefs or an image might. I assume that notions are constituents of beliefs, but I do not assume the reverse. Now, there are some interesting issues about individuative relations between the beliefs a notion is involved in and the notion itself. It might be held, for instance, that if a notion was involved in certain beliefs at its formation, then having been involved in those particular beliefs at its formation is essential to it. It might even be held that for every notion there are some beliefs involving it whose continued existence is always necessary for the existence of the notion. But if we want to be able to formulate these questions without begging them, it is useful to start by thinking of a notion as a representational *simple* with respect to the things that involve it as constituents, such as beliefs and intentions. In fact I think that we can get far in explaining what notions are without answering the difficult questions about whether it is essential to a notion to be involved in any particular beliefs.

At first glance, a view treating notions (as well as some ideas) as concrete particulars and not presupposing representational complexity can seem to be impoverished, compared to an account on which the role of a way of thinking is played, say, by a cluster of descriptions. But exactly the opposite is the case. A notion can be described by enumerating a group of beliefs it is involved in, or by specifying when it was formed, or by noting any of the following: the individual it is of, the actions it helped to motivate, the natural language expressions and modes of recognition tied to it, and so on. There need be no canonical kind of answer to a question like 'What is Ann's notion of Joe?' any more than there is to the question 'What is Ann's left kidney?' A notion may have *lots* of features we can use to describe it; to focus on, say, a cluster of descriptions determined by some beliefs it is involved in (even if we end up agreeing that these beliefs somehow help individuate the notion) is to abstract away what we have no reason to ignore. This point will be important in the following discussion of our epistemic access to others' notions.

3.3   Contents of Notions

Since I believe that we quite standardly think about and talk about each
other's particular mental representations, I need to address the natural
concern as to whether this is even *possible*, given that we are not in
relations of direct acquaintance with representations inside each other's
heads. Now, since I hold that being able to think about a thing amounts
to having a notion of the thing, what is in question is the plausibility of
our ordinarily having notions of each other's notions and ideas. And to
establish the plausibility of this, I need to show that a correct account
of the contents of our notions—of what determines a notion to be *of* a
thing—entails that we are often related to each other's representations in
ways appropriate for forming notions of them. So, the right place to start
is with a general account of notion content. Inconveniently, however, I
do not have one. I do have sympathies with a sort of account on which
content is fairly easy to come by, and I will sketch this account below,
but I will focus instead on deflecting intuitions and arguments that are
behind the appeal of acquaintance restrictions on content. Having done
that, I will address the question of whether we are typically in a position
to think and talk about each other's representations.

   We are not truly acquainted with much of anything, Russell once
thought, beyond patches of perceived color, our own thoughts and feelings, and certain properties and relations.   One reason this troubled
him was that it appeared to follow that we cannot, strictly speaking,
talk or even think about any individuals except such things, since "every proposition which we can understand must be composed wholly of
constituents with which we are acquainted" (Russell 1959, 58). Russell
finally acquiesced in the view that everything we can say and believe is
at bottom a complex proposition about sense data (as well as thoughts,
feelings and universals); we are literally unable to think about chairs,
mountains, other people, and other ordinary things.

   While few philosophers remain attached to Russell's narrow conception of what we are acquainted with, many retain his basic idea that,
to understand a proposition about a thing, one must be in one way or
another directly acquainted with it.[1] Though Russell drew the line in
the wrong place, there is an intuitive distinction between two kinds of

---

1. For recent defenses of versions of this principle, see Ackerman 1987 and Evans

thoughts "about" things: thoughts about things with which we have direct enough knowledge or other contact to count as being acquainted, and thoughts about things with which we have insufficient direct knowledge, or none.

Consider Kaplan's 1969 example of "the shortest spy." It is a safe bet that, of all the spies, there is a shortest. Suppose that the spy is named 'Ortcutt', and that you know Ortcutt well, though I do not know him at all. Then, we would be likely to view your thought about Ortcutt's shortness as having the following singular proposition (singular propositions have individuals as constituents) as its content:

$$\langle\!\langle \, Short; Ortcutt \, \rangle\!\rangle \, . \tag{1}$$

Since I am not acquainted with Ortcutt, I can have only a thought with the following content (I use predicate logic to express propositions when it would be cumbersome to use an angle-bracket notation of the kind that is used in (1) and explored in detail in chapter 4):

$$\exists x[Spy(x) \ \& \ \forall y(Spy(y) \ \& \ x \neq y \ \rightarrow \ Shorter(x,y)) \ \& \ Short(x)]. \tag{2}$$

This is a *general* proposition (one not containing particular individuals, but only properties and relations) to the effect that there is a spy shorter than all other spies, who is short. It is in a loose sense "about" Ortcutt, since it is his shortness upon which its truth actually hangs; but Ortcutt is not a constituent of this proposition, and it might have been true even if Ortcutt had never donned the trench coat.

So, in a very loose sense of "about," there are at least two ways a proposition might be about a thing. It might contain the thing as a constituent, and the thing might bear on its truth in a more indirect, contingent way. As a matter of terminology, I will say that, strictly speaking, only (1), and not (2), is *about* Ortcutt. The proposition (2) is about the properties of being a spy and being short, but it is not about Ortcutt. Propositions are about only the individuals they contain as constituents.

What characteristic of a thought determines its propositional content to be about a thing (like Ortcutt), rather than just about properties (like spyhood and shortness)? I have suggested that the content of an

---

1982. A rejection of the criterion motivated, I believe, by concerns similar to mine, can be found in Kaplan 1978 and Kaplan 1989.

ideational belief is a singular proposition about an individual just in case it involves a notion that is *of* that individual. So the question is, what is needed for an agent to have a notion of an individual? Must the agent be acquainted with the individual in some more or less direct way? Is it conceptually impossible for me to form a notion of Ortcutt without being acquainted with him more directly than I am in virtue of believing (2)?

I will approach this question without giving a detailed characterization of just what acquaintance is, because I am not satisfied that there is a very clear notion of acquaintance that is at all suited to the tasks of restricting singular thought. Acquaintance must of course be some sort of relation to an entity that permits the agent to form a representation of the entity. Beyond this, all I will rely on is that, whatever acquaintance is, purely general knowledge of propositions like (2) does not suffice for it. I assume that any reasonable account on which acquaintance is required for singular thought will involve a notion of acquaintance looser than Russell's but with enough bite to exclude me from thinking about Ortcutt.

I find four kinds of reasons for holding that acquaintance is required for thought about individuals.

First, as Russell saw, acquaintance can delimit a foundation for an empiricist picture of knowledge, and, if so, there are consequences for what we can think about:

If ... we say 'The first Chancellor of the German Empire was an astute diplomatist', we can only be assured of the truth of our judgement in virtue of something with which we are acquainted—usually a testimony heard or read. Apart from the information we convey to others, apart from the fact about the actual Bismarck, which gives importance to our judgement, the thought we really have contains the one or more particulars involved, and otherwise consists wholly of concepts.

... we should like, if we could, to make the judgement which Bismarck alone can make, namely, the judgement of which he himself is a constituent. In this we are necessarily defeated, since the actual Bismarck is unknown to us. (Russell 1959, 56–57; see also Russell 1956b)

I suspect that Russell has in mind here an argument of the following sort. Suppose we accept these principles:

1. When one is acquainted with a thing, one has direct knowledge about it, including knowledge that it exists; all other knowledge comes through inference from previous knowledge.

2. One must understand a proposition before one can know through inference that it is true.

3. To understand a proposition about a given individual (including the proposition that it exists), one must be able to think about the individual.

4. If one can think about an individual, one must know that the individual exists.

If these are true then a proposition known through inference can be about only individuals such that one already knows that they exist. So, one cannot come to know through inference that an individual exists, but only through acquaintance. Therefore, one can think about only objects of acquaintance.

Perhaps the argument can be questioned at a number of points. But the first (foundationalist) premise seems to me the most dubious. If we do not accept a clean distinction between direct and inferential knowledge, we can hold onto the other premises without the consequence that all the propositions one knows are cobbled only from objects of one's acquaintance. For instance, if we adopt a "reliablist" account of what we know (Armstrong 1973; Goldman 1976, 1986), a belief's status as knowledge depends on its having been formed through a reliable process—one that reliably produces true beliefs. If this sort of view is right, then there may be belief-forming processes other than acquaintance that can expand one's cognitive reach, enabling one to think about a new thing. Such a process must, on my account of what it is to think about a thing, involve forming a notion that is involved in beliefs that (reliably often) are true.

Consider a process that takes as "input" a general belief that there is a unique P (such a belief involves an idea i_P of the property of being the unique P) and produces a new notion and also a belief that involves both this notion and the idea i_P. On a reliablist account of knowledge, it would be open to us to hold that this process produces a notion of a thing (namely, the thing a that actually is the unique P) that one previously had been unable to think about. For if we hold that the new notion formed by this process really is about a, then the new belief (that a is the unique P) has been formed in a way that reliably forms true singular beliefs on the basis of true general beliefs. It is consistent with this picture of knowledge, that is to say, that all one needs to think about a thing a that happens to be the unique P is the knowledge that there is a unique P (and one needs to actually form the notion and the belief). On this promiscuous view about notion-content, I can form a notion of Bismarck simply on the basis of my knowledge that there was a unique German Chancellor named 'Bismarck'. Further, even if I am not acquainted with Ortcutt, I can form a notion of him simply on the basis of my knowledge that there is a shortest spy. I have not argued that the promiscuous view is correct, but only that it is not in conflict with one version of a reliabilist account of knowledge, which I find more plausible than Russell's. The point is simply that Russell's dubious foundationalist picture of knowledge is crucial to the argument for the acquaintance restriction on thought.

A related argument for acquaintance restrictions turns on the fallibility of indirect connections to individuals. If one can promiscuously form a notion on the basis of a general belief that could conceivably be false, then there is the peril that one's thoughts involving the notion are not about anything at all—that one has thoughts with no content. This may seem troubling for various reasons, none of which, I think, holds up under scrutiny. For instance: 'if there is *nothing* that one thinks, one does not have a thought'. If we keep in mind the distinction between a mental entity (a notion, a belief, an episode of thinking) and its content (an individual, a proposition), this concern loses its force. Another: 'in a case where there is a notion and no appropriate individual for it to be *of*, there not only is a mental episode involving the notion, but there also is *something* one is thinking about (say, descriptions or memories); so it is plausible that in the successful case (where there is an appropriate individual) what one thinks about is not the remote individual, but rather only these things about whose existence one cannot be mistaken'. Certainly, one often has thoughts about descriptions or memories *at the same time* as thoughts involving a notion; but this does not entail that these associated descriptions and memories are what a thought involving the notion is *about*. Finally, 'if it is conceivable that there is no individual for one's notion to be *of*, then even if there happens to be one, one does not truly *know* that it exists'. It may be plausible that in order to have a belief about a thing you must know that it exists (though it can be argued that a suspicion of existence is all that is required); but the brand of knowledge that makes this plausible is weaker than infallible certainty. You can know that a thing exists, even if it is conceivable that your belief is mistaken.

Another reason that philosophers have felt the need for a restrictive condition of acquaintance has to do with intuitions about "*de re*" attitude reports, and the behavior of quantifiers (really, of anaphora) across belief contexts. Consider these sentences:

Jenny believes that Cicero was loud.   (3)

Jenny believes that Tully was loud.   (4)

Jenny believes of Cicero that he was loud.   (5)

There is someone such that Jenny believes that he was loud.   (6)

There is a tradition of regarding (5) as importantly different from (3), in that it alone licenses the inference to (6) (Quine 1966a; Hintikka 1962; Kaplan 1969). The difference, it is held, is that (5) really reports a relation to the individual Cicero, while (3) and (4) report relations only to names or descriptions or modes of presentation or intensions. The problem with allowing the first two sentences to report relations to Cicero is that it seems that they must then report the *same* relation to Cicero; but surely they can have different truth values. Thus, neither of these two sentences can support the truth of (6), which claims that there *is* some individual related to Jenny in the 'believing that he was loud' way.

This generates a motivation for distinguishing between two kinds of beliefs: those reportable *only* with "*de dicto*" reports like (3) and (4), and those reportable with "*de re*" reports like (5). Beliefs of the latter sort, but not of the former, are genuinely about the individuals referred to in the reports. A criterion of acquaintance is a tool ready-made for carving this distinction. We are relatively unwilling to use a *de re* report like (5) in cases where, for example, the subject has merely heard the name of the individual used. We are much more likely to use such a sentence if there has been close contact between the believer and the object of belief. The implicit argument here runs as follows: first, there are belief locutions that seem to assimilate naturally to certain formulas in predicate logic that involve relations to, and quantification over, individuals; second, we seem unwilling to use these locutions except when a criterion of acquaintance is met; therefore, believers are genuinely related to *individuals* via their beliefs only when they are acquainted with the individuals. This argument makes the following mistake: we canvass *typical* cases in which beliefs really are about specific individuals (these are simply beliefs involving notions), and we notice that in each of them the agent stands in a somewhat intimate relation to the individual in question, leading us to suspect that this sort of relation is what makes the belief truly about the individual. All we are entitled to conclude is that we typically form beliefs truly about individuals only when we are related to them in an intimate manner. The right way to think about this fact is as arising from a constraint on the *usefulness* of forming a notion about an individual, as I will explain in a moment.

I will leave issues about quantification into belief contexts, uses of *de re* constructions and substitution failures for later chapters, but I want to point out that the data are more complicated than many have understood. As is often the case in semantics, the intuitions one gets by contrasting sentences in isolation from described contexts are liable not to reflect entirely general features of actual statements. Are sentences (5) and (3) as clearly different as the argument requires? In fact I think that they are something like stylistic variants; intuitions of difference in what they claim arise, I think, *only* in situations in which we explicitly contrast them—and this cries out for an explanation not by semantic differences but by contextual features of uses of belief sentences. The facts about belief reporting do not clearly motivate a criterion of acquaintance as a prerequisite for having beliefs with singular propositions as their contents.

Perhaps the strongest consideration threatening a liberal view of what it takes to have a notion *of* a particular individual is the clear intuition that, whatever notion-forming processes take place, one *cannot* think about Ortcutt, who happens to be the shortest spy, simply in virtue of knowledge on general grounds that there is a shortest of all spies. The best explanation of this sort of intuition is that there *are* restrictions of acquaintance on what we are in a position to think about.

But I think a promiscuous view of notion-content can be reconciled with such intuitive qualms in two ways. First, there are constraints of *cognitive practicality* on what kind of notions actually are formed and retained. Even if we can very promiscuously form notions with informationally remote individuals as their contents, practicality moderates our appetites. I will expand on this shortly. Second, there are constraints of *conversational pragmatics* on what kinds of notions we are concerned with when we discuss an agent's representations and beliefs. These latter constraints (as I will explain in chapters 5 and 6) drive our specification of "how" information in belief reports. The truth of an ordinary belief report depends on more than whether the agent has a belief with the specified content; it typically also depends on what kinds of representations are involved in such a belief. Our conversational interests typically exclude notions conceived in representational promiscuity from making belief reports true (as well as reports that an agent knows an individual, or knows who an individual is).

Notions are useful to believers for all the same reasons that the FBI finds it useful to keep all the information and plans it has concerning a person of interest to the Bureau in a single file folder.[2] When the file is used for research and as a basis for action, it is useful to have all available information about the person in question within reach.

The FBI typically opens a file only when it discovers, through whatever means, an individual who is *of interest* to the Bureau. The FBI finds people interesting when information about them or actions toward them are likely to be useful in furthering the Bureau's goals. A file will not be opened in just any case in which there is reason to believe that there is a person of interest to it. The FBI might open a file now for 'the heaviest person who will commit murder next year', without knowing who that will be; but of course they will not—the file would be useless. Suppose an FBI agent recalls thinking about a person, and thinking that the person was of great interest to the FBI, though the agent cannot remember anything else about the person, including where, when, and why he had thought about the person. The FBI, on the basis of evidence that there is *someone* of interest to them, *could* open a file (and perhaps write in it 'is a person of interest'). But assuming that the

---

2. I borrow the analogy with files from Perry 1980b; the analogy has been used also by Grice, Evans, and Forbes. Like the analogies with proper names and with real individuals, however, the helpfulness of the image in understanding notions can be defeated by taking the analogy too seriously. Though files have their information literally *inside* them, *containing* this information, it may be misleading to think of notions as *containing* information. Notions are *parts of* beliefs. The file analogy can lead one to get the issue of what-contains-what backwards.

agent does not remember whom he was thinking about, there is no conceivable way that the file could see use; it is idle. There is no way that further information about the person could find its way into the file, or that the Bureau could direct an action toward the person. In order for the file to be useful, the FBI needs to be able to spot new information about a person as belonging in the file (call this passive recognition) and needs to be able to direct actions at the person whose file it is (active recognition).

In the same way, the significant possibility of recognition—of connecting new beliefs, perceptions, intentions and actions to a pre-existing notion—is an important practical constraint on the formation of notions. There is no reason to form an idle notion: a notion that one is not significantly likely to connect in the future to the thing it is a notion of. Notice that this is not a conceptual restriction about what is required for having a notion that is truly *of* a thing. It is undeniable that we typically form beliefs truly about individuals only when we are related to them in a more or less intimate manner. And *this* fact falls out directly from a simple constraint on the usefulness of forming a notion of an individual. There is no reason to deny that the idle FBI files just discussed are truly *about* the individuals in question, so long as we understand the force of the practical constraint: they are useless files. I want to suggest that the same is true of notions formed promiscuously.

If we separate questions of content from those of usefulness, the explanation of what it is for a notion to be *of* an individual need not be burdened by intuitions about typical or paradigm cases, which naturally are nearly all cases of *useful* notions.[3]

Given that these arguments and intuitions do not motivate acquaintance restrictions on notion-content, the difficulty in formulating such a restriction in a principled way takes on added importance. This difficulty is to be expected, on a promiscuous view, since the kinds of connections agents have to *useful* notions do not form a very natural family. So it is

---

3. Evans (1982) argues that a notion cannot really be *of* a thing unless it is potentially *useful*—unless, that is, the agent has the ability to "identify" the thing (that is, distinguish it from all other objects). Evans's case for this claim rests finally on his intuition that it must be right, an intuition that I do not share, since I see the conceptual possibility of idle notions as a harmless by-product of a form of representation that in general issues in useful notions, just as the possibility of empty names is a by-product of our practices of reference.

not surprising that it is hard to formulate a criterion that allows for the obvious cases of thinking about things while excluding the promiscuous cases. Adopting a promiscuous view allows us to avoid the slippery slope of restricting the kinds of acquaintance appropriate for thought being "truly about" particular individuals.

I do not plan to develop a promiscuous account of notion-content in detail, but I will sketch what seem to me to be some defensible principles. First, one can form notions of what one knows to exist. Depending on one's account of knowledge, this principle would seem to be compatible with more than one kind of notion-forming process, including some processes that do not require direct acquaintance. On a reliabilist view it may be compatible with the "promiscuous" process discussed above, in which the general belief that there is a unique P leads to a new notion involved (at first) only in a belief attributing the property of being the unique P. The content of a notion formed by such a process would (at least at first) be the individual that is the unique P, if there is one. To have a notion of a thing, arguably, is to have an at-least-tacit belief that it exists (not necessarily that it exists *now*), and (on a reliabilist theory of knowledge) this belief will count as knowledge that the thing exists if the original general belief itself counts as knowledge.

Let me give some examples of notions that might actually be formed by this kind of process. Though we had only indirect reasons for thinking that there was a planet (Neptune) in a certain part of the sky, we nonetheless formed notions of it. I have strong reasons for thinking that Mary will always have a dog named 'King' (adopting a new one when necessary), so I have formed a notion of the dog she has now, despite my lack of any causal acquaintance with it. The notions of King and Neptune are potentially useful despite their being formed in the absence of acquaintance with their contents. In contrast, although one can form a notion of Newman, the first child born in the twenty-first century (Kaplan 1969), notions of that kind rarely are useful (though might be if, say, we were planning a party for Newman). Similarly, if one forms a notion of the shortest spy, it is unlikely to pull any cognitive weight.

Certainly, in any of these cases the agent can get by without forming a notion. And this possibility can tempt one to hold that the agent really must not have beliefs specifically about the individuals in question, but only about related descriptions. But of course the possibility of being moderate does not conflict with promiscuity in fact—let alone with promiscuity that does not make a practical difference. Being able to get by without a notion is clearly a fact about its usefulness; and there is no reason to suppose that there are no marginally useful or even useless representations of things. There *may* be good reasons to hold that a belief-forming process cannot *usually* yield useless beliefs, if what makes things *beliefs* has to do with their function in reasoning. But this is consistent with there being belief-forming processes that generally yield useful beliefs, but which can also yield useless ones. What makes useless beliefs *beliefs* may be their status as idle members of an industrious family.

Also, it is clear that because of conversational constraints, in some of the more promiscuous cases—especially in the shortest spy case—one cannot truly and cooperatively *report* that the agent has a belief about the individual. But this is relevant to deciding whether a notion has a certain content only if we think belief reports are simply reports of content (*and* that our intuitions about the truth values of belief reports are accurate). If, as I will argue, belief reports specify more than the content of an alleged belief, then a report to the effect that I believe that Ortcutt has a difficult life can be false, even if I do in fact have a belief with that content, involving a notion of Ortcutt (the shortest spy).

The principle that we can form notions of whatever we know to exist might also allow a process that forms notions and attaches them only to modes of recognition (such as face-recognition abilities), if that process (reliably often) selects modes of recognition that are ways of recognizing unique individuals. The content of a notion formed in this way is (at least at first) the individual that would activate the mode of recognition—at least in those cases where there is such an individual related to the notion-forming process in the way that explains its reliability.[4] Thus,

---

4. The reason for this hedge is the following sort of case: you disguise yourself just once as Fred, whom I have never met, and I form a notion attached to a face-recognition skill. It will be Fred who activates this mode of recognition—so without the hedge I would be committed to the awkward view that Fred is the content of my notion from the start, when I have encountered only you in disguise. The hedge eliminates Fred as the content of this notion, since he does not figure in the way that explains the reliability of this process; it was not his face that I encountered when I developed the face-recognition skill. This goes along with the intuition that I do not know that Fred exists merely on the basis of having seen you. However, the principle without the hedge may not be quite as implausible as it seems. Holding that the notion as first formed, attached to nothing but a face-recognition skill, is about

one can form a notion of a person encountered in perception in virtue
of attaching a recognitional ability to a notion.

A second plausible, if vague, principle relates not only to notion
formation but also to notion maintenance: A notion is *of* an individual if it is maintained in order to organize information about it and
to guide actions toward it. This principle invokes a criterion of purpose, and leaves it unspecified whether the purpose in question must
arise from intentions of the agent or from natural function, and whether
the "purposiveness" must be specific to the notion in question, or can
be a consequence of general purposes or global functional properties of
cognitive "architecture."

For all its vagueness, this criterion clearly places importance on
the basis for the formation of a notion: if a notion is formed because
of evidence that there is an individual of interest, then it is formed
to organize information about, and action toward, the individual that
the evidence is evidence of. This may be an individual that caused
a certain perceptual experience, or one whose existence is inferred in
a more indirect way. But it is also clear that, on this criterion, such
considerations of origin are defeasible. Suppose that I see a person once
only, briefly, and at a distance (forming a notion of her), and mistakenly
take her to be the same person as someone I am introduced to later
and come to know well. My numerous beliefs arising from my contact
with the second person involve the notion that originally was *of* the first
person; but this notion is now maintained primarily in order to organize
my information and action relating to the second woman—she is now
the content of that notion. (This case is much like some in Evans 1973.)

I hope that a satisfactory account of notion-content can be given
along roughly these lines, one that would cohere with a general account
of the representational functions of items in complex systems. I hope
also that this task will seem less imposing when we are careful about the
relevance of the *usefulness* of representations, as well as the relevance
of conversational phenomena affecting our reports of representational
content.

Fred is consistent with holding that it becomes a notion of you in a very short time.
Perceptual beliefs and other beliefs about the encounter will soon overwhelm the mere
recognitional skill in determining the individual of which the notion is maintained in
order to keep track (I will discuss this sort of content change soon).

The considerations about acquaintance are important not only to the plausibility of a liberal account of notion-content in general, but also to the particular case of our thought about each other's thoughts. If thought involves private, particular representations, then other agents' thoughts are beyond our acquaintance. But on a liberal view of content, all we need in order to think about another agent's representation is solid evidence that it exists.

The "credo" about ideas and notions above suggests many different ways we can know about other agents' representations. For instance, we know that agents normally attach representations to words they use. So if we know that an agent has used a certain word, we know about one of her representations; we do not necessarily know much about what beliefs it is involved in, or much else about it, but we know that it exists and that a certain utterance was attached to it. An agent who engages in an object-directed action is certain to have a notion of it involved in the beliefs and desires that motivate the action. We can therefore know that the notion exists, that it is a notion of the object in question, and that it helped motivate the action. An agent who is in a situation in which an object is perceptually salient and relevant to the agent's interests is extremely likely to have a notion of it involved in beliefs that are based on the perception. Agents who are normal members of our society are almost certain to have notions of very famous individuals and to have ideas of properties and relations that are expressed with common words in our language.

Thus, on a plausible view of the contents of our notions, other agents' representations are very much within our cognitive reach, despite our often not knowing very much about them.

3.4   Contents of Ideas

Though there are real, as well as merely apparent, disanalogies between notions and ideas, I believe that essentially the same sort of account should be given of the contents of the two sorts of representations.

One disanalogy turns on the fact that at least some properties and relations are universally important for agents to represent, while few or no individuals have that status, since agents in different circumstances encounter largely distinct sets of individuals. There is a tremendous overlap in the sets of properties different agents confront and represent in thought. There are perceptual properties like *being cold*, and other properties and relations that are important for survival, such as *being safe to eat* and *being an enemy*; it is not implausible to suppose that our minds have built-in mechanisms for representing such properties—and that the mechanisms are the same from person to person.

Also, the evolution of a society involves the development of a shared set of *concepts*—concepts of properties and relations that the society finds important. Our society has the concepts of war, of animals, and of labor. In order to understand the words 'war', 'animal', and 'labor', each of us must grasp the concepts that the words stand for. So there are two good reasons to think that, unlike notions, many of our ways of representing properties and relations are public. We share ways of dealing with properties and relations possibly in virtue of shared innate structures and abilities, and certainly in virtue of a shared arsenal of concepts.

Though our countenancing notions as particular, unshareable representations was supported by the possibility of misrecognition of individuals (as in the Cicero-Tully case), such possibilities are at least remote, and perhaps nonexistent, for a significant class of properties and relations. Cases of natural kind properties like *being gold* and *being an elm* may be relatively susceptible to misrecognition, but properties and relations like *being a friend*, *being taller than*, and *not being true* seem far less likely to be confused. One can perhaps understand the property of *being water* in two ways without recognizing that one has two ways of thinking about the same property. But it would be a bizarre case indeed in which an agent really understands the relation of *being taller than* in two ways without realizing that they are ways of thinking about the same property. Such properties, unlike natural kind properties, are apparently grasped in a way that prohibits their unknowingly being grasped twice.

These points of disanalogy between our ways of thinking about things and our ways of thinking about properties and relations can make the strategy of treating notions and ideas in parallel ways seem poorly motivated. But here again I think that the distinction between representational content and our conversational interests in discussing it is crucial. When we attribute to an agent a belief in a proposition involving a property or relation, we usually are interested not in just *any* way the agent might represent the property or relation, but only in a *normal* idea of it. Many of our ordinary ways of discussing the contents of ideas, I will claim, involve restrictions of normality on ideas.

To make this point, I will explore a device we have for talking about the contents of ideas. The ordinary expression 'having the concept of *P*' may seem closely related to what I am calling 'having an idea of *P*', but I wish to argue that they are importantly different. When we are willing to say that an agent 'has the concept of *P*', it is always a case in which the agent has an idea (in my sense) of the property or relation expressed by '*P*'. But the converse does not hold—'having the concept' is typically stronger than 'having an idea'. One can have an idea *of* a property or relation without having the concept, and so one can have beliefs that are *about* a property or relation without having the concept.

Consider an example. The property of *being cold*, science tells us, is just the property of having a low mean molecular kinetic energy. Does everyone who has an idea of this property count as having the *concept* of being cold? Imagine a scientist who lives in a world where there is no variation in temperature, though she does understand what mean molecular kinetic energy is and has made the discovery that everything (nearby, at least) has the same mean molecular kinetic energy—nothing higher, nothing lower. The scientist has an idea of the property of being cold; but we would not be very likely to attribute to her the *concept* of being cold. Why not? Before we attribute the concept of being cold to someone, we require that she have an idea of that property and also that her idea function in her cognitive life *in the normal way*. We require, roughly, that her idea be associated with the usual sensory methods of recognition, that she have a sense of what cold things *feel* like, that she would realize on entering a cold room that it is cold, and perhaps some other things.

'Having the concept', I suggest, is simply having a *normal* idea. Typically, this means that one needs, among other things, normal beliefs and recognitional abilities to count as having the concept. Knowing about the potent solvent 'H_2O' is not sufficient for having the concept of water. One must know that water is a clear, more or less tasteless, colorless liquid at room temperature, that it is safe to drink, and so on.[5]

---

5. Notice that I have contrasted having *an* idea, not with having *a* concept, but with having *the* concept. Coud the same sort of distinction not be made between having

Certainly, what counts as a *normal* idea is a vague, society-relative *and* purpose-dependent matter. Normality is of course not a simple matter of averages; consider what it is to have a normal human eye—our interests are crucial in fixing what counts as normal. It follows that there are no fixed conditions for having the concept of a given property or relation. In this way, 'having the concept of P' is like 'knowing who a is'. Both are locutions that make perfect sense, as long as we understand the intents and purposes of the attributions—as long as the background is rich enough to tell us what counts as a normal or relevant idea or notion. (For an account of the purpose-dependence of 'knowing who', see Böer and Lycan 1985.)

This account of 'having the concept of P' explains one of the apparent asymmetries between notions and ideas. We noted that it seems much more difficult to imagine cases of multiple, unconnected ideas of the same property or relation than to imagine multiple, unconnected notions of individuals. In fact, I think it is rarely impossible to imagine such cases of multiple ideas. In the case of *being taller than*, take the following example.

I am employed as an admissions officer at a school that has done poorly in recent volleyball seasons. I have been instructed to base my judgments on the results of an interview in which I take no part. What I see, for each applicant, is a name, a written recommendation, and a mysterious number labeled 'stature'. Not knowing that term, I follow instructions to admit well-recommended applicants of superior 'stature'. Of course, the result is that I admit many applicants of impressive height.

---

a concept and having *the* concept? Is this not just a case of the context-dependence of a definite description? I do not think so. First, as used here, 'idea' is a technical term; I am not making any claims about how it is used or what it means—I am not analyzing the locution 'having an idea'. But I am not defining 'concept' in a technical way—I am analyzing the locution 'having the concept' as it is used in ordinary English. It may be that what we normally mean by 'having a concept' is much like what what I use 'having an idea' to say. I am, however, skeptical about this. In fact, I suspect that we usually talk about 'concepts' as if they are public entities, unlike what I have defined as 'ideas'. The ways normal ideas are propagated (which I discuss below) explains the usefulness of this way of talking. For instance we ask whether *the Egyptians* had a concept of love—not whether each Egyptian had such a concept. Facts like this hint at a system behind many of the different ordinary uses of 'concept'; still, for now I prefer to make no claims beyond the analysis of the phrase 'having the concept'. I pursue the relation between ideas and concepts further in Crimmins 1989a; much of the material in this section is adapted from that paper.

In this example, I am cognitively connected in *some* way to the relation of *being taller than*. I have an idea, to which I attach the phrase 'being of greater stature than'. This idea gets involved in a belief about two applicants when I notice that the numbers in the 'stature' column by their names differ. The relation that explains the *truth* of my beliefs involving this idea is the property of *being taller than*. It is this relation, also, that was involved in the *formation* of my idea, since *height* is what the admissions interviewers measure when they fill in the 'stature' column, and I formed the idea to keep track of which applicants have this feature to greater degrees than others. And it is this relation that explains my actions of admitting applicants who are taller than their competition.

There is, despite all this evidence that my idea is an idea *of* the relation of *being taller than*, a strong intuition that it is not enough—that my idea is really not a genuine idea *of* that relation. I think this intuition is just a bit off target. My 'greater stature' idea really is an idea *of* the property. But it is not an idea that, for everyday purposes, would constitute my *having the concept* of the relation. My idea of 'being of greater stature than' is not a normal idea of *being taller than*. For it to be a normal idea, I would have to be able to apply it simply by looking at two upright objects next to each other—and I cannot do this. It would have to be hooked up with normal ideas of *height* and *size*, as well. So it is right to be reluctant to count me as having the concept of *being taller than*. I have only an abnormal idea of that relation.

Normal ideas of properties and relations often propagate from agent to agent by the teaching of *words and phrases* that express the properties and relations. By this I mean not that agents literally come to share ideas with others—that would be like sharing a left arm—but that they lead others to create ideas with the features required to count as normal ideas. When a child learns the use of the word 'water' in the usual way, the facts about the teaching situations determine not only that the child forms an idea *of* water, but also that the idea is involved in the requisite normal beliefs about water and that the idea is connected to the normal modes of recognizing water. The phenomenon of the linguistic propagation of normal ideas, makes it a good bet that any speaker of our language has a normal idea about any property or relation that is expressed by a common word or phrase. This fact supports Geach's 1957 contention that having a *word* for so-and-so is the central case of having a concept of so-and-so.

One other important feature of 'having the concept' is that in most cases it is almost inconceivable for an agent to have *two* normal ideas of a given property or relation at a single time. The admissions officer example showed that one can have two ideas *of* the relation of *being taller than* at one time (if we suppose that the admissions officer also has the usual concept of being taller than), but I cannot concoct an example in which someone has two unconnected *normal* ideas of this relation, or of many others.[6] The beliefs and modes of recognition required for ideas to count as normal typically preclude the possibility of multiple unconnected normal ideas. You cannot have the concept *twice*.

I indicated in passing that 'having the concept' is much like 'knowing who' (as applied to an individual "*de re*"; knowing who it is that meets a description is another matter). The former involves a condition of normality on ideas, the latter involves a similar condition on notions. Just as nearly every member of our linguistic community has a normal concept of *being hungry*, nearly every citizen of the United States has a normal notion of Ronald Reagan. It is a notion that is involved in beliefs about the former President, one that is associated with a large subset of the properties of *being tall*, *being an actor*, *being a Republican*, *being called 'Reagan'*, and so on. Such a citizen is extremely unlikely to have *two* notions of Reagan that are normal in this way. There are few individuals who, like Reagan, are almost certainly known (via a normal notion) to everyone we deal with. But there are many cases in which, among members of a certain group, everyone has a normal notion of some individual. Among academics at Cornell, it is safe to assume that everyone has a normal notion of President Frank Rhodes. Among analytic philosophers, it is safe to assume that everyone has a normal notion of W. V. Quine.

---

6. There are some properties, like *being an elm tree*, of which I can imagine having two unconnected ideas, such that the ideas are both more or less "normal" for the general population. There are very weak standards of recognition and information needed to count as having a normal idea of such a property. But this isn't the sort of case where we are likely to talk about 'having the concept' of the property. Cases in which we *are* likely to talk of that are ones in which the possibility of multiple ideas is almost nonexistent. We certainly can, as I have pointed out, have two unconnected ideas of a property or relation that count as normal in different contexts.

If it is obvious that someone has a normal notion of an individual, we can think and talk about that notion. We can talk about basketball star Larry Bird's normal notion of Reagan, not because we have seen it, or even because we have seen its effects, but simply because it is *obvious* that he has such a notion. We needn't talk in generalities about 'whatever notion it is that is Bird's normal notion of Reagan, if he has one'; we can just talk directly about Bird's notion, asking, for instance, whether Bird thinks Reagan knew about the Contra scandal. That this is what we in fact do in belief reports is certainly contentious; I will argue for this view at length in chapters 5 and 6.

4 Structure, Propositions, and Beliefs

Now I will develop some tools that will find work in characterizing beliefs and in analyzing belief reports. In section 4.1 I will sketch accounts of the structures of beliefs and of the propositions that are their contents. Most importantly, this overview will introduce (largely by example) the notation I will use in chapters 5 and 6 and will exhibit the central concepts. Reading this section is all that is required to understand the main points of the following chapters.

But I want to show that the accounts can be filled in more rigorously and to make one way of doing so available to the interested reader. So, at the very real risk of dressing things more formally than the occasion demands, in sections 4.3 and 4.4 I will give details of the account of structured propositions, which are marshaled for service as contents of both statements and beliefs, and then details of the account of "thought maps," which are structural types of explicit ideational beliefs an agent is in principle capable of forming, given an initial stock of notions and ideas. The accounts of beliefs and propositions are unfortunately not without artificiality, but they may serve as a useful starting point for further work. In section 4.6 is a sketch of a fanciful system with all the structural features needed to instantiate a system of ideational representations. I sketch this example to ward off some natural but incorrect "sententialist" assumptions concerning how a system about which the account of section 4.4 is right must look.

4.1 Overview

I argued in chapter 1 that naïve semantics for belief reports is implausible and that the considerations that have seemed to support it ignore a genuine possibility: that information about *how* a proposition is believed comes into the truth conditions of a belief report, but through *tacit* means—the "how" information is not encoded by words used in the report. Since I think this possibility is more than idle, I need to show how such information is systematically incorporated into the truth conditions of belief reports.

The two main difficulties in developing a non-naïve account of belief reports are (i) to specify just what kind of information this "how" information *is* without invoking an implausible account of mind, and (ii) to explain how such information is expressed in belief reports without invoking an implausible account of language. The results of the last two chapters have cleared the path toward a solution to the first difficulty. An instance of believing is individuated not merely by the believed proposition, but also by the concrete particular representations employed by the agent to represent objects, properties and relations that the proposition is about. The "how" information conveyed by a belief report, then, must constrain the representations involved in the alleged belief. Thought maps, as they are defined below, fit this need; they specify the logical arrangement of representations in a belief—they are in a certain sense maximal encapsulations of "how" information about an instance of believing.

Ideational beliefs (from here on, simply *beliefs*) are structured concrete particulars, involving ideas and notions as constituents. I will suppose that a belief has as immediate constituents a single *main idea* and a number of other ideas and notions, which, as they occur in that belief, are *associated* with *argument places* of the main idea. Ideas have argument places; some ideas are one-place ideas, some are two-place ideas, and so on. My idea of the relation of being taller than has three argument places, for two individuals and a time; my idea of having good taste in clothing has just two, for an individual and a time. In a belief, each argument place of the main idea must be associated with a notion, with another idea, or with a thought (on which more soon).

For example, my belief (b_{JR}) that Joe is taller than Rob has as constituents an idea and two notions (ignoring the time, as I will do often for simplicity): my idea i_T of *being taller than*, which has argument places pl_T^+ (for the taller individual) and pl_T^- (for the shorter), and my notions n_{Joe} and n_{Rob} of Joe and Rob. The notions n_{Joe} and n_{Rob} are both immediate constituents of b_{JR}, but they fill different roles in its structure. In my belief, n_{Joe} is associated with pl_T^+ and n_{Rob} with pl_T^- (equivalently, n_{Joe} fills a role in b_{JR} that *corresponds* to pl_T^+ and n_{Rob} fills one corresponding to pl_T^-; the connections among roles, filling, correspondence, association, and argument places will be made clearer soon and will be fully explained in the following sections). These broad features of my belief are encoded in the depiction of its structure given in figure 4.1. A less perspicuous but more compact depiction of the same information is given in this notation:

$$(i_t; f),\tag{1}$$

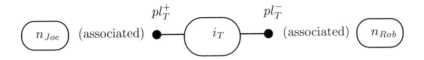

Figure 4.1
My belief that Joe is taller than Rob

where $f = \{\langle pl_T^+, n_{Joe}\rangle, \langle pl_T^-, n_{Rob}\rangle\}$. (I adopt the usual definition of
a function as a set of ordered pairs, such that function f contains the
ordered pair $\langle a, b\rangle$ just in case $f(a) = b$.) This notation suffices because
we can give the internal, structural details of a belief by giving its main
idea and the function from its argument places to the notions and ideas
that are associated with those argument places in the belief. This is
to give the immediate constituents of the belief and to specify just how
those constituents are related within it. In fact, I have a belief (b_{JR})
characterized by the depiction in (1), but I would not have had one had
I not believed (in the particular way I do) that Joe is taller than Rob.
Thus, (1) is best regarded as representing a *type* of beliefs. I actually
have, but might not have had, a belief of that type. Since a belief of the
type depicted by (1) must involve n_{Joe}, which is a concrete particular
representation that belongs to me alone, no one but myself can have a
belief of this type—that is, it is an *agent-bound type*.

The agent-bound types of beliefs that can be represented by depictions of the form (1) are what I call *thought maps* (I will use the symbols
'$\tau, \tau_1, \ldots$' to stand for thought maps). A thought map is uniquely determined by a main idea and a function from that idea's argument places
to further notions and ideas.

Where there is no chance of confusion, I will abbreviate the notation
used in (1) as follows:

$(i_T; n_{Joe}, n_{Rob})$.

This is an ambiguous shorthand, since it does not specify explicitly which
argument places are associated with which notions, so I will use it only
in contexts where the correct resolution of the ambiguity is clear.

The content of a belief is determined compositionally from the contents of its immediate constituents. It is the proposition attributing the

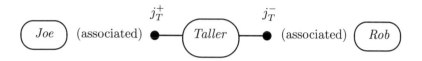

Figure 4.2
The proposition that Joe is taller than Rob

property or relation the belief's main idea is *of* to those individuals, properties and relations that the notions and ideas associated with the argument places of the main idea are *of*. My idea i_T is of the relation *Taller*, and my notions n_{Joe} and n_{Rob} are notions of Joe and Rob. Taking *ContentOf* to be the relation between cognitive entities and their contents, we have (if it is now t):

$ContentOf(\,Taller, i_T, t)$ & $ContentOf(\,Joe, n_{Joe}, t)$ &
$\quad ContentOf(\,Rob, n_{Rob}, t)$.

So the content of my belief b_{JR} is the proposition (p_{JR}) that Joe is taller than Rob. This proposition is itself an entity with constituent structure—it involves as constituents a *main relation* (*Taller*) and two individuals (Joe and Rob). Of course, Joe and Rob, though both immediate constituents of p_{JR}, fill different roles in its structure. In p_{JR}, they are associated with two different *arguments* of the relation *Taller*. Call these arguments j_T^+ and j_T^-. The proposition p_{JR}, in which Joe is associated with j_T^+ and Rob with j_T^-, can be depicted as in figure 4.2. The astute reader will sense a structural similarity between this proposition and the belief b_{JR} depicted above. The concrete belief represents this abstract proposition in part because of this isomorphism. A less perspicuous but more compact depiction of the same proposition is given in this notation:

$$p \;=\; \langle\!\langle\,Taller; f\,\rangle\!\rangle \tag{2}$$

where $f = \{\langle j_T^+, Joe\rangle, \langle j_T^-, Rob\rangle\}$. The function f assigns to each argument of *Taller* the individual associated with that argument in p (equivalently, the individual filling the role in p that *corresponds* to the argument).

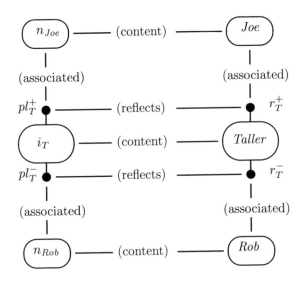

Figure 4.3
Relations between the belief and its content

The two arguments of the relation *Taller*, j_T^+ and j_T^-, bear an important relation to the two argument *places* of my idea i_T. My belief b_{JR} is such that in its content Rob is associated with the argument j_T^-, only because in b_{JR}, my notion n_{Rob} is associated with the argument place (pl_T^-) in i_T that, as I will say, *reflects* the "shorter" argument of the relation *Taller*. The relation $Reflects(pl, j)$ is a relation between argument places of ideas and arguments of relations. Figure 4.3 should help clarify these notions.

To connect this to $Believes(a, t, p, \tau)$ (posited in chapter 2), this instance of believing is one in which (where I am A and it now is t):

$$Believes(A, t, \langle\!\langle\ Taller;\ Joe,\ Rob\ \rangle\!\rangle, (i_T; n_{Joe}, n_{Rob})).$$

The facts depicted in (2) about which entities are associated with which arguments determine p_{JR} uniquely. In general, a proposition can be uniquely characterized by the facts specifying the entities associated with arguments of its relations (since, really, the only relation we need consider is the proposition's main relation), but a look at more complex propositions will demonstrate that a bit more sophistication will be useful for describing the internal structure of propositions.

A complex proposition contains entities that occur below the surface of its constituent structure—it has constituents that are not among its immediate constituents. One way in which propositions can be complex involves structure introduced by logical relations. For instance, there are propositions that are negative, conjunctive, disjunctive, or conditional in form. Disjunction, as I will treat it, is a relation (Or) that holds of two propositions just in case at least one of them is true. Similarly, Not holds of a proposition just in case it is not true. The proposition (p_k) that Dave kicked Joe or Joe did not kick Rob can be written as follows:

$$p_k \;=\; \langle\!\langle\, Or; \langle\!\langle\, Kicked; Dave, Joe \,\rangle\!\rangle\,, \langle\!\langle\, Not; \langle\!\langle\, Kicked; Joe, Rob \,\rangle\!\rangle \,\rangle\!\rangle \,\rangle\!\rangle\,.$$

(To give the remaining logical relations on which I will rely: the relations All, $Some$, and $Most$ hold between two properties just in case all (some, most) entities having the first property also have the second. The relation The holds between two properties just in case there is just one entity having the first property, and it also has the second.[1])

The point of looking at logical relations now is to introduce the notion of a *role* filled by one entity within the structure of another; this notion is crucial to my accounts of propositions and beliefs. Within p_k, it seems that both Dave and Joe are associated with the argument j_K^+ (for the kicker) of $Kicked$, and both Joe and Rob are associated with j_K^- (for the one kicked). In order to describe the innards of p_k completely, we cannot rely merely on these facts about who is associated in p_k with which arguments of which relations, but we need to distinguish more finely among the different roles entities fill within propositions. One relation can fill multiple roles within the constituent structure of a proposition, and so multiple roles within the proposition can arise from a single argument. In proposition p_k, the relation $Kicked$ occurs twice—it itself fills two distinct roles in the structure of p_k; Joe also fills two roles in p_k. Now, it happens that the two roles Joe fills in p_k arise from different arguments of $Kicked$, but it is possible also for a single individual to fill two different roles in a proposition arising from the

---

1. This is one version of a generalized quantifier strategy for treating determiners; while it makes for a particularly simple theory, other treatments are by no means excluded by the present general strategy for characterizing propositions.

same argument. For example, Joe fills two such roles in the proposition that Rob kicked Joe or Dave kicked Joe.

When we want to talk about specific "occurrences" of an individual within a proposition, arguments of relations do not give us a direct means of doing so. This is one among several reasons for developing carefully the notion of a *role* within a structured entity like a proposition or a belief. Certainly, the roles that the constituents of a proposition fill within its structure often have close connections to the arguments of relations occurring in it. But since relations can fill multiple roles within a proposition, there can be more than one role in a proposition arising from a single argument of a relation. So roles within a proposition— the roles that can individuate different occurrences of things within the proposition—are not simply arguments of relations occurring in it. For any type of structured entity that can have constituents occurring more than once, it is useful to have a notion of the different roles within the entity that can distinguish among the different occurrences.

I will leave most of the specifics about propositional roles for following sections. Here, I will give the essentials mostly by example.

I will characterize the notion of propositional roles so that for every occurrence of an entity within a proposition, there is exactly one role. Since individuals, relations and propositions can be among the constituents of a proposition, these will fill various roles in the proposition. Every proposition has at least (i) a role filled by its main relation, and (ii) roles corresponding to the arguments of the main relation. The proposition $\langle\!\langle$ *Taller*; *Joe*, *Rob* $\rangle\!\rangle$ has three roles (r_T, r_{Joe}, r_{Rob}), filled by the relation *Taller*, Joe and Rob. The role r_{Joe} corresponds to the argument j_T^+, and the role r_{Rob} corresponds to the argument j_T^-. In the simple case, an entity fills a role in a proposition just in case it either is the proposition's main relation or is associated with an argument of the main relation. This is because, in the simple case, the only constituents of a proposition are immediate constituents.

A complex proposition contains entities that occur below the surface of its constituent structure—it has constituents that are not among its immediate constituents. For every occurrence of a constituent within a proposition, there is exactly one role. The eleven roles in the proposition that Dave kicked Joe or Joe did not kick Rob are shown in the following diagram:

$$p_k = \langle\!\langle \underbrace{\underbrace{Or}_{r_1}; \underbrace{\langle\!\langle \underbrace{Kicked}_{r_4}; \underbrace{Dave}_{r_5}, \underbrace{Joe}_{r_6} \rangle\!\rangle}_{r_2}, \underbrace{\langle\!\langle \underbrace{Not}_{r_7}; \langle\!\langle \underbrace{Kicked}_{r_9}; \underbrace{Joe}_{r_{10}}, \underbrace{Rob}_{r_{11}} \rangle\!\rangle \rangle\!\rangle}_{r_8}}_{r_3} \rangle\!\rangle .$$

In general, if one proposition is an immediate constituent of another proposition, then for each of the roles in the former, there is a role in the latter *derived* from it (though, I will hold, not identical with it). So, the role r_9 in p_k is derived from a role in the proposition $\langle\!\langle \textit{Not}; \langle\!\langle \textit{Kicked}; \textit{Joe}, \textit{Rob} \rangle\!\rangle \rangle\!\rangle$, and that role is derived from the role filled by the relation *Kicked* in $\langle\!\langle \textit{Kicked}; \textit{Joe}, \textit{Rob} \rangle\!\rangle$.

Though the concept of a role, as I use it, goes hand in hand with that of an occurrence of one entity within the constituent structure of another, I have chosen to frame my account in terms of roles rather than occurrences for two reasons. It seems odd, first of all, to talk of an occurrence of Joe as being a thing other than Joe himself. Secondly, so far as I have been able to determine, the best accounts of propositions containing complex relations, and of the contents of certain beliefs and statements, involves positing *partial* propositionlike entities with roles that are unfilled and so do not correspond to occurrences of any entities. I will return to complex relations shortly.

Being able to talk about the roles entities fill within structured propositions gives us a neat way of specifying partial information about how an agent believes a proposition. If there are two occurrences of an entity in a proposition (that is, if it fills two roles in the proposition), then it is possible for an agent to believe the proposition by having a belief that contains two different representations of the entity, one for each role the entity fills in the proposition. Consider Tom's belief that Cicero kicked Tully. The proposition Tom believes is this one (with all roles indicated):

$$p_{CT} = \langle\!\langle \underbrace{Kicked}_{r_1}; \underbrace{Cicero}_{r_2}, \underbrace{Cicero}_{r_3} \rangle\!\rangle .$$

This proposition has two distinct roles filled by Cicero, and Tom believes the proposition in a way such that two of his notions are, as I will say, *responsible* for those roles. His notion n_C, that is connected to the name 'Cicero', is responsible for r_2, and his 'Tully' notion n_T is responsible for r_3.

The technical term 'responsible' expresses what I take to be a concept central to our commonsense understanding of structured representation. Suppose one is told, of a certain ancient inscription

$\mp \; \lhd \; \angle$

containing three symbols, only that it contains two different symbols for Venus and expresses the proposition that Venus is brighter than Venus. One can ask, just which symbol-inscription represents just which occurrence of Venus in that proposition? One wants to know which representation is *responsible* for filling (with Venus) which role in the proposition. If one knows only that the two symbol-inscriptions represent Venus, then one clearly lacks certain information about *how* the inscription represents the proposition it represents. This information connects the symbol-inscriptions to the different occurrences of Venus in the proposition—to the different roles Venus fills in it. If responsibility sounds like an unfamiliar concept, that is only because we seldom know that a representation represents a certain proposition, without also knowing which constituents of the representation are responsible for which roles in the proposition.

The commonsense status of responsibility is important for my project, since I will claim that, in reporting beliefs, we often give information about which representations are responsible for which roles. The particulars of my account of thought maps and structured propositions may be found unsatisfactory in various ways, but as long as we accept a notion of representational responsibility everything else about the account of belief reports can survive intact.

Now, it clearly is possible for Tom to believe both that Cicero kicked Tully and that Tully kicked Cicero. This would be for Tom to believe p_{CT} in two ways, such that in one of those ways, the facts about responsibility are as we have just seen, while in the other way, the notion n_T is responsible for r_2 and n_C is responsible for r_3. Thus, responsibility is not a relation simply between a representation and a role, but is relative to a belief or to a way of believing (that is, on my account, it is relative to a thought map). Thus I will posit the relation $Responsible(n, b, r)$, which holds when n is responsible for r in an actual belief b. And by extension I will say that $Responsible(n, \tau, r)$ holds between a representation, a thought map, and a propositional role just in case, in a belief mapped by map τ, n is (or would be, if such a belief existed) responsible for r.

A thought map, since it shares a structure with the proposition believed, determines (together with facts about the contents of simple representations) just which representations in a belief mapped by the map are responsible for each role in the proposition. That is because the roles filled by representations in the constituent structure of a thought map have a direct correspondence to the roles filled by entities in the proposition. But we can also *partially* detail the innards of a belief simply by specifying certain representations as responsible for certain roles in the proposition. Since I think this is precisely what we do in belief reports, it is worth giving a few examples.

Suppose the following is a fact about Tom at t:

$$\exists \tau \ [\ Believes(\mathit{Tom}, t, \langle\!\langle \underbrace{Loud}_{r_1} ; \underbrace{Cicero}_{r_2} \rangle\!\rangle , \tau) \ \& \ Responsible(n_T, \tau, r_2) \ ].$$

Then, Tom believes at t that Cicero is loud, in the way that involves his 'Tully' representation n_T.

Suppose the following is true:

$$\exists \tau \ [\ Believes(\mathit{Tom}, t, \langle\!\langle \underbrace{Taller}_{r_1} ; \underbrace{Cicero}_{r_2}, \underbrace{Cicero}_{r_3} \rangle\!\rangle , \tau) \ ].$$

Then, Tom believes in some way or other that Cicero is taller than Cicero. Suppose in addition, with respect to some such τ, that the following is true:

$$Responsible(n_T, \tau, r_2) \ \& \ Responsible(n_C, \tau, r_3).$$

Then, Tom believes the proposition in a way he would express by saying 'Tully is taller than Cicero', rather than 'Cicero is taller than Tully'.

Before moving on to the more rigorous presentation of the accounts of structured propositions and beliefs, I will briefly explain how I take complex relations to be composed and represented and introduce the notation I will use for complex relations and the complex ideas that represent them.

If *Taller* is a relation with two arguments, and Joe is an individual, then there is a complex property (call it R_1) of *being such that Joe is taller than one*. An even more complex relation (R_2) is one that holds between two individuals just in case *either [the first] is taller than Joe or [the second]* *is not taller than Dave.* Complex properties and relations like these are *abstracted* from *partial propositions.* A partial proposition is an entity with the structure of a proposition, except that it may have "gaps," which are unfilled roles. In the shorthand we can depict the partial propositions from which R_1 and R_2 are abstracted as follows (indicating only the unfilled roles):

$$p_{R_1} \; = \; \langle\!\langle \; Taller;\, Joe,\, \underbrace{\quad}_{r_1} \; \rangle\!\rangle \, ,$$

$$p_{R_2} \; = \; \langle\!\langle \; Or;\, \langle\!\langle \; Taller;\, \underbrace{\quad}_{r_2},\, Joe \; \rangle\!\rangle \, , \; \langle\!\langle \; Not;\, \langle\!\langle \; Taller;\, \underbrace{\quad}_{r_3},\, Dave \; \rangle\!\rangle \; \rangle\!\rangle \; \rangle\!\rangle \, .$$

These two partial propositions have roles that are not filled by any entities. Unfilled roles can be *bound* by arguments of complex relations. The complex property R_1 has a single argument (call it j_{R_1}) that binds the unfilled role r_1 in p_{R_1}, and R_2 has two arguments, one ($j_{R_2}^1$) that binds r_2 and one ($j_{R_2}^2$) that binds r_3. In my official notation, these relations are depicted as follows:

$$R_1 \; = \; [\{j_{R_1}\} : p_{R_1}],$$

$$R_2 \; = \; [\{j_{R_2}^1, j_{R_2}^2\} : p_{R_2}].$$

In the official depiction of a complex relation, we specify two things: the set of the relation's arguments, and the partial proposition from which the relation is abstracted. On the account of arguments I give in following sections, this determines the relation uniquely, since an argument is an argument of only one relation—the facts about which roles it binds are essential to its identity. There is nothing about this *notation* that indicates which roles are bound by which arguments, so the official notation is in a way unhelpful; while it displays the essentials of an abstracted relation (its arguments, and the proposition from which it is abstracted), it gives no depiction of facts about what binds what.

A slightly more perspicuous notation would specify the set of arguments of a relation only indirectly, by specifying the set of those sets of propositional roles that are bound by the arguments. That is, instead of specifying the set $\{j_{R_2}^1, j_{R_2}^2\}$, we would specify the set $\{\{r_2\}, \{r_3\}\}$. But this would be unhelpful in a similar way, absent a helpful depiction of just which propositional roles r_2 and r_3 are (we might use the underbracket notation for this).

A perspicuous and familiar shorthand notation for these relations is this:

$$R_1 = [x : \langle\!\langle\, Taller; Joe, x \,\rangle\!\rangle\,].$$

$$R_2 = [x, y : \langle\!\langle\, Or;\, \langle\!\langle\, Taller; Joe, x \,\rangle\!\rangle\,,\, \langle\!\langle\, Not;\, \langle\!\langle\, Taller; y, Dave \,\rangle\!\rangle \,\rangle\!\rangle \,\rangle\!\rangle\,].$$

In the shorthand, we can write the proposition that a and b stand in the relation R_2 as follows:

$$\langle\!\langle\, [x, y : \langle\!\langle\, Or;\, \langle\!\langle\, Taller; Joe, x \,\rangle\!\rangle\,,\, \langle\!\langle\, Not;\, \langle\!\langle\, Taller; y, Dave \,\rangle\!\rangle \,\rangle\!\rangle \,\rangle\!\rangle\,];\, a, b \,\rangle\!\rangle\,.$$

Notice that a complex relation, like a proposition, is a structured entity in which constituents fill roles. For instance, Joe fills a role in relation R_1. This should make clear the distinction between a relation's arguments and its roles; its roles are filled by its own constituents; its arguments are never *filled*, but correspond to roles in any proposition of which the relation is the main relation—roles that are filled by entities which need not be constituents of the relation.

To give another example, this is the proposition that Mary has the property of being either at home or in her own car:

$$\langle\!\langle\ [x : \langle\!\langle\, Or;\, \langle\!\langle\, Home; x \,\rangle\!\rangle\,,$$
$$\langle\!\langle\, The; [y : \langle\!\langle\, And;\, \langle\!\langle\, Owns; x, y \,\rangle\!\rangle\,,$$
$$\langle\!\langle\, Car; y \,\rangle\!\rangle \,\rangle\!\rangle\,]\,,$$
$$[y : \langle\!\langle\, In; x, y \,\rangle\!\rangle\,]\,\rangle\!\rangle \,\rangle\!\rangle\,]\,\rangle\!\rangle \,\rangle\!\rangle\,]\,;$$
$$Mary \,\rangle\!\rangle\,.$$

While the shorthand is quite useful, it gives the misleading impression that in partial propositions roles are filled by "variables" or some kind of thing that can be referred to by 'x' or 'y' in the notation. Really, unfilled roles in a partial proposition are not filled by anything at all (even in a complex relation abstracted from it), and there is no difference between complex relations corresponding to a mere consistent difference in the choice of a variable in the shorthand notation. The reader who is concerned about such issues will find in following sections detailed explanation of partial propositions, complex relations, and binding.

I will give a parallel treatment of complex ideas in beliefs. If a single idea occurs twice within a complex belief, then one of its argument places can give rise to more than one role in the belief. In my belief that Dave is taller than Rob or Rob is taller than Joe, both Dave and Rob are associated in some way with pl_T^+, since both fill roles arising from the argument place pl_T^+. So, as in the case of propositions, it is useful to have a notion of the different roles an idea or notion can fill within a particular belief. And, as in the case of propositions, complexity can arise from abstraction. Just as there is a property of *being such that Joe is taller than one*, I can form a complex idea i_{JT} of that property that has as constituents my idea i_T and my notion n_J. I will leave the details for the following sections, but the end result is that the structures of complex ideas are similar to the structures of complex relations. Thus, my idea i_{JT} is characterized by the *idea map* depicted (in shorthand notation) as follows:

$$(x : (i_T; n_J, x)).$$

To give a final example, one that should convey the similarity of the accounts of the structures of beliefs and propositions, the following depicts the thought map that characterizes my belief that Mary is either at home or in her car:

$$(\ (x : (i_{Or}; (i_{Home}; x),$$
$$(i_{The}; (y : (i_{And}; (i_{Owns}; x, y),$$
$$(i_{Car}; y))) \ ,$$
$$(y : i_{In}; (x, y)))))) \ ;$$

$$n_{Mary}).$$

4.2   Constituent Structure

I will give accounts of structured propositions and beliefs that employ some concepts that apply to many kinds of entities with constituent structure, including sets, sequences, and sentences. So I will present first these general structural concepts, and then develop the more topic-specific accounts of proposition and belief structure.

An entity with constituent structure of the kind I will consider here has other entities that fill roles in it. These entities are its constituents. For some kinds of structured entities, including sets, sentences, sequences, and (on the present account) propositions, there is a clear distinction between the entity's immediate constituents and constituents that occur below the surface in the entity's structure. Thus, the set $\{1, \{2, 3\}, 4\}$ has the number 1 as an immediate constituent and the number 2 as a constituent, but not an immediate one. In the set $\{1, \{1, 2\}\}$, the number 1 is both an immediate constituent and a non-immediate constituent; it fills one role that is an *immediate-constituent role* and one that is not. In the sequence $\langle 1, 2, 1, 3 \rangle$ (if we do not presuppose a particular set-theoretic account of sequences), the number 1 is an immediate constituent, in a sense, twice over; it fills two immediate-constituent roles.

(I use '$\langle x, y, z \rangle$' to denote the sequence containing x, y and z in that order, and '$\frown$' to denote the concatenation operation on sequences, so that, for instance,

$$\langle x, y \rangle \frown \langle y, \langle x, z \rangle \rangle = \langle x, y, y, \langle x, z \rangle \rangle.)$$

The role (call it r_1) that 1 fills in the sequence $\pi_1 = \langle 2, \{1, 3\} \rangle$ bears a close relation to the role (r_2) it fills in the set $S_1 = \{1, 3\}$. The sequence π_1 has role r_1 only because it has the set S_1 with role r_2 as an immediate constituent. I will say that r_1 is *derived from* r_2. Any role filled by a constituent of any sequence (or set) either is an immediate constituent role or is derived from a role in some entity that fills an immediate constituent role in the sequence (or set). I will assume that this is true of all entities with the sort of constituent structure in question here.

Now, a derived role is not identical to the role from which it is derived. To see this, consider the sequence $\pi_2 = \langle \langle 1, 4 \rangle, \langle 1, 4 \rangle \rangle$. This sequence has two distinct roles (r_a and r_b) filled by 1, both of which are derived from the single role (r_c) that 1 fills in the sequence $\pi_3 = \langle 1, 4 \rangle$. The difference between r_a and r_b is not a difference in the roles from which they are derived, nor a difference in which immediate constituent *entity* has the roles from which they are derived: they are both derived from role r_c in sequence π_3. Rather, the difference is between the two immediate-constituent roles *through which* r_a and r_b are derived. The sequence π_3 fills two different immediate-constituent roles in π_2, call them r_d and r_e. Then, r_a is derived *from* r_c, *through* r_d, while r_b is derived *from* r_c, *through* r_e.

$$\pi_3 \;=\; \langle \underbrace{1}_{r_c}, 4\rangle.$$

Thus, role derivation is a relation among three roles, and it holds if the first role is derived from the second through the third.

Consider another example:

$$S_2 \;=\; \{\langle 1, \{\underbrace{2}_{r_f}, 3\}\rangle\},$$

$$\underbrace{\phantom{\langle 1, \{2, 3\}\rangle}}_{r_g}$$

$$\underbrace{\phantom{\langle 1, \{2, 3\}\rangle\;\;}}_{r_h}$$

$$\pi_4 \;=\; \langle 1, \{\underbrace{2}_{r_i}, 3\}\rangle,$$

$$\underbrace{\phantom{\langle 1, \{2, 3\}\rangle}}_{r_j}$$

$$S_3 \;=\; \{\underbrace{2}_{r_k}, 3\}.$$

In this example, r_i is derived from r_k through r_j, and r_f is in turn derived from r_i through r_h (also, r_g is derived from r_j through r_h). Thus there is a clear sense that r_k is an *ancestor* of r_f. I will restrict the concept of derivation to immediate derivation—derivation through an immediate-constituent role. (We can define the concept of a role's ancestors easily enough, given the concept of immediate role derivation.)

It is clear that some roles in different entities have a lot in common. For instance, the role played by 1 in $\langle 1, 4\rangle$ is quite similar to that played by 2 in $\langle 2, 4\rangle$. However, on the account I will develop each role is a role in just one entity. Similarities between roles, then, must be explained not by identity but by various features roles can share. The word 'role' has a type-ish connotation that makes this decision seem arbitrary and even odd. But if we keep in mind the connection between my use of 'role' and the intuitive idea of an *occurrence* of one entity within the structure of another, the decision seems natural. Certainly, the occurrence of 1 in $\langle 1, 4\rangle$ is not the same occurrence as that of 2 in $\langle 2, 4\rangle$. Also, the first occurrence of 1 in $\langle 1, 2\rangle$ is not the same occurrence as the first occurrence of 1 in $\langle 1, 3\rangle$. Occurrences, and the roles I use to explain them, are entity-bound.

That said, we can allow that there are often natural *types* we can use to classify roles. In a sequence, types of immediate-constituent roles might correspond to ordinal positions: first, second, and so on. And roles below the surface might be typed by a sequence of such positions: a certain role might be described as that of the third member of the second member of the fourth member of the sequence. Thus we may have use for an abstract entity 'third-second-fourth' that characterizes the role. I will develop a similar notion for propositions below, which I will call the notion of a role's *pedigree*.

The central notions of constituent structure that will find use below are now out on the table.[2] I will next display them in more formal dress. Where important for clarity I will use the standard predicate calculus with equality, and notions from an unspecified set theory. I will use the variables $S, T, \ldots$ for sets, f, g, $\ldots$ for functions, $r, s, \ldots$ for roles, and x, y, z for any entities whatever. The explanations in the following list are informal; I give official axioms below.

4.2.1 Basic Structural Concepts

$\underline{Roles(x) = S}$ means: S is the set of roles in entity x.

$\underline{Fills(x, r)}$ means: entity x fills role r.

> There is no need for an argument in this relation for the entity in which x occurs, since, according to the theory, a role is a role in just one entity.

$\underline{ICRole(r)}$ means: r is an immediate-constituent role.

> If such a role of an entity x is filled, then what fills it is an immediate constituent of x.

$\underline{Derived(r_1, r_2, r_3)}$ means: role r_1 (in entity x) is derived from role r_2 through r_3. The relation *Derived* holds if the presence of r_1 among the roles in an entity x is due to role r_2's being a role in the entity that fills immediate-constituent role r_3 in x.

Based on these concepts, we can define some others, which will come in handy:

---

2. These notions apply only to a certain kind of constituent structure; others, including no doubt physical parthood, are not elucidated by what follows. I make no claim to have discovered features of structure-in-general; I have my sights on a kind of structure that the account in the text serves to identify.

ImmConst(x, y) means: x is an immediate constituent of y. That is, x fills a role r of y such that *ICRole*(r).

S = *UnfilledRoles*(x) means: S is the subset of *Roles*(x) containing the roles r such that for no x, *Fills*(x, r).

A *partial* entity may have unfilled roles (this is the definition of 'partial entity'); an entity that is *properly* partial does have unfilled roles. We will encounter properly partial propositions below; these can occur within the constituent structure of a genuine, complete proposition. In the account of the next section, they will perform some of the jobs of non-sentential well-formed formulae or propositional functions or parametric objects in other systems, but they contain no variables, parameters, or arbitrary objects.

4.2.2   Axioms for Constituent Structure

Now I will give the basic principles about structure that will be used in the accounts of propositions. I take these to be plausible rigorous formulations of the preceding informal characterization of these notions (the more complex axioms are given a brief italicized slogan followed by the official formulation).

S1   A role is a role in only one entity.

S2   A role is filled by at most one entity.

S3   Roles are immediate-constituent roles or derived roles, but never both.

S4   Derivation is immediate, unique, and preserves the filling.

That is:

1.   A derived role in an entity is derived *through* one of its immediate-constituent roles, *from* a role in what fills that immediate-constituent role.

2.   If role r_1 is derived from r_2 through r_3, then no other role is derived from r_2 through r_3, and r_1 is derived from no role other than r_2 and through no role other than r_3.

3.   A derived role is filled by the thing, if any, that fills the role from which it is derived.

4.3   A Simple Theory of Propositions

On to the account of structured propositions and relations. Before I
begin I want to deflect an objection to the present account based on its
complexity. One might ask, if there are alternative accounts of structured propositions in terms of sets or sequences or formulae in some
formal language, and these can be given more concisely, does their simplicity not argue strongly for them over this account? I am not sure
about the role in general of differences in simplicity in deciding among
competing explanations, but here I think the question does not arise.
To give a thorough account of structured propositions, one needs to give
explanations of substitution, abstraction, well-formedness and so on. It
happens that much of this groundwork, for accounts of propositions as
sequences or as formulae, is familiar from work in set theory or in the
foundations of logics involving formal languages; so it need not be re-
hashed each time use is made of sequences or of logical formulae. But
when such accounts of propositions are presented from the ground up,
the presentations are as complex as what follows. In any event, much of
the apparent complexity of the present account is due to its unfamiliar-
ity.

The account is as far as I know novel in its use of empty roles in
abstraction (in order to avoid the assumptions that there are variables or
parametric objects in propositions, and that the arguments of relations
are ordered). It is otherwise similar to some accounts of states of affairs
in situation theory (Barwise and Perry 1983; Barwise and Etchemendy
1987)—especially in the adoption of distinctive, non-set-theoretic modes
of constituency for propositions and relations. My account is meant to
fill out the sometimes sketchy notion of a Russellian proposition, but
the novel aspects may be useful in formulating a situation theory. I
should note from the start that the simple account I will give of the
truth of these propositions is "naïve" in that it does not escape semantic
paradoxes if, for example, the relation of *holding* (between any relation
and assignment of entities to its arguments) is taken to be within its
purview (I will explain why below).

In what follows I will use variables $p, p', \ldots$ for (partial) propositions, $R, R_1, \ldots$ for (partial) relations, and $j, j_1, \ldots$ for the arguments of
relations.

4.3.1 Basic Logical Concepts

As before, the following explanations are informal, and the official axioms will be presented shortly.

$Prop(p)$ means: p is a partial proposition. (Recall that a partial entity may, but need not, have unfilled roles.) I will often omit the 'partial' in discussion of partial propositions and relations.

$Reln(R)$ means: R is a partial relation. A partial relation with a nonempty set of roles (including any properly partial relation) must be a complex relation, abstracted from a partial proposition. A simple relation, though of course it has arguments, has no roles (and so cannot be properly partial).

$Args(R) = S$ means: S is the set of arguments on which R is a relation.

$MainRelRole(r, p)$ means: r is the main-relation role in proposition p.

$Corresponds(r, j)$ means: role r is the role in a proposition corresponding to argument j of its main relation.

The entity that fills r, if there is one, is associated with argument j of the main relation in the proposition. Correspondence thus applies only to immediate constituent roles in a proposition.

$Abstracted(R, p)$ means: relation R is a complex relation abstracted from proposition p.

$Binds(j, r)$ means: argument j (of a complex relation) binds role r (in the proposition that is abstracted over in forming that relation).

A complex relation is formed from a properly partial proposition (the sole immediate constituent of the relation) by binding unfilled roles in the proposition. The arguments of the complex relation do the binding; each binds a nonempty set of roles.

We can define:

$MainRel(R, p)$ means: R is the main relation of proposition p—it fills p's main-relation role.

$Associated(x, j, p)$ means: entity x fills the role in p that corresponds to argument j, which is an argument of p's main relation.

And here are some notational conventions I adopt (they were introduced informally above):

$\langle\!\langle R; f \rangle\!\rangle$ means: the (partial) proposition with main relation R, such that for each argument j of R, it has a corresponding role filled by the entity (if any) given by $f(j)$. According to the theory below there is exactly one such (partial) proposition for a given R and f. I will call this function the proposition's *assignment*.

$[\{j_1, \ldots, j_n\} : p]$ means: the relation abstracted from proposition p with the set of arguments $\{j_1, \ldots, j_n\}$. According to the theory, there is a distinct set of arguments (belonging to a distinct abstracted relation) for every truly different way the unfilled roles in p might be bound by arguments. That is, there is one n-ary relation abstracted from p for each collection of n disjoint, nonempty subsets of *UnfilledRoles(p)*.

4.3.2   Axioms for Structured Propositions

P1 Propositions have relation-argument structure.

That is, the immediate-constituent roles in a (partial) proposition are a single main-relation role, which is filled by a relation, and for each argument of that relation, a single corresponding role (a distinct role for each argument).

P2 There exists a unique proposition for any assignment to arguments.

That is, for any relation R and any partial function f from its arguments to any entities whatever, there is a unique proposition $\langle\!\langle R; f \rangle\!\rangle$. That is, a proposition is uniquely determined by a main relation and an assignment from the relation's arguments to the entities (if any) that fill the roles in the proposition corresponding to those arguments. (This is not a notation of operator-application.)

P3 A proposition has roles derived from all roles in its immediate constituents.

That is, for every immediate constituent role r_3 in a proposition, and role r_2 in the entity that fills r_3, there is a role r_1 in the proposition, derived from r_2 through r_3 (that is, $Derived(r_1, r_2, r_3)$).

P4 An argument is an argument of only one relation.

P5 A complex relation has the unique proposition from which it is abstracted as its only immediate constituent.

P6 There is a unique, distinct relation for any partial proposition p and any way of grouping some of p's unfilled roles into co-bound sets.

That is, for any proposition p and set $\{S_1, \ldots, S_n\}$ of disjoint, nonempty sets of p's unfilled roles, there is a distinct, unique relation abstracted from p, with arguments $j_1, \ldots, j_n$, such that each j_i binds exactly the roles in S_i.

P7 A complex relation has roles derived from all the unbound roles in the abstracted proposition.

That is, if $R = [S : p]$, then for each role in p not bound by any member of S, there is a role in R derived from it.

These axioms yield a simple theory of propositions and relations, allowing proposition formation from any relation and any assignment to its arguments, and allowing relation abstraction from any partial proposition and grouping of some of its unfilled roles.

The principles about abstracted relations may bear more explanation. Consider a proposition with some unfilled roles:

$$\langle\!\langle R; \cdots \underline{\quad} \cdots \underline{\quad} \cdots \underline{\quad} \cdots \underline{\quad} \cdots \rangle\!\rangle .$$

The idea is that there is a different relation for each way of grouping some of the unfilled roles together. So, for instance, there is a relation abstracted from this proposition as follows (where lines from arguments to unfilled roles indicates binding):

The identity of the arguments in this relation (call them j_1 and j_2), by axioms P4 and P6, is determined by the grouping of the proposition's unfilled roles into co-bound sets.

4.3.3 Roles and Pedigrees

I want now to define the function $Ped(r)$, which for any role in a proposition or relation yields a certain sequence we will call its *pedigree*. This function will be useful in two ways. First, as I mentioned earlier, it will give us a systematic way to characterize structurally, or to "type," the roles in propositions and relations. Second, it will aid in the characterization of the truth conditions of arbitrary propositions. For that task we will need a notion of *completion*: a completion of a partial entity is another entity identically structured except for having specified entities fill some roles that structurally correspond to unfilled roles in the partial entity (since roles are roles in just one entity, unfilled roles can never themselves literally be filled). Considerations about pedigrees guarantee that an appropriate completion function exists.

A pedigree is simply a sequence, each of whose members is either an argument of a simple relation, one of the two arbitrarily chosen entities ϕ_R and ϕ_p, or a set of pedigrees. We can choose any two entities whatever to be ϕ_R and ϕ_p (so long as they are not arguments or sets of pedigrees); they serve as flags of main-relation roles (in any proposition) and abstracted proposition roles (in any complex relation), respectively. Since *Ped* is a defined notion—a tool as opposed to a basic concept—the arbitrariness of the choice of ϕ_R and ϕ_p is no cause for deep concern.

The sequence $Ped(r)$ traces the way in which a role r in entity x is derived through the constituent structure of x; it determines a path down the constituency tree of the structured entity.

Definition of $Ped(r)$:

1. If r is a main-relation role then $Ped(r) = \langle \phi_R \rangle$ (that is, the singleton sequence containing ϕ_R).

2. If r is the role in proposition p corresponding to argument j of p's main relation R, then

    a. if R is simple, then $Ped(r) = \langle j \rangle$, and

    b. if R is complex, then $Ped(r) = \langle S \rangle$, where S is the set of the pedigrees of the unfilled roles in the proposition abstracted over in R that are bound by j.

3. If r is the role in relation R of the proposition from which R is abstracted, then $Ped(r) = \langle \phi_p \rangle$.

4. If $Derived(r_1, r_2, r_3)$, then $Ped(r_1) = Ped(r_3) \frown Ped(r_2)$. (Recall that '$\frown$' is the concatenation operator on sequences.)

    Define $Peds(x)$ to be the set containing $Ped(r)$ for each $r \in Roles(x)$.

    To see how the concept of pedigree works, the reader should verify the following claims:

- In the proposition $\langle\!\langle$ *Taller*; *Tom*, *Ann* $\rangle\!\rangle$, in which Tom and Ann fill roles corresponding to the arguments j_T^+ and j_T^-, there are three roles, with the pedigrees $\langle \phi_R \rangle$, $\langle j_T^+ \rangle$ and $\langle j_T^- \rangle$.

- The partial proposition $\langle\!\langle\, Taller; x, Ann \,\rangle\!\rangle$ has three roles with exactly the same pedigrees as those in $\langle\!\langle\, Taller; Tom, Ann \,\rangle\!\rangle$. (This hints at the use pedigrees will see in defining a notion of completion on which the latter proposition is a completion of the former.)

- The relation $[x : \langle\!\langle\, Taller; x, Ann \,\rangle\!\rangle\,]$ has three roles, with pedigrees $\langle \phi_p \rangle$, $\langle \phi_p, \phi_R \rangle$, and $\langle \phi_p, j_T^- \rangle$. It does not have a role derived from the role with pedigree $\langle j_T^+ \rangle$ in $\langle\!\langle\, Taller; x, Ann \,\rangle\!\rangle$, because that role is bound by the sole argument of this relation.

- In the proposition $\langle\!\langle\, [x : \langle\!\langle\, Taller; x, Ann \,\rangle\!\rangle\,]; Tom \,\rangle\!\rangle$, the role filled by Tom has the pedigree $\langle \{ j_T^+ \} \rangle$.

- Finally, a relatively complex example. Consider the proposition p that Ann and Tom are such that the thing between them has Fred between it and Joe. This is the following proposition (with all roles indicated; B is the relation among three things of [the first] being between [the second and the third]):

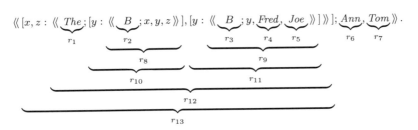

Table 4.1 gives the pedigree π_i of each role r_i in this proposition (where j_{The}^1 and j_{The}^2 are the arguments of the relation The, and j_B^1, j_B^2, and j_B^3 are the arguments of B).

For the present purposes, I will make two simplifying assumptions. First, I assume that the only structured constituents of propositions are propositions and relations. Second, I will assume that all roles have finitely long pedigrees.

Define the notion of the completion of a partial proposition as follows:

$p^+ = Completion(p, f)$ means: (where f is a function on a finite set S of p's unfilled roles) p^+ is the unique proposition such that

Table 4.1
Pedigrees of roles in the proposition

π_1	$=$	$\langle \phi_R, \phi_p, \phi_R \rangle$	π_8	$=$	$\langle \phi_R, \phi_p, j^1_{The}, \phi_p \rangle$
π_2	$=$	$\langle \phi_R, \phi_p, j^1_{The}, \phi_p, \phi_R \rangle$	π_9	$=$	$\langle \phi_R, \phi_p, j^2_{The}, \phi_p \rangle$
π_3	$=$	$\langle \phi_R, \phi_p, j^2_{The}, \phi_p, \phi_R \rangle$	π_{10}	$=$	$\langle \phi_R, \phi_p, j^1_{The} \rangle$
π_4	$=$	$\langle \phi_R, \phi_p, j^2_{The}, \phi_p, j^2_B \rangle$	π_{11}	$=$	$\langle \phi_R, \phi_p, j^2_{The} \rangle$
π_5	$=$	$\langle \phi_R, \phi_p, j^2_{The}, \phi_p, j^3_B \rangle$	π_{12}	$=$	$\langle \phi_R, \phi_p \rangle$
π_6	$=$	$\langle \{\langle j^1_{The}, \phi_p, j^1_B \rangle\} \rangle$	π_{13}	$=$	$\langle \phi_R \rangle$
π_7	$=$	$\langle \{\langle j^1_{The}, \phi_p, j^3_B \rangle\} \rangle$			

a. For every role in p there is a role in p^+ with the same pedigree. That is, $Peds(p) \subseteq Peds(p^+)$. In this sense, they are structurally similar.

b. Roles in p and p^+ that share pedigrees are filled by the same entities, if any, except for the differences entailed by the following: each role r^+ in p^+ with the same pedigree as a member r of S is filled by $f(r)$.

Then, the following holds:[3]

THEOREM 1 For any proposition p and function f on a finite set S of p's unfilled roles, there is a proposition p^+ such that $p^+ = Completion(p, f)$.

4.3.4 Truth and Holding

Given the notion of a completion, we can now interdefine truth for propositions and the relation of *holding* between a relation and an assignment to its arguments. We take facts about holding for simple relations and assignments of simple entities, as given; the effect of these definitions is to define truth and holding, for arbitrary propositions and relation/assignment pairs, inductively from this given basis.

A proposition $\langle\!\langle R; f \rangle\!\rangle$ is *true* just in case its main relation R *holds* of the entities assigned to its arguments by assignment f.

A complex relation $[T : p]$ *holds* of the entities assigned to its arguments by assignment f just in case the proposition $Completion(p, g)$ is *true*, where g is the function that takes each unfilled role in p bound by an argument j in T, to $f(j)$.

---

3. I omit the proof, which is not brief. I prove a similar theorem in Crimmins 1992b.

This account is "naïve" in that it does not escape semantic paradox if, for example, the relation of holding is taken to be within its purview. To see this, note that it is straightforward to define from that relation the property *HoldsOfSelf*, which is the property of being such that one does not hold of oneself assigned to one's sole argument. Then, simply consider the Grelling's Antinomy relation,

$$R \; = \; [\, x : \langle\!\langle \, Not; \, \langle\!\langle \, HoldsOfSelf; x \,\rangle\!\rangle \,\rangle\!\rangle \,].$$

On the present account, the proposition $\langle\!\langle R; R \rangle\!\rangle$ is true if and only if it is not true. The account of the truth of these propositions (though not the account of what propositions there are) is thus inconsistent, though I suspect that many techniques for resolving the paradoxes, including that of Barwise and Etchemendy (1987), can be adapted to this account.

We will consider an example in the next section that demonstrates the effect of the definitions of truth and holding.

4.3.5 Logical Relations

Since I treat logical relations as relations like any others, they play no distinguished role in the account of truth. Here are characterizations of some logical relations.

$\langle\!\langle \, Not; p \,\rangle\!\rangle$ is true iff p is not true.

$\langle\!\langle \, And; p, q \,\rangle\!\rangle$ iff p and q are true.

$\langle\!\langle \, Or; p, q \,\rangle\!\rangle$ is true iff at least one of p and q is true.

$\langle\!\langle \, Some; P, Q \,\rangle\!\rangle$ is true iff at least one entity x such that P holds of x, is such that Q holds of x.

$\langle\!\langle \, All; P, Q \,\rangle\!\rangle$ is true iff every entity x such that P holds of x, is such that Q holds of x.

$\langle\!\langle \, The; P, Q \,\rangle\!\rangle$ is true iff there is exactly one entity of which P holds, and Q holds of everything of which P holds.

Now for the example. Consider the proposition (whose thirteen roles are indicated above) that Ann and Tom are such that the thing between them has Fred between it and Joe. This is true if the relation filling the role r_{13} holds of Ann and Tom. The relation holds of them just in case the following completion of the proposition filling r_{12} is true:

$$\langle\!\langle \, The; [y : \langle\!\langle \, B; Ann, y, Tom \,\rangle\!\rangle \,], [y : \langle\!\langle \, B; y, Fred, Joe \,\rangle\!\rangle \,] \,\rangle\!\rangle \,.$$

This proposition is true if there is just one thing of which the property

$[y : \langle\!\langle B; Ann, y, Tom \rangle\!\rangle]$

holds, and it is such that the following property holds of it:

$[y : \langle\!\langle B; y, Fred, Joe \rangle\!\rangle]$.

This is the case just in case (i) there is just a single individual who is such that B holds among Ann, this individual and Tom, and (ii) B also holds among this individual, Fred, and Joe.

4.4   Structured Beliefs and Thought Maps

The account of structured ideational beliefs is similar to the account of propositions just given in that both accounts classify entities by structure, and in that the structures of beliefs and propositions are similar. For instance, in both accounts abstraction is explained in terms of the binding of unfilled roles in partial entities. However, there is a key difference. Since ideational beliefs are concrete particulars, it is not the case that (in analogy to axiom P2) for any idea and assignment of representations to its argument places, there *really is* a belief in which those argument places are associated with those representations. Instead, there is at least a *potential* for a belief with that structure. Supplying an idea and an assignment yields not a belief but a thought map—a structural type of belief that an agent is equipped to form. This difference will make the treatment of structured beliefs more than just an echo of the account of propositions.

What is crucial about this account as it fits into the rest of my project is that it licenses a notion of representational responsibility. I do not think that the acceptibility of (what I take to be) the commonsense notion of representational responsibility turns on this being a correct account of belief structure. In fact I am not as confident as I would like to be about what would count as a correct account of belief structure (partly because of considerations discussed in chapter 2 about tacit belief). The following account is one way in which a systematic account of representational structure can be given; the strategy of presentation is certainly adaptable to different views about belief structure.

The task is to characterize the structural types of the beliefs an agent is in principle capable of forming given a stock of notions and ideas. In the case of structures having enormous complexity, the "potential" for beliefs having those structures falls short of practical possibility, since, for one thing, brains can get only so big. The obstacles here are much like those restricting the class of assertions an agent can make using a given vocabulary. We recognize an unlimited class of sentences as in some sense potential objects of utterance for an agent, and yet we recognize that many of these sentences actually cannot be uttered by the agent due to resource limitations. Sentences are (or determine) utterance maps; they play a role in structurally characterizing potential utterances very like the role that thought maps will play here in characterizing potential beliefs. The structural principles that govern which arrangements of words can be asserted, and those that govern which arrangements of representations can occur in a belief, do not themselves limit the complexity of sentences or of beliefs. Recall that an important difference between beliefs and utterances is that different beliefs of a single agent often involve the same representation, while different utterances cannot (ordinarily, at least) involve the same token utterances of words.

The thought map that maps a given belief contains specifications (or maps) of the belief's main idea and of the representations that are associated with the idea's argument places. So we can structurally describe the potential beliefs of a given agent by identifying the thought maps that map them.

I will introduce an apparatus to set-theoretically model thought maps, and then characterize the set-theoretic entities that model thought maps of potential beliefs for the agent in question. It will be important to keep in mind that there are three kinds of entities involved in the account: actual concrete representations (which include notions, ideas and beliefs); maps, which are structural types of representations; and set-theoretic entities (called *depictions*), which I use to model maps. My task has two parts: I will say what it is for a depiction to model (or "depict") a given map, and then I will generate a class of depictions using simple set-theoretic definitions, in a way such that this class contains exactly the depictions that depict maps of potential beliefs for the agent.

To depict the thought map that maps a belief in which certain representations are associated with the argument places of the main idea i, we generate a depiction—a set-theoretic entity—that contains in its constituent structure in a uniquely decodable way (i) the main idea, and (ii) the function f from the argument places of that idea to the representations associated with them. We can do this with an ordered pair of the idea and the function, or with an ordered triple of these and a specific "flag" entity to mark the triple as a thought map depiction, or in any number of other ways (so long as we are consistent and choose suitably different such devices for depictions of idea maps, thought maps, and so on; more on these below). However we choose to do it, we can denote the resulting thought map depiction as follows:

$(i; f)$.

For any belief with the structure that this depiction models, i is its main idea and, for each argument place pl of i, the representation $f(pl)$ is associated with pl in the belief. In just this way we can model the structures of many potential beliefs, namely, ones that involve an actually existing main idea and actually existing representations associated with the argument places of the idea.

Given some ideas and representations, agents can form others; many potential beliefs involve not only actual but also merely potential ideas and representations, ones that are structurally cobbled from simpler actual ideas and representations. For instance, you have the potential to form a belief that every Russian is either tall or rich, which would involve a complex idea of *being either tall or rich*, which you probably do not have in your repertoire of persistent representations. If you were to form this belief, you would need to form the complex idea from your simpler ideas of *being tall*, *being rich*, and *Or* (the relation that holds of two propositions just in case at least one is true). In modeling the structures of potential beliefs, then, we need also to model the structures of the potential ideas that can be involved in the beliefs.

In addition to modeling the structures of beliefs and of complex ideas, we will need to model the structures of the complex representations of propositions I will call *thoughts*. I assume that if an agent is capable of forming a belief with a given proposition as its content, then the agent is also capable of forming beliefs *about* the proposition, in a certain sense of 'about'. A belief about a proposition, in this sense, has as its content a proposition that contains the given proposition as a constituent. In this sense, a belief that p or q is about the propositions p and q. And a belief that Joe hopes that p is about p. Having such a belief involves having a concrete particular representation of a proposition. But not all representations of propositions are alike: while some representations of propositions are articulate, having structure like that of a belief, others may be simple *notions*. Someone may have a notion representing Goedel's Theorem, or antidisestablishmentarianism (pretending for the moment that these are specific propositions), that does not articulate the structure of these propositions. Thoughts are articulate, concrete representations of propositions; thus, like notions, thoughts are token representations rather than episodes of thinking. But a thought has logical structure; like a belief, a thought has a main idea and other representations associated with the argument places of that idea. Thus, it is reasonable to hold that an agent's potential thoughts stand in a one-to-one structural correspondence to her potential beliefs, and so to take thought maps to be structural types equally of beliefs and thoughts.

First some notation. I will use h's with various subscripts and superscripts for thoughts, i's for ideas, n's for notions, m's for representations generally, and x's as variables. The boldface version of a symbol will be used for *depictions* of maps of the kind of entity for which the nonbold symbol is used. That is, I will use $\mathbf{h}$'s, $\mathbf{i}$'s, $\mathbf{n}$'s, and $\mathbf{m}$'s for depictions of maps of thoughts, ideas, notions, and any representations, respectively; μ's will be used for the maps themselves, and τ's specifically for thought maps.

4.4.1   Depiction of Actual Representations

Now I will offer some principles connecting depictions, maps, and actual representations.

There is exactly one depiction of every representation map, exactly one map depicted by every depiction and exactly one map of every representation (for brevity I will include both beliefs and argument places as representations, as well as ideas, notions and thoughts). Because of this, we can use the following notational device to talk about maps: if $\mathbf{m}$ is a depiction of a map of a representation, then the term '$\overline{\mathbf{m}}$' stands for the map itself.

Simple representations: Every notion, simple idea, and argument place of a simple idea depicts a map of itself (for example, a simple idea depicts the idea map that maps the idea itself). The way depictions of thought maps and idea maps (for complex ideas) specify particular ideas and notions as involved in the representations they map is by containing the ideas and notions themselves as constituents.

Beliefs and Thoughts: The thought map $\overline{(\mathbf{i}; f)}$ maps m (a belief or thought) just in case

a. $\bar{\mathbf{i}}$ maps the main idea i of m, and

b.   there is a representation m_1 associated in m with an argument place pl of i, just in case there is a map $\overline{m_1}$ and an argument-place map depiction $\mathbf{pl}$ belonging to $\mathbf{i}$ such that $\overline{m_1}$ maps m_1, $\overline{\mathbf{pl}}$ maps pl, and $f(\mathbf{pl}) = \mathbf{m_1}$. (I will define below the notion of an argument-place map depiction *belonging to* an idea map depiction.)

Complex Ideas: The idea map $\overline{(S : \mathbf{h})}$ maps a complex idea i just in case $\bar{\mathbf{h}}$ maps the partial thought from which i is abstracted, and the members of S depict the maps of i's argument places.

To define what it is to map an argument place of a complex idea requires a brief detour, in which I will introduce the notions of *roles* in mental representations and of the *pedigrees* of these roles, in much the same way as these notions were introduced for propositions. Since the territory here is very similar to the account of propositions, I will be brief; an understanding of that account is necessary here. Recall that thoughts and complex ideas have constituents, which play roles in the structure of these entities. There can be partial thoughts and ideas, in which roles go unfilled. These are cognitively real representations that are components of more complex, complete thoughts and ideas. In what follows I will often omit the 'partial' when discussing thoughts and ideas that may be either complete or properly partial.

A thought (or a belief) has immediate-constituent roles for its main idea and for each argument place of its main idea, each role of the latter kind being filled by the representation, if any, associated with that argument place in the thought (or belief). A thought (or belief) has roles derived from all roles in its immediate constituents; these roles are derived through its immediate constituent roles. These two sorts of roles exhaust the roles in a thought (or belief).

A complex idea contains as its only immediate constituent a partial thought. It has argument places (all of which belong only to that idea), each of which binds one or more of the unfilled roles in that partial thought. Apart from the role filled by the thought, the only roles in a complex idea are roles derived from each role in the thought that is not bound by an argument place of the idea.

Given two arbitrarily chosen objects ϕ_i and ϕ_t we can define the pedigree of a role in a belief, thought, or idea. The pedigree of a main-idea role is $\langle \phi_i \rangle$. That of an abstracted-thought role is $\langle \phi_t \rangle$. The pedigree of a role in a thought or belief corresponding to an argument place pl of its main relation i is $\langle pl \rangle$ if i is simple, and otherwise is $\langle S \rangle$, where S is the set of the pedigrees of roles bound by pl. The pedigree of a role derived through a second role from a third role is the concatenation of the pedigrees of the second and third roles.

Argument Places: $\overline{pl}$ maps an argument place pl of an idea i abstracted from a thought h, just in case $\mathbf{pl}$ is a set containing exactly the pedigrees of the roles in h bound by pl. The argument-place map depictions *belonging to* an idea map depiction are just the argument places of $\mathbf{i}$ if $\mathbf{i}$ is a simple idea, and, if $\mathbf{i} = (S : \mathbf{h})$, are the members of S.

4.4.2 Maps of Potential Representations

Now we can state the following principles about the maps of the agent's potential representations; every map will be a distinct structural type of (potential) representation.

Since thoughts and complex ideas can mingle structurally just like propositions and complex relations, I will give simultaneous characterizations of the depictions of thought maps and of idea maps for an agent.

Thought maps: For any simple idea i and function f from the argument places of i to any representation-map depictions, there is a thought map $\overline{(i; f)}$. And for any idea map $\overline{(S : \mathbf{h})}$ and function f from S to any representation-map depictions, there is a thought map $\overline{((S : \mathbf{h}); f)}$.

Before we can state the principle about what idea maps there are, we need to extend the notion of pedigree to depictions of representation maps in addition to representations themselves, so that a depiction $\mathbf{m}$ is assigned the set of pedigrees that a representation would have if it were mapped by $\overline{\mathbf{m}}$. We will define at the same time a relation of one depiction being *at* a pedigree within another depiction:

1. A thought map depiction $\mathbf{h} = (\mathbf{i}; f)$ has

   a. a pedigree $\langle \phi_i \rangle$ such that $\mathbf{i}$ is at that pedigree within $\mathbf{h}$, and

   b. for each argument-place map depiction $\mathbf{pl}$ belonging to $\mathbf{i}$, a pedigree $\langle \mathbf{pl} \rangle$ such that $f(\mathbf{pl})$ (if f has a value at $\mathbf{pl}$) is at that pedigree within $\mathbf{h}$.

2. An idea map depiction $\mathbf{i} = (S : \mathbf{h})$ has a pedigree $\langle \phi_h \rangle$ such that $\mathbf{h}$ is at that pedigree within $\mathbf{i}$.

3. Say that $\mathbf{m_1}$ is an immediate constituent of $\mathbf{m_2}$ if

    a. $\mathbf{m_2} = (S : \mathbf{h})$, and $\mathbf{m_1}$ is $\mathbf{h}$, or

    b. $\mathbf{m_2} = (\mathbf{i}; f)$, and $\mathbf{m_1}$ is either $\mathbf{i}$ or a value of f.

    If $\mathbf{m_2}$ is an immediate constituent of $\mathbf{m_1}$ at pedigree π_1 within $\mathbf{m_1}$, and $\mathbf{m_2}$ has a pedigree π_2, then $\mathbf{m_1}$ has a pedigree $\pi_1 \frown \pi_2$; and if a depiction $\mathbf{m_3}$ is at π_2 within $\mathbf{m_2}$, then $\mathbf{m_3}$ is also at $\pi_1 \frown \pi_2$ within $\mathbf{m_1}$.

If a depiction $\mathbf{m}$ has a pedigree π such that no depiction is at π within $\mathbf{m}$, then π is an *empty* pedigree for $\mathbf{m}$. A depiction $\mathbf{m}$ has an empty pedigree just in case a representation mapped by $\overline{\mathbf{m}}$ would have an unfilled role with that pedigree. Thus, empty pedigrees in thought map depictions correspond to bindable roles.

Idea maps: For any thought map $\overline{\mathbf{h}}$ and nonempty set S of disjoint, nonempty sets of empty pedigrees for $\mathbf{h}$, there is an idea map $\overline{(S : \mathbf{h})}$.

All of this yields a system of thought maps that assigns an agent potential beliefs of arbitrary complexity, cobbled from simple ideas and notions by way of unrestricted mental "predication" and abstraction.

4.5   Content and Responsibility

The structural features given by thought maps are not the only important properties of beliefs. For instance, beliefs have causes and effects, time-segments of existence, and perhaps strengths or intensities. I have two major reasons for being especially interested in the structural features given by thought maps. First, as I claimed in chapter 2, instances of at-least-tacit believing can be individuated in part by these structural features. Second, the content of an ideational belief (or of a merely "potential" belief) is determined by the thought map mapping it, together with the contents of the structurally simple ideas and notions occurring in the map. In this section, I will spell out this third claim, and characterize the notion of representational responsibility that will figure prominently in the semantics for belief reports.

The upshot of the account will be that the content of a belief (or potential belief) is the proposition with a structure isomorphic to the belief's, containing the contents of the belief's constituent representations in the roles structurally corresponding to the roles filled by those representations in the belief. We saw examples of this representation-content isomorphism in section 4.1. The idea is plausible enough, and elaborating it will not require a great deal of space.

To start, I want to extend the notions of representational content and of (argument) reflecting to maps (not depictions) as well as concrete representations. Ideas, thoughts, notions, and beliefs have content; derivatively, we can assign to a map the content that a representation mapped by it would have. Similarly, we can take the relation *Reflects* to hold between an argument-place *map* and an argument when any argument place mapped by it would reflect the argument.

I assume that we are given the contents of the agent's notions and simple ideas, as well as the facts about which arguments are reflected by which argument places of the agent's simple ideas. From this starting point, we will build up the contents of beliefs, thoughts, and complex ideas based entirely on their structure; we will assign the contents to the structures (the maps) themselves.

Beliefs and Thoughts: The content of a thought map $\overline{(\mathbf{i}; f)}$ is the proposition $\langle\!\langle R; g \rangle\!\rangle$ where (i) R is the content of $\bar{\mathbf{i}}$, and (ii) g is the function on $Args(R)$ that takes an argument j to the entity, if there is one, that is the content of $\overline{f(\mathbf{pl})}$, where $\mathbf{pl}$ belongs to $\mathbf{i}$ and $\overline{\mathbf{pl}}$ reflects j.

To characterize the contents of complex idea maps, it is necessary to define a relation $Trans(\pi_1, \pi_2)$, read 'π_1 translates π_2', that relates pedigrees of roles in propositions or relations with pedigrees of roles in thoughts or ideas (and also relates sets of such pedigrees). We define:

1. $Trans(\langle\langle\phi_R\rangle, \langle\phi_i\rangle\rangle)$. A main-relation pedigree translates a main-idea pedigree.

2. $Trans(\langle\langle\phi_p\rangle, \langle\phi_h\rangle\rangle)$. An abstracted-proposition pedigree translates an abstracted-thought pedigree.

3. If $Reflects(\overline{\mathbf{pl}}, j)$, then $Trans(\langle j\rangle, \langle\mathbf{pl}\rangle)$. The pedigree of a role corresponding to an argument place of an idea is translated by the pedigree of a role corresponding to the argument (of a relation) that the argument place reflects.

4. If $Trans(\pi_1, \pi_2)$ and $Trans(\pi_3, \pi_4)$, then $Trans(\pi_1 \frown \pi_3, \pi_2 \frown \pi_4)$.

The translation of a concatenation of pedigrees is the concatenation of their translations.

5. $Trans(S, \{\pi_2 | \exists \pi_1 (\pi_1 \in S \ \& \ Trans(\pi_1, \pi_2))\})$. The translation of a set of pedigrees is the set of their translations.

Ideas: The content of an idea map $\overline{(S : \mathbf{h})}$ is the relation $[T : p]$, where p is the content of $\overline{\mathbf{h}}$ and the arguments in T bind together those sets of unfilled roles in p whose pedigrees are grouped together in the set T' that is such that $Trans(T', S)$. (T' is a set of sets of pedigrees of unfilled roles in p). This relies on the fact that the pedigrees of unfilled roles in a thought are translated by pedigrees of unfilled roles in the content of the thought.

Argument Places: If $\overline{(S : \mathbf{h})}$ is an idea map whose content is relation R and $\mathbf{pl} \in S$, then $\overline{\mathbf{pl}}$ reflects the argument j of R that is such that the set of pedigrees of roles bound by j translates $\mathbf{pl}$.

Finally, we can give the definition of representational responsibility. We will characterize the relation $Responsible(m, \mu, r)$ among actual representations, representation maps, and roles in propositions:

1.   If $\mu = \overline{(\mathbf{i}; f)}$, and p is the content of μ, then

   a.   if $\mathbf{i}$ is an actual (simple) idea i, then, where r_R is the main-relation role in p, $Responsible(i, \mu, r_R)$; and

   b.   for any argument-place map depiction $\mathbf{pl}$ belonging to $\mathbf{i}$, if $f(\mathbf{pl})$ is an actual representation m, then where r_{pl} is the role in p corresponding to the argument of its main relation reflected by $\overline{\mathbf{pl}}$, $Responsible(m, \mu, r_{pl})$.

2.   If $\mu = \overline{\mathbf{m_1}}$ and

   a. $\mathbf{m_2}$ is an immediate constituent of $\mathbf{m_1}$ at a pedigree π_1,

   b.   there is a role r_2 in the content of $\overline{\mathbf{m_2}}$ and an actual representation m such that $Responsible(m, \overline{\mathbf{m_2}}, r_2)$, and

   c. r_1 is the role in the content of μ derived from r_2,

   then $Responsible(m, \mu, r_1)$.

This gives the characterization of responsibility for immediate-constituent roles as well as derived roles. We can now characterize responsibility in actual beliefs:

$Responsible(m, b, r_1)$ *iff* $\exists \tau (Maps(\tau, b)$ & $Responsible(m, \tau, r_1))$.

On this account, the examples of responsibility given in section 4.1 are straightforward examples of responsibility for immediate-constituent roles. I will close this section with an example of responsibility for a derived role.

I do not believe that someone hates Al, but I might have. If I were to form that belief, I would have a belief b with the following structure (τ_b) and content (p_b):

$$\tau_b = \overline{\mathbf{h}} = \overline{(i_{Some}; i_{Person}, (\{\langle pl^1_H \rangle\} : (i_{Hates}; \underline{\quad}, n_{Al})))},$$

$$p_b = \langle\!\langle Some; Person, [x : \langle\!\langle Hates; x, \underbrace{Al}_{r_{Al}} \rangle\!\rangle] \rangle\!\rangle$$

(where i_{Some}, i_{Person} and i_{Hates} are my ideas of the relations *Some*, *Person* and *Hates*, pl^1_H is the "hater" argument place of i_{Hates}, and n_{Al} is my notion of Al). Note that the first of the following representation-map depictions is an immediate constituent of the second, which is an immediate constituent of $\mathbf{h}$:

$$\mathbf{m_1} = (i_{Hates}; \underline{\quad}, n_{Al})$$

$$\mathbf{m_2} = (\{\langle pl^1_H \rangle\} : (i_{Hates}; \underline{\quad}, n_{Al}))$$

By the first clause in the definition of *Responsible*, my notion n_{Al} is responsible, in $\overline{\mathbf{m_1}}$ for the immediate-constituent role filled by Al in $\langle\!\langle Hates; \underline{\quad}, Al \rangle\!\rangle$ (the content of $\mathbf{m_1}$). By the second clause, that notion is also responsible in $\overline{\mathbf{m_2}}$ for the derived role filled by Al in $[x : \langle\!\langle Hates; x, Al \rangle\!\rangle]$ (the content of $\mathbf{m_2}$). By the second clause again, n_{Al} is responsible in τ_b for the derived role r_{Al} in p_b. As desired, the occurrence of n_{Al} in my potential belief is responsible for the occurrence of Al in the structurally parallel role in the content of that potential belief.

4.6 Systems of Ideational Representation

The account I have given describes only very simple structural properties of a system of ideational beliefs. It is a relatively minimal account, in that it ascribes to beliefs features that are needed to account for what is obvious—that beliefs share notions and ideas—as well as enough structure to distinguish in a principled, systematic way among potential beliefs, ideas and thoughts that need to be distinguished. For example, we must distinguish between two beliefs that differ only in which argument places of their main idea are associated with which constituent notions; my potential beliefs that Joe is taller than Rob and that Rob is taller than Joe need to be distinguished. My goal has been to pre-judge in the account of beliefs as little as possible, while giving a characterization of their structure and contents that meets these desiderata.

The assumptions I have made about the simple idea/assignment structure of ideational beliefs do not entail that there are no further important structural facts about beliefs. There may well be good reasons to consider general beliefs, for example, to be structurally different from particular beliefs (beliefs about things), rather than as differing simply in their main ideas and constituent assignments. Nonetheless, many accounts of mental representation given by researchers in cognitive science are compatible with a single-structure way of looking at things. Ray Jackendoff (1983), for instance, posits "conceptual structures" of many different kinds; but each of these can with little violence be squeezed in to our normal form, given a liberal view about what counts as a thing or property. Jackendoff's project, of deducing features of the human representational system from subtle facts about our linguistic resources and data from experimental psychology, is quite interesting, and suggests directions for systematizing and filling out the simple account given here. Of course, the structural aspects of ideational belief on which I wish to rely heavily should be facts that we need no laboratory evidence or linguistic theory to discover. My claim is that such facts as that beliefs are complex entities containing simpler representations, and that these representations are responsible for filling roles in the contents of beliefs, are deliverances of common sense—they are common (if tacit) knowledge to all who use belief reports. Jackendoff's work supports the literal truth of this part of common sense, and, of course, goes far beyond.

The account I have given certainly places substantive constraints on what can count as a system of ideational representations. The constraints, however, may seem more severe in some ways than they in fact are. For instance, it may seem that the account could be right about only a system in which each explicit belief involves a wholly distinct token sentence-inscription in a mental language. But while my account is compatible with such a language-of-thought system of representation, it does not require that ideational representation work that way. For instance, while there are many interesting points of comparison between notions and names, notions need not be names. To make this point vividly, I will give an example of a system of representations without names but with all the structural features needed to be a system of ideational representation.

A language-of-thought representational system creates a logically interrelated space of ideas, notions, and thoughts by exploiting a system of words and sentences in a way such that each notion, idea, or thought corresponds to a single expression-type of that internal language. A belief (which corresponds to a token inscription of a complex sentencelike expression) involves a particular notion if the inscription contains a token of the name-type corresponding to the notion. Thus, in a language-of-thought system there is a type-token distinction: different beliefs involving the same notion contain *different* tokens of the same representation-type.

Now onto the example of a system of structured representations in which, since there is no such type-token distinction, there is no language of thought (I will return to this claim). This system bears close similarities to the *semantic nets* discussed in cognitive science and AI literature (Quillian 1967).

In our "blocks and string" system, notions and simple ideas are balls of string, each with a large number of loose ends that can be taken and tied to posts anywhere in the system, while the other end remains tied to the notion or idea, that is, to the ball.

A simple belief with the structure

$$\overline{(i; n_1, \ldots, n_k)}$$

consists of a block of wood with a line of posts, one large "idea post" on the left and k small "assignment posts" to its right; the idea post is tied to ball i and, for each j, the jth assignment post from the left is tied to ball n_j (see figure 4.4). (I assume that the ordering of the argument places of simple ideas, like the contents of notions and simple ideas, is given by some aspect of the system that I will not describe.)

A thought with the structure

$$\overline{(i; m_1, \ldots, m_k)}$$

is just like a belief, except that it has an eyelet screwed into a side, to

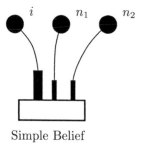
Simple Belief

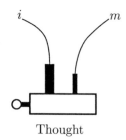
Thought

Figure 4.4
A belief and a thought

enable it to be tied to posts elsewhere in the system—so that the thought may become a constituent of other thoughts, beliefs, and complex ideas. A properly partial simple thought has at least one assignment post that is not tied to anything (there are other ways for complex thoughts to be partial, as we will see).

We will say that one block is an immediate constituent of another if the eyelet of the first block is tied to a post on the second block. One block has another block as a constituent if there is a sequence of blocks that starts with the one block, ends with the other, and is such that each member has the next as an immediate constituent.

A complex idea is a block with a number of "argument posts," which are small posts to the left of a large "thought post." The thought post of a complex idea is tied to the eyelet of the partial thought from which the idea is abstracted. Each argument post binds one or more unfilled roles in the thought by being tied to as-yet-untied argument posts on the thought block and its constituents.[4] The idea with structure

$$\overline{(x, y : (i; \_\_, x, y, m, y))}$$

---

4. This system recalls two points due to Quine: first, that variables of quantification can be replaced with simple lines connecting the "positions" in predicates that are bound together (Quine 1951); and second, that variables are not needed for a language as powerful as a quantified predicate calculus with abstraction (Quine 1966b). His technique for doing away with variables relies heavily on the fact that the argument places of predicates have a definite order (because of this, the way I do without variables in the above account of propositions is importantly different).

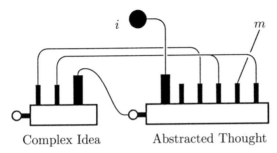

i m

Complex Idea   Abstracted Thought

Figure 4.5
A complex idea and the thought from which it is abstracted

is represented in figure 4.5. The order of the argument places in a complex idea is given by the order of the argument posts.

In this system of blocks and string we can form any potential beliefs, thoughts, and ideas countenanced by the account given above. Consider a belief that Michael either is a child of Edward and Beth or is tall. The realization of this belief in the block system is shown in figure 4.6, along with a list of depictions of the structures of each complex constituent of the belief, and of the belief itself.

In this belief, there is a thought $thought_2$, corresponding to the depiction $(i_{Tall}; \_\_)$—a properly partial thought that has a post bound by an argument post in $idea_2$, as we will see.

There is a complex idea, $idea_1$, that corresponds to the depiction $(y, z : (i_{ChildOf}; \_\_, y, z))$. This idea has two argument posts, each of which binds an assignment post in the constituent thought $thought_1$. The remaining assignment post of $thought_1$, like that of $thought_2$, is bound by the argument post of $idea_2$, of which both thoughts are constituents.

The thought $thought_3$ has as its main idea $idea_1$ and has n_E and n_B (notions of Edward and Beth) associated with the argument places of that idea. The order of the constituent pegs in $thought_3$ reflects the order of the binding pegs in $idea_1$. Thus, n_E is associated with the second argument post of $idea_1$, and n_B is associated with the third. So $thought_3$ is the properly partial thought that [gap] has Edward and Beth as parents (here, I use '[gap]' to signal an unfilled role).

The thought $thought_4$ is a disjunctive thought; it disjoins $thought_3$

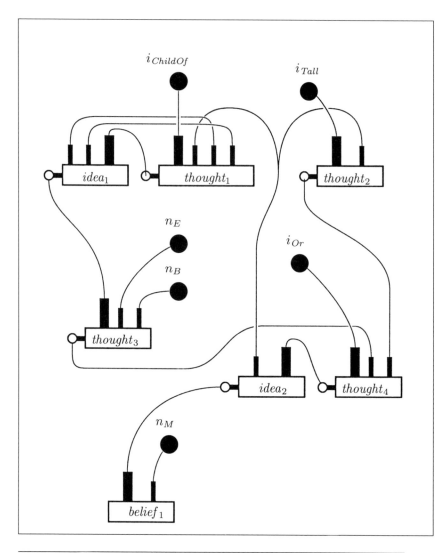

$$
\begin{array}{lll}
thought_1 & : & (i_{ChildOf};\underline{},\underline{},\underline{}) \\
idea_1 & : & (y,z:(i_{ChildOf};\underline{},y,z)) \\
thought_2 & : & (i_{Tall};\underline{}) \\
thought_3 & : & ((y,z:(i_{ChildOf};\underline{},y,z));n_E,n_B) \\
thought_4 & : & (i_{Or};((y,z:(i_{ChildOf};\underline{},y,z));n_E,n_B),(i_{Tall};\underline{})) \\
idea_2 & : & (x:(i_{Or};((y,z:(i_{ChildOf};x,y,z));n_E,n_B),(i_{Tall};x))) \\
belief_1 & : & ((x:(i_{Or};((y,z:(i_{ChildOf};x,y,z));n_E,n_B),(i_{Tall};x)));n_M)
\end{array}
$$

Figure 4.6
A belief that Michael either is a child of Edward and Beth or is tall

and *thought$_2$*. This makes it the thought that either [gap] has Edward and Beth as parents, or [gap] is tall (the two unfilled roles in this thought are not inherently co-indexed—a complex idea other than *idea$_2$* might have bound only one of them or have had different arguments binding the two roles).

Since *idea$_2$* binds the two unfilled roles in *thought$_4$* together, it is the idea of being either the child of Edward and Beth, or tall. In *belief$_1$*, the notion of Michael is associated with the single argument place of *idea$_2$*. So it is the belief that Michael either is the child of Edward and Beth, or is tall.

Of course there are lots of ways in which the blocks and string system differs from spoken and written languages. I think that one of these ways is crucial to a false presupposition that language-of-thought theorists themselves have had about what a system of ideational representations must be like. The crucial difference is that with the balls and blocks there are no symbol-tokens that are distinguished by syntactic type (unless strings that are tied to a thing are tokens of the thing!). It is reasonable to assume that token-type distinction is a crucial one to any representational system that can count as a language—or at any rate, so I will assume, and so it has been assumed by many proponents and critics of the language of thought picture. If this is right, then the 'structured representation = language' identity is unfounded, though it often has been assumed in cognitive science and artificial intelligence.[5]

Now, there are those who would want to claim that, since there are representations in this system, despite the lack of a type-token distinction they *must* be linguistic items, or at least close enough to make a good analogy. And certainly there is enough in common between any two systems of compositional, structured representations to make for lots of good analogies. The point of my denial that there is a language of thought here is to stress that to hold to such an analogy would be to miss at least one important way the system differs from paradigm languages—both natural and formal languages. A language of thought analogy *can* be used to cover almost any representational system, but if it is stretched that far, then it is bound to be misleading. The proof of this is simple—*lots* of critics of the language of thought picture have nat-

---

5. See, for example, the introduction and many of the essays in Brachman and Levesque 1985.

urally assumed that a representational system of that kind must share more features with natural or formal languages than simply being a system of structured representations. Rather than chide these critics for misunderstanding what a language of thought must be like, clearly we should dispense with the analogy and adopt a vocabulary for talking literally about systems of structured representations.

5 Belief Reports

5.1   The Truth about Giorgione

Some of Quine's best ideas have fallen to his decrees of conceptual banishment: any locution that does not quite fit the eternal paradigm of predicate logic does not cut the muster for "limning the true and ultimate structure of reality." Quine passes one such judgment in *Word and Object*, where he tries to come to terms with a troublesome two-sidedness of attitude reports, concluding that although they are practically indispensable, they are, strictly speaking, too infested with vagueness and circumstantiality to make any real sense (Quine 1960, 221). However, he notes elsewhere in the book that vagueness is not such a big deal, as long as you are not out in the penumbra where truth values cannot be found. And neither is circumstantiality much of a flaw: demonstratives like 'that' and 'this', which drip the stuff, still get his applause for their utility.

The analysis of belief reports I will give in this chapter is antagonistic to many aspects of Quine's program, but nonetheless, the semantic account follows upon two of Quine's ideas: first, his brief remarks that *circumstantiality* is a crucial feature of belief reports:

... even if we eternalize the contained sentence [in a belief sentence] and also rid the containing sentence of such sources of truth-value variation as inadequate descriptions, indicator words, and the like, still the whole may remain capable of varying in truth value from occasion to occasion. . . . (Quine 1960, 218)

(An eternal(ized) sentence is one whose significance and truth value do not vary from context to context.) This, of course, is just what Kripke (1979) takes great pains to demonstrate with respect to the sentence 'Pierre believes that London is pretty' (we encountered this example in chapter 1). Like Quine, Kripke sees this fact of apparently varying truth value as a sign that belief reports may be somehow substandard—that they work fine for many purposes but can "break down" if pushed too hard.

Normally, the fact that different uses of a single sentence (like 'it is raining') can have different truth values is taken to be a sign not of any semantic weakness, but of the semantic flexibility that comes with context sensitivity. Belief reports, I will suggest, exhibit a context sensitivity analogous to a use of 'it is raining' or of the term 'you'; the same expression can serve to express different things in different utterances. Explaining how 'you' works involves characterizing how the referent of a use of 'you' depends systematically on the circumstances in which it is used. Similarly, an analysis of belief reports must clarify the effect of circumstances on the claim that a belief sentence is used to make.

The second idea of Quine's that finds its way into this account is his suggestion that, in certain troublesome locutions, proper names can play a role in addition to their usual, primary one of standing for objects. He considers this sentence:

Giorgione was so-called because of his size.   (1)

Quine notes (1960, 153) that the name 'Giorgione' plays two *roles* in this statement. First, it stands for the subject of the claim—the man who was so-called because of his size. And second, it provides *itself* as the name that Giorgione is alleged to have been called because of his size. Quine claims that this two-role phenomenon is what accounts for failures of substitutivity in belief sentences as well. For instance,

Tom believes that Cicero denounced Catiline,   (2)

can be true while at the same time,

Tom believes that Tully denounced Catiline,   (3)

is false, since the two names 'Cicero' and 'Tully', though they refer to the same man, provide different names with which to classify Tom's beliefs.

Quine claims that (1) can be paraphrased as follows:

Giorgione was called 'Giorgione' because of his size.   (4)

This sentence indeed seems to get across what (1) would express in the obvious kinds of circumstances. But a happier paraphrase would be:

Giorgione was called that because of his size.   (5)

Here, 'that' functions as a demonstrative referring to the name that, according to the speaker, Giorgione was called because of his size. The reason this is a better paraphrase than (4) is that there are circumstances unlike the ones Quine means for us to imagine, in which (1) and (5) express the same claim, while (4) expresses something different. If the speaker were to preface his remark with 'Giorgione was called *Mr. Big*', a use of (1) would make the claim that the artist was called 'Mr. Big' because of his size, as would (5). In the same context, (4) would make the claim that Giorgione was called 'Giorgione' because of his size. More evidence that (5) is a better paraphrase is that it suggests the correct analysis of 'He was so-called because of his size' (what, 'he'?).

The locution '*A* is so-called because ...' is more interesting than Quine lets on. This is how it works: every such use of 'so-called' is about a name (usually a name that the subject is called); but the name can be provided *either* by the surrounding circumstances, or, as in Quine's example, by a name used in the very sentence in which 'so-called' occurs. This illuminates the sense in which 'Giorgione' plays a dual role in both (1) and (5), given the circumstances Quine has us imagine. The name plays both a *semantic* role—referring to Giorgione—and a *pragmatic* role—determining the name presupposed by 'so-called' in (1), or referred to by 'that' in (5).

Notice that (1) and (5) can be used to make the same claim by a speaker who is pointing at the name 'Giorgione' on a blackboard. In such a case, the blackboard inscription contributes the name to the statement in virtue of the *pragmatic, contextual* fact that it is being pointed out. In Quine's original case, I believe, the second role played by 'Giorgione' is pragmatic and contextual in the same way. It is the lack of any other relevant name in the circumstances surrounding the use of (1) that makes for the contextual salience of 'Giorgione', the name used in that very sentence.

Since a use of (1) can be about a name other than 'Giorgione' in different circumstances, it cannot be a *semantic* fact about the sentence itself that it is about the name 'Giorgione'—that fact cannot be a consequence simply of what the sentence *means*. And yet, it is part of what the sentence is used to *claim* in the ordinary sorts of circumstances Quine envisions.

In a statement of 'Giorgione played chess', the man Giorgione plays a role quite different from the name 'Giorgione'. The man is part of the subject matter, and the name is a part of the sentence. Both the man and the name contribute to the claim made in a statement of the sentence, but the name contributes only semantically, by representing a constituent of the claim. In contrast, the name 'Giorgione' in (1) is both part of the sentence *and* part of the subject matter of the statement; the name contributes to the claim both semantically (by representing Barbarelli) and pragmatically (by becoming a part of the claim made in context).

The phenomenon of a word contributing both semantically and pragmatically to the claim made in a single statement seems much less surprising in the case of (5). There, the demonstrative 'that' can be used to refer to any name, so why not a name used in (5) itself? And (1) is really no different.[1]

I have gone on about 'so-called' because it is a simple expression that exhibits two features I wish to attribute to belief reports. I think that the claim made in a statement of a given belief sentence can depend in subtle ways on the total circumstances of the report, primarily because the claims made in belief reports involve objects of contextually determined reference (in this case, tacit reference). And second, following Quine, I think that a name or other expression used in a belief report can play two roles—the semantic role it plays in simpler sentences, plus a pragmatic, contextual role that helps to nonreferentially determine a constituent of the claim being made. The difference between (2) and (3), I believe, is no semantic difference in meaning or overt reference, but a contextual, pragmatic difference that results in different claims being made.[2]

An account that recognizes these two features of belief reports will

---

1. An appearance of a sharp difference might come from the fact that 'so-called' is used much more frequently in other ways, as in 'the so-called graduate students are playing volleyball again'. In such cases, it is a good bit more difficult to override the presumption that it is the term used in that sentence ('graduate students') that is presupposed by 'so-called' (though shifts of stress can help). It may be plausible to suppose that in this turn of phrase, 'so-called' has acquired a second meaning by picking up an idiomatic immunity to the normal flexibility of 'so-called'. This would explain why we often write 'The so-called graduate students...'—in which a name is not only used (if indeed it is), but also referred to. This would also explain why paraphrases can recoup the pragmatic flexibility: 'There go the lazy ones. The graduate students so-called are playing volleyball again'. 'So-' should be treated as an operator that does roughly the same things in 'so-called', 'so-defeated', and 'so-learned', which mean 'called in that way', 'defeated in that way', and 'learned in that way'.

2. After I wrote this Graeme Forbes sent me a draft of Forbes 1990 in which he proposes that some belief reports be paraphrased as '*A* so-believes that *s*', a proposal with obvious similarities to the present one in the case of *de dicto* reports (see more on this below). Loar (1972) and Cartwright (1971) also have stressed the usefulness of this example.

go a long way toward explaining the many puzzling cases of belief reporting that have appeared in the philosophical literature since Frege, including Quine's puzzle about Tom and Kripke's about Pierre. In what follows I will offer a semantic and pragmatic account of the claims made in belief reports that honors Quine's two insights, exploits the account of ideational beliefs given in the last two chapters, reflects our ordinary intuitions about the truth of such reports, and allows us in good conscience to "limn" with belief reports as much as we like.

5.2   Semantics

However novel the account of belief reports may be, the style of the semantic framework will be traditional. In this section I will describe the conception of semantics I will adopt and explain how I will treat three sorts of phenomena that are wrapped up in belief reporting: simple predication, context sensitivity, and underarticulation.

A *statement* is an assertive utterance of a sentence intended to make a claim. If everything goes well in a statement and there are no reference failures or other failures of presupposition, a claim is made; this claim is the propositional content of the statement.[3] Claims are

---

3. As Jon Barwise has pointed out in discussion, not every successful assertive utterance of a sentence makes only a single claim. Consider the exam proctor who says to a hall full of students: 'You have by now finished writing your name at the top of every sheet'. The proctor has made a different claim for each student. Another case would be the following sly move to arouse a neighbor's jealousy and a spouse's respect: on a certain morning, the spouse expects the agent to head off to work at a savings bank, while the agent has led the neighbor to believe that the real destination is a fishing spot on a river; in front of both hearers, the agent says 'I'm off to the bank'. These cases are interesting, but for the present purposes it is best to legislate that these utterances are not statements, but things that work by exploiting certain features of statements. Take the announcer's utterance of 'we do it all for you'. How many claims does it make? Suppose it is recorded and played over and over on the radio; does it then make a different class of claims each time it is played? Better that we decide to exempt these kinds of utterances from classification as claim-making statements, and treat them as meaningful assertive utterances of a different kind.

There is a more important sense in which a statement might express more than one proposition, namely, if the rules of the language do not uniquely determine a single proposition as a statement's content, but rather a set or cluster of related propositions. It might be that the ordinary category "claim" picks out not just single propositions but also clusters of them (which would explain fuzzy intuitions about claim identity). These are of course different points if the technical concept of

propositions; they are the timelessly true or false, structured, abstract objects explored in chapter 4.

On the conception of statement semantics outlined in chapter 1, the semanticist's goal is a systematic account of which propositions are expressed in which utterances. For instance, a plausible result of a semantics for simple statements would be that my statement of the sentence 'You are tired', made at time t, addressed to person a, expresses the claim that a is tired at t:

$$\langle\!\langle\, Tired; a, t \,\rangle\!\rangle\,.$$

Singular belief reports are statements made with belief sentences—sentences of the form:

$$A \text{ believes that } s. \tag{6}$$

The 'A' slot holds a singular term referring to the alleged believer, and the 's' slot contains a "content sentence." The verb 'believes' need not be in the present tense, as it happens to be in (6). This class of sentences is syntactically legitimate, but it is also unwieldy. The reason is that there is no restriction on the sentences that can be substituted for the s in (6)—for every English sentence, there are belief sentences that include it as a content sentence. One way of restricting our project would be to consider only belief sentences that contain simple content sentences of certain kinds. This would in fact be adequate for many of the puzzling examples, since they concern belief sentences with only very simple content sentences like 'London is pretty' and 'you are in danger'. But I will not restrict my account in that way. I will hold that for any singular belief report, the only feature of the content sentence that is directly semantically relevant is its propositional content—the proposition that the utterance of that sentence expresses. So what I will do is explain how that proposition together with other features of the report determine the claim made in the report—I will give the "belief-report clause" of a recursive semantics.

In giving the account of the content of a statement u of 'A believes that s', I will assume that we are given the content of the subutterance u_s of the content sentence s. Let $Cont(u)$ be the function yielding the

---

content and the ordinary concept of claim do not coincide. In the text I assume they do coincide, but this assumption is not essential to what follows.

content of an utterance u; my task can be seen as giving a constraint on $Cont(u)$ for utterances of belief sentences. The account of belief reports will have the following structure: for a report u of a belief sentence of the form 'A believes that s',

$$Cont(u) = \cdots p \cdots,$$
   where $p = Cont(u_s)$.

I will assume the thesis of direct reference (discussed in chapter 1), which entails that the function $Cont(u)$ yields *singular* propositions for utterances of simple sentences containing demonstratives and proper names (a singular proposition has individuals as constituents). The proposition expressed by an utterance of a simple sentence with names and demonstratives has among its constituents the objects referred to by the uses of those expressions; the objects are the contents of the uses of the terms. Also, I will assume for simplicity that there is a natural class of "simple predications," in statements of which a relation (expressed by a verb) is claimed to hold among various entities. In utterances of these sentences, the use of the verb has as its content that relation, and the proposition expressed in such a statement has the relation as a constituent.

Consider the propositional content of an utterance of

Wellington defeated Napoleon.   (7)

I will take this proposition to have as constituents the men Wellington and Napoleon, and the relation of defeating. (Of course, the past-tense construction also contributes to the proposition expressed. For simplicity, rather than assume a particular account of tense, I will ignore tense altogether.) The content of a use of (7) is this proposition:

$\langle\!\langle\, Defeated;\, Wellington,\, Napoleon\, \rangle\!\rangle$.

Different utterances of context-sensitive expressions can have different contents. So the form of a correct semantics for such an expression ϕ is not going to be:

For any utterance u of ϕ, $Cont(u) = a$.

Instead, we need something of this form:

For any utterance u of ϕ, $Cont(u) = x$, where x is the unique y (if there is one) such that $R_\phi(y, u)$.

For example,

For an utterance u of 'you', $Cont(u) = x$, where x is the person to whom u is addressed.

Notice that while the condition of *being the person addressed (in u)* plays a role in the semantics for an utterance of 'you', that condition is not part of the content of the utterance. Instead, the condition provides the entity that meets it as the content of the utterance; it is what I will call a *providing condition*.

Consider now 'so-called':

For an utterance u of 'so-called',

$$Cont(u) = [x : \langle\!\langle Called; x, \phi \rangle\!\rangle],$$

where ϕ is a singular term provided in the circumstances of u.

That is, an utterance of 'so-called' expresses a property of being called a certain name—a name that is provided in context. I will come back soon to just what it means for something to be provided in context.

Let 'so-called' reports be statements of sentences of this form:

A is so-called because f. (8)

Such a report makes a claim that an individual is called some name in virtue of some fact. So the following is a good candidate for the semantics of so-called reports (this would not be a *basic* semantic principle but a consequence of other principles, perhaps including that just given for 'so-called'):

For an utterance u of a sentence of the form (8),

$$Cont(u) = \langle\!\langle Because; \langle\!\langle Called; a, \phi \rangle\!\rangle, p \rangle\!\rangle, \qquad (9)$$

where $a = Cont(u_A)$ is the individual referred to by the utterance (u_A) of 'A', $p = Cont(u_f)$ is the content of the utterance of f, and the name ϕ is provided in the circumstances of the utterance.

This proposal provides an (approximately) acceptable semantic rule for 'so-called' reports, because it explains which claims are made by statements of such reports, and it exhibits the dependency of such claims on circumstantially varying facts. There is nothing in the semantic rule to indicate that a 'so-called' report typically is about the very name used in the report. According to the rule, the name is simply supplied by context. Of course, in understanding how to use and interpret 'so-called' reports, we know a good bit more than is reflected in the rule itself. In particular, we know that which name gets supplied in context by a cooperative speaker depends on criteria of salience and relevance. The name used in the report becomes salient in virtue of its use; so a speaker who wishes to provide a different name for the report to be about must take pains to make that name extremely salient (as a name for the subject of the report) and relevant (as a name that makes sense given what is claimed about it).[4]

The semantics for these reports needs to presuppose a name supplied by the context, but it does not provide the rules that determine which names are supplied in which contexts; that important task is left to our account of the pragmatic workings of the reports. In a similar way, our semantics needs to assume a referent for the subject-term 'A', but it does not specify any principles that determine which uses of names refer to which things. It is no failing of the semantics that these questions about presupposition and reference are bracketed; but the viability of the semantics rests on their not being impenetrable. The semantics are acceptable only insofar as there are acceptable accounts of the phenomena that have been shuffled into the pragmatician's hand—reference and presupposition.

In simple predications, we are assuming, proper names and demon-

---

4. There are cases in which no name is uniquely salient, but in which things go fine anyway. Consider: "Barbarelli was called 'Gigantor' or 'Largione' or something. Anyway, he was so-called because of his size." Here, no name is available to the speaker or hearer in the usual way (such that they can utter it or write it down). But I am not certain whether (i) the report is nonetheless *about* the name 'Giorgione' (since that name is what is at some level *driving* the use of 'so-'), or (ii) the use of 'so-' is anaphoric on (or bound by) something in the previous sentence (there is a name the artist was called, which is 'Gigantor' or 'Largione' or something similar, and which he was called because of his size), or (iii) the use of 'so-' stands for, not a name, but a *kind* of name (so that a paraphrase would be 'he was called a name of that kind because of his size', where the kind is expected to be clear enough from the examples in the previous sentence. Examples like this, and similar phenomena involving underarticulation, make it difficult to give a simple account of the "specificity" of these constructions.

stratives serve the sole semantic function of standing for objects, and verbs stand for properties and relations. The propositions that are the contents of such statements are *about* the individuals and properties that the expressions contribute semantically—the propositions contain these entities as constituents. These individuals and properties are *articulated* constituents of the claim, since they are the contents of expressions uttered in the statement.

But recall from chapter 1 that articulated constituents are not always the only things that statements are about. Examples of statements that exploit *un*articulated constituents—constituents of the propositions expressed that are not articulated by overt expressions—may include the following:

It is raining.   (10)

It is two o'clock.   (11)

David is at home.   (12)

The acceleration due to gravity is 9.8 m/sec^2.   (13)

Meg agrees.   (14)

The first two examples are sentences that are used to talk about a place—usually, though not always, the place of utterance—without containing a word for the place. Since the contents of statements of these sentences will be *about* particular places, these places are unarticulated constituents of the claims made. Similarly, 'home' is used to talk about *someone's* home. The sentence (12) would be most naturally used to claim that David is at his own home. But if David is my house guest, I can use the sentence to claim that he is at my home, rather than his. The person or persons whose home it is, is an unarticulated constituent of the claim made with (12). Example (13) seems on the surface to make an entirely general claim, as does 'If you turn the ignition key in a car, it will start'. But both sentences are used to make true, restricted claims *about* certain kinds of circumstances. The last example, 'Meg agrees', is a sentence that can be used in different circumstances to claim that Meg agrees to almost anything. What Meg is claimed to agree to is an unarticulated constituent of the claim.

When we know what we are talking about, we need not always bring it into our statements overtly. This is why most examples of underarticulation are ones in which the subject matter of a statement is left unarticulated. The notion of subject matter is closely bound up with what is salient and relevant to the discourse; all of these examples can be seen as following a single pattern: the unarticulated constituent in each case, if the speaker is being cooperative, is what is salient and relevant to the discourse. Salience and relevance are pragmatic requirements that affect not only the implications of what is said, but in these cases also the very proposition expressed. Our deciphering the claims made with sentences (10) through (14) depends crucially on our knowing which places, time zones, claims, and so on are salient and relevant to the discourse. In a typical use of 'it is raining', only the location of utterance is salient and relevant, so we decide easily that the statement makes the claim that it is raining *there*. These are not the only pragmatic conditions that are important in determining what is talked about in these cases, but they clearly are important ones. For each of the examples, if the listener knows that there *is* a constituent playing a certain role in the expressed proposition, she is able to deduce what it is by relying on general pragmatic rules and other items of common knowledge.

There is nothing in the least unusual or epistemologically suspect involved in the claim that hearers standardly interpret underarticulated constructions by relying only on common knowledge and general pragmatic rules, with only the thinnest of semantic rules to go on. For first, this is how hearers deduce unstated conversational implicatures—and no one supposes that these are generally epistemically unavailable. And second, this is how we standardly discern the referent of a use of a common proper name like 'John'. A speaker can refer to lots of individuals with that name, but we nearly always know which individual is intended. How? By relying on common knowledge and general pragmatic rules, including criteria of salience and relevance.

For an example of a semantic rule for an unarticulated construction, consider 'David is at home'. The predicate 'is at home' expresses the relation $AtHome(x, y, t)$, which holds if x is at y's home at t. So we have:

For an utterance u of 'David is at home', at time t,

$$Cont(u) = \langle\langle\, AtHome; d, a, t\, \rangle\rangle,$$

where d is the content of the utterance of 'David', and a is provided in context.

Certainly, this is not a basic semantic principle but should follow from a broader principle that yields similar treatments of 'at school', 'at work', and so on. Also, even this broader principle may be a consequence of two different kinds of rule: one that determines a syntactic structure of which the overt form 'David is at home' is a projection (this structure might involve a covert expression referring to the person a), and one that determines the content of this structure. As I pointed out in chapter 1, underarticulation can always be assimilated to covert reference if we are willing to posit covert expressions. If we phrase semantic accounts of underarticulated constructions in terms of the propositions expressed by utterances of *overt* forms (as I do here), we can remain neutral on whether there are covert expressions involved.

5.3   Reporting Beliefs: Semantics

When we utter a belief sentence, we are talking *about* an agent's ideas and notions, and these notions and ideas become unarticulated constituents of what we say. Specifically, we are talking about the ideas and notions allegedly involved in the instance of believing we claim to exist. What we claim is that the agent believes a certain proposition in a way such that certain ideas and notions are responsible for representing certain constituents of the proposition. In this section, I will make these ideas explicit; in the following sections and in chapter 6, I will argue for their plausibility and defend them from several objections.

Recall from chapter 2 that while instances of explicit believing are individuated by concrete particular beliefs, instances of (ideational) believing in general—of at-least-tacitly believing—are individuated by "ways of believing," which, on my account are given by thought maps. A thought map is a structural type such that a particular belief is of that type just in case the belief involves certain actually existing representations (notions and ideas) in a certain structural arrangement. Thus we posited $Believes(a, t, p, \tau)$, which holds if agent a at t at least tacitly believes p in the way given by map τ. I adopted the strategy of analyzing at-least-tacit believing in terms of hypothetical explicit beliefs: an agent believes a proposition in way τ if she is cognitively disposed as if she has a particular explicit belief in p of type τ.

Consider the statement I make using this sentence:

Susan believes that Dean Smith fired Tom.   (15)

In this statement, I claim that Susan has a belief with a certain proposition (about firing and Tom and the Dean) as its content, and with certain notions (one, n_{Tom}, of Tom and one, n_{Dean}, of the Dean) and a certain idea (i_{Fired}, of firing) in its constituent makeup. If everything goes right and my report is true, it is because Susan has a belief with that content, involving the notions and the idea that I am talking about. So here is a first approximation to the proposition I express in (15):

$$\exists \tau \, [Believes(Susan, t, p, \tau) \; \& \qquad\qquad\qquad\qquad (16)$$

$$Involves(\tau, n_{Dean}) \; \& \; Involves(\tau, n_{Tom}) \; \& \; Involves(\tau, i_{Fired})],$$

where p is the content of my utterance of 'Dean Smith fired Tom', and t is the time of my utterance.

The gist of (16) is that Susan, at t, believes the proposition p, in a way that involves her representations n_{Dean}, n_{Tom}, and i_{Fired}.

The "how" information conveyed in a belief report, on this approximation, concerns the agent's particular representations of individuals and relations. In report (15), I claim that the way Susan believes the proposition in question involves certain specific notions and a certain idea. She may or may not believe that proposition in other ways—in ways that involve different representations—but that is irrelevant to the claim I make.

Certainly, there is a lot left to explain about (16), including just how it is determined which specific notions and ideas are claimed to be involved in Susan's belief, and how those mental entities buried deep within Susan's cranium manage to get into my claim. But before I venture into those waters, I want to point out a different reason that (16) is not quite a satisfactory account of the content of my use of (15). Susan, we are supposing, has two notions, n_{Dean} and n_{Tom}. Suppose further that, though she does not recognize this, these notions are really *of* the same man, Dean Tom Smith. Now, there are two different kinds of belief she might have involving these notions and her idea i_{Fired};

the structures of these beliefs are given in the following way (using the notation developed in chapter 4):

$$\tau_1 = \overline{(i_{Fired}; n_{Dean}, n_{Tom})},$$

$$\tau_2 = \overline{(i_{Fired}; n_{Tom}, n_{Dean})}.$$

Susan would express a belief of the former type, if she had it, by saying, 'Dean Smith fired Tom'; she would express the latter with 'Tom fired Dean Smith'. Surely, my report (15) is true only if Susan believes the proposition (that Smith fired Smith) in the way mapped by τ_1. But the claim (16) is true whether she has that belief or instead a belief mapped by τ_2, since either belief would have the content that the Dean (that is, Smith) fired Tom (that is, Smith).

Something, then, is missing in (16). The claim I make with (15) specifies the content of Susan's alleged belief, and it specifies which notions and ideas are claimed to be involved; but it does more than that: it specifies which notion is *of* the firer and which is *of* the firee. My claim is that Susan has a belief with the content that Smith fired Smith, such that (i) her notion n_{Dean} is responsible for determining the firer in the content of her belief, (ii) her notion n_{Tom} is responsible for determining the firee, and (iii) her idea i_{Fired} is responsible for determining that the main property is *Fired*.

What is missing from (16) is information about representational responsibility. If all we know about Susan's belief is what is given in (16), then we are in the same position as the archaeologist who knows that an inscription of '⊤ ◁ ∠' expresses the proposition that Venus is brighter than Venus, but does not know which symbol is responsible for which occurrence of Venus in the proposition. The "how" information expressed in belief reports includes information of this kind, about which representations are (allegedly) responsible for which roles in the proposition (allegedly) believed.

Recall that the relation $Responsible(n, \tau, r)$ holds of a representation (a notion or idea), a thought map, and a propositional role, just in case in τ the representation is responsible for filling (with its content) the propositional role, which is a role in the content of any belief mapped by τ. This relation is just what we need to point out the distinction between the two types of beliefs τ_1 and τ_2. A belief of either type would have the following content:

$$\langle\!\langle \underbrace{Fired}_{r_1}; \underbrace{Smith}_{r_2}, \underbrace{Smith}_{r_3} \rangle\!\rangle \ .$$

But in τ_1 the notion n_{Dean} is responsible for filling the first, firer role (r_2) in p, while in τ_2 the notion n_{Tom} is responsible for filling that role. Similarly for the firee role (r_3). A better approximation to the content of my utterance of (15), then, is the following proposition:

$$\exists \tau \ [\ Believes(Susan, t, \langle\!\langle \ Fired; Smith, Smith \rangle\!\rangle, \tau) \ \& \qquad (17)$$

$$Responsible(n_{Dean}, \tau, r_2) \ \&$$

$$Responsible(n_{Tom}, \tau, r_3,) \ \&$$

$$Responsible(i_{Fired}, \tau, r_1) \ ],$$

where t is the time of my utterance.

The clause that contains the conjunction of '$Responsible(m, \tau, r_i)$' claims in (17) will be called the *responsibility clause* of the semantics. Without the responsibility clause, (17) would be a version of the "naïve" semantics discussed in chapter 1. Without this clause, the proposition would be simply that Susan has *some* belief with the content expressed by the content sentence. The responsibility clause in (17) adds to this in two ways. First, it places some *internal* requirements on the alleged belief: it must involve certain notions and ideas. Second, it places *relational* requirements on the belief with respect to its content: the notions and ideas in the belief must be appropriately related, via ties of responsibility, to the roles in its content. This belief report specifies three things about the agent's alleged belief: its components, its content, and the connections between its components and its content. Appearances aside, there really is nothing terribly complicated about a proposition of the form (17). The information about responsibility given by that proposition can be much more simply depicted; figure 5.1 shows how (read the arrows as indicating responsibility).

Now, there may well be belief reports in which the representation allegedly responsible for a certain role is neither uniquely specified nor left entirely open, but is described as meeting a specified condition—as having a given property. Thus, a belief reporter might claim that Susan has a belief in the proposition that Smith fired Smith, in which *some* notion to which Susan associates the name 'Tom' is responsible for the firer role r_2. Here the property of *being a notion associated with the name*

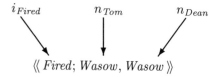

Figure 5.1
Graphical depiction of information about responsibility in (17)

'*Tom*' becomes a constituent of what is claimed in the belief report. So I will allow that belief reports can specify either a representation or a condition on a representation for any role in the proposition that is alleged to be the content of the agent's belief. In fact I think it can be difficult to determine, in a given belief report, whether a representation is specified or merely described. I will return to this "specificity" issue in the discussion of "*de re*" belief reports.

Also, a speaker may allege that a representation of a certain sort is responsible for multiple roles in the content proposition. For instance, I may report that

Ann believes that Sue hired Tom and gave Tom a higher (18)

salary than Bob's.

Suppose the content of the embedded sentence is the following proposition (with selected roles indicated):

$$p \;=\; \langle\!\langle \cdots ; \cdots \underbrace{Sue}_{r_1} \cdots \underbrace{Tom}_{r_2} \cdots \underbrace{Tom}_{r_3} \cdots \underbrace{Bob}_{r_4} \cdots \rangle\!\rangle .$$

Here, there are two roles (r_2 and r_3) filled by Tom. Now, it is plausible to suppose that, for (18) to be true (in ordinary circumstances), Ann must represent the two occurrences of Tom with the same representation (one representation must be responsible for both roles). Suppose that in this report, Ann's representation of Tom is not specified but only described as having a specified property P. Then, the claim made in the report is not simply that there is some representation having P responsible for r_2 and some representation having P responsible for r_3. Instead, it is that there is a single representation having P responsible for both roles. If we suppose that in uttering (18) I specify Ann's representation n_{Sue} of Sue and I describe Ann's representation of Bob as having property Q,

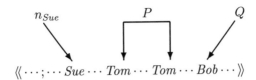

Figure 5.2
Graphical depiction of information about responsibility in (19)

we might most perspicuously represent the information about representations and responsibility in this report as in figure 5.2. More formally, the content of the report is:

$$\exists \tau \; [\; Believes(Ann, t, p, \tau) \; \& \tag{19}$$

$$\exists m_1, m_2, m_3 \; (\; m_1 = n_{Sue} \; \& \; P(m_2) \; \& \; Q(m_3) \; \&$$

$$Responsible(m_1, \tau, r_1) \; \&$$

$$Responsible(m_2, \tau, r_2)) \; \&$$

$$Responsible(m_2, \tau, r_3)) \; \&$$

$$Responsible(m_3, \tau, r_4) \;) \;].$$

In general, I suggest, the content of a singular belief report, a statement u of 'A believes that s', is of this form:

$$\exists \tau \; [\; Believes(a, t, p_s, \tau) \; \& \tag{20}$$

$$\exists m_1, \cdots \exists m_k \; (\; P_1(m_1) \; \& \; \cdots \; \& \; P_k(m_k) \; \&$$

$$Responsible(m_{i_1}, \tau, r_1) \; \& \; \cdots \; \&$$

$$Responsible(m_{i_n}, \tau, r_n) \;) \;],$$

where a is the agent referred to with the subutterance u_a of 'A'; t is the time of u, p_s is the content of the subutterance u_s of the embedded sentence s; the properties $P_1, \ldots, P_k$ are provided in context; $r_1, \ldots, r_n$ are roles in p_s; and each 'm_{i_j}' is one of the variables $m_1, \ldots, m_k$.

The guiding idea behind this formal statement is simply that in making a belief report an agent can, as pictured in figure 5.2, specify or describe the representations that allegedly are responsible for various roles in the allegedly believed proposition. As far as the semantics determines, the contextually supplied properties $P_1, \ldots, P_k$ may be any properties whatever, from the property of being identical to a certain representation (this being how particular representations are specified) to the property of being a notion attached to a certain name, to the vacuous property of being self-identical. Let me stress at this point (since (20) may be misleading in this regard) that I will hold that, usually, representations are *specified* rather than merely described. The notions and ideas (or the properties of them) that occur in the responsibility clause of the content of a belief report are unarticulated constituents of that report—there are no overt expressions uttered in the belief report to refer to them or stand for them. Instead, they are provided by the total circumstances of the statement. To show the variety of ways in which these constituents are provided, and to show how the semantics works for different kinds of belief report, I will next consider a number of examples.

5.4   Providing Representations: Pragmatics

5.4.1   Normal Notions and Ideas

I suspect that the majority of our belief reports are about an agent's *normal* notions and ideas. For notions and ideas, being normal typically involves being involved in normal sorts of beliefs and being tied to normal modes of recognition (see section 3.4 above). What counts as normal depends at least on the intents and purposes of the discourse, and the community among which the agent is being considered by the participants in the dialogue. It is a vague condition, but usually the presupposition that an agent has a normal representation of a certain relation or individual is unproblematically obvious.

Consider this sentence:

Sarah believes that Jackson will be President.   (21)

Suppose that Sarah is an acquaintance of those listening to me, that it is recognized that I mean Jesse Jackson (an American political figure), and that I mean President of the United States. Like nearly all adult U.S. residents, Sarah has a normal notion of Jackson, to which she attaches the properties of *being a politician*, *being a Democrat*, *being called 'Jesse Jackson'*, and so on. Neither I nor the background of the statement has provided any reason to suspect that Sarah has multiple, unconnected notions of Jackson that might be relevant to my report. My claim, then, is that Sarah's belief involves her ordinary, normal notion ($n_{Jackson}$) of Jackson. More formally, my claim is of this form:

$$\exists \tau \ [\ Believes(Sarah, t, p, \tau) \ \&$$
$$\exists m \ (\ m = n_{Jackson} \ \& \ Responsible(m, b, r_{JJ}) \ ) \ ],$$

where t is the time of the utterance, and r_{JJ} is the role that Jackson fills in p, which is the content of my utterance of 'Jackson will be President'.

My claim will be false, for example, if Sarah would deny that 'Jesse Jackson will be President' and yet recalls having told the fortune of a man whose palms bespoke future greatness in the Oval Office—without realizing that he was Jackson. Though she would then have a belief with the content that Jackson will be President, it would not satisfy the conditions laid out in my report, since it does not involve her notion $n_{Jackson}$. She would in that case believe the proposition, but not in the way that I meant.

I am able to talk about Sarah's normal notion simply because I know her to be an informed adult resident of the United States. It is an extremely good bet that she has a normal notion of Jackson, in the sense just described. And when all parties to the dialogue know that it is an extremely good bet that a certain notion exists, and such a notion is relevant, then it can be talked about with a belief report. Of course, we can imagine an example in which, through a series of coincidences, Sarah has never heard of Jackson. In that case there would be a presupposition failure leading to a failure of tacit reference. I will discuss such cases in chapter 6.

When a friend phones me long distance, and I ask what time it is, I am inquiring about the time zone she is in. That time zone is an unarticulated constituent of my question, and of her answer. My assumption—an extremely good bet—is that she is on earth, and is in a single time zone throughout the conversation (rather than, say, on a spinning carousel at the North Pole). Since this is a safe bet, I need not make my assumptions explicit, by asking, "What time is it in the time zone where you are, assuming you in fact are in a single time zone?" Ordinary talk about what time it is presupposes a determinate time zone as subject matter. In normal phone conversations, each participant is in a single (perhaps different) time zone; this is an obvious fact to all involved. So these time zones are salient as objects of discussion, and we can talk about them without making the presupposition, that there *are* such time zones, explicit. In the same way, we can use the name 'Jackson' to talk about Jesse Jackson without making explicit the presupposition that there is a single individual we refer to with that name. All of these presuppositions can go wrong, but they do so only very rarely. So we do not often hedge our bets by raising the assumptions into explicit caveats, like 'given that there is a unique person we have been calling *Jesse Jackson*, ... ' And we do not often make belief reports like 'Assuming Sarah knows who Jackson is in the normal way you and I do, she believes of him (in that way) that he will be President'; instead, I suggest, we justifiedly assume that she has a normal notion, and we simply talk about it.

For a case in which what counts as normal is not based on such a large community, suppose now that (21) is uttered in different circumstances: Sarah, myself, and my hearer are participants in a church retreat. None of us knows that another man participating in the retreat is the political figure Jesse Jackson. If I were to utter (21) in such circumstances, my claim would be, still, that Sarah has a belief that Jackson will be President, which involves a certain notion: her *normal* notion of Jackson. But in these circumstances, what counts as normal is *not* the notion $n_{Jackson}$ that she has of the political figure. Instead, it is the notion $n'_{Jackson}$ that she has of the man involved in the retreat (it is associated with ideas of *participating in the retreat*, and so on). My claim is true just in case Sarah believes the proposition in the way I lead my hearer to expect: via her notion $n'_{Jackson}$.

The condition of normality is even more pervasive, in belief reports, as a condition on agents' ideas of properties. It is unusual to find a belief report in which it is *not* an agent's normal ideas that are being talked about. In addition, what counts as being normal varies much less frequently in the case of ideas than in the case of notions—it is unusual for an idea that counts as normal in one set of circumstances not to count as normal in another. But there *are* cases in which other than normal ideas are implicated, so it is important to understand that in the lion's share of reports, the agent's normal ideas really are being discussed. To understand the unusual, abnormal cases, we have to be clear about the more usual ones, like a typical report of

Ann believes that Herbert is tall. (22)

In the obvious kinds of circumstances in which this sentence could be asserted, the claim would be that Ann has a belief that, among other things, involves a certain idea: her normal idea of *being tall*.

What counts as a normal idea of *being tall* is fairly constant across different circumstances. However, there are properties with more variation in what counts as normal. For instance, there is a great difference in what is needed for a normal idea of *being nylon* in the communities of hosiers and rock climbers. One can easily imagine a person, call him Wright, having two, unconnected ideas of nylon, each of which counts as a normal idea in one of these communities. Depending on which community is relevant, and hence on which idea is part of the subject matter, the following report might be true or false:

Wright believes that nylon does not tear easily. (23)

5.4.2 Notions Linked to Action and Perception

Often, an agent's actions set the stage for a belief report about that agent—and about the notions and ideas implicated in the actions. When we see a person bite painfully into her pen, we can say,

She believed that it was a pretzel. (24)

The person has at the time of action at least two notions of the pen. One is a "stable" notion of it that is associated with her ideas of *being a pen, being blue, being nearby*, and so on. The other is a perceptual notion, associated with her ideas of *being a pretzel, being in hand*, and so on. Clearly, the report is about the latter notion—we claim that she believed the proposition that that pen was a pretzel, via a certain notion—her perceptual notion of the thing she believed to be in her hand. This notion alone is both salient and relevant to the discourse, since we present ourselves as explaining her action.

In cases like this, there is a salient *object-directed* action that is part of the common background knowledge of the speaker and the audience. There is a direct "backward" connection from such an action to that notion of the object that is involved in the attitudes that have guided the action. If the speaker presents the report as being relevant to the action (which may, as in the case of (24), take very little effort), then the report makes a claim *about* the notion that the agent links to his action.

For us to be able to talk about the notion linked to an action, it suffices to have evidence of an action that is of a sort that is plausibly object-directed. If a person kicks a rock absentmindedly, her action may or may not have been directed toward the rock—she may or may not have a notion of the rock linked to the action. In that case, we are not on safe grounds presupposing that she has such a notion. But if the person throws a rock in the air, it is extremely likely that she knows what she is doing—that she has a notion of the rock linked to her action. In this case, when we claim that she believed the rock would miss the window, we are talking about the notion linked to the rock in that action. We need not even have witnessed the action to have sufficient referential access to the notion linked to it. If we see a shattered window, and see the agent standing sheepishly near a pile of rocks, we may have plenty of evidence that she threw a rock at the window, and hence that she has a notion of the rock that was linked to her action. We may know very little indeed about this notion; but we know what is obvious—that it was linked to the action and is a notion of the rock.

When a boy is kneeling with a lizard in front of him and looks fascinated, we can make the report 'He believes that the lizard is asleep'. In doing so, we are talking about the notion, which we assume to exist, that is perceptually linked to the lizard. We can unproblematically presuppose that he has such a notion, since we can assume that he has normal perceptual faculties, and we see that his eyes are open and that the lizard is in clear view.

A notion linked to action and/or perception is provided as an unarticulated constituent of a belief report only when it is both salient in the circumstances and relevant to the report. An example where a notion that is salient but not relevant does not count is the following. Fred is moving all the books in his office up one shelf in order to clear space on the bottom shelves. He is doing this quickly, without noticing the titles of the books he moves. Watching him, we see that he is moving his copy of *Oliver Twist*. Susan remarks, "Fred believes that that book once belonged to Dickens." Here, it is clear that Fred has a perceptual notion of the book, which is associated with ideas of *being in hand*, *being a book*, and so on. But it cannot be *this* notion that Susan is talking about, since it is obvious to us that Fred does not know which book he has in his hand as he moves it. Instead, it is clear in the circumstances that Susan is talking about Fred's stable notion of the book, which is no doubt associated with ideas of *being a copy of* Oliver Twist, *being a first edition*, and, if Susan is right, *being owned at one time by Dickens*. We give Susan the benefit of the doubt by assuming that there is something she is talking about—that there *is* a relevant notion; the notion becomes salient in part because Susan's statement leads us to suppose that there is a relevant notion she is talking about. This case is similar to Strawson's 1956 example in which a speaker approaches, hands cupped as if holding something, saying, "This is a fine red one." The hearer assumes that there is something the speaker is talking about; the object, if there is one, becomes salient because of that very assumption. More on this phenomenon of "referential bootstrapping" below.

We have enough tools now to give a very straightforward solution to Kripke's 1979 puzzle about Pierre, which we encountered in chapter 1. We know through Kripke's explanation of Pierre's experiences in France that Pierre has a notion formed through reading travel brochures about London, and this notion is salient when Kripke reports truly that 'Pierre believes that London is pretty'. The report is true because Pierre does have a belief in the proposition that London is pretty, involving the notion we are talking about. When Kripke describes Pierre's reactions to his new hometown (London), we know that Pierre has a different notion involved in his perceptions, attitudes, and actions relating to hometown situations. This notion is salient when Kripke reports truly that 'Pierre does not believe that London is pretty'. This report is true because Pierre does not have a belief in the proposition that London is pretty, involving the notion we are talking about.

5.4.3 Self-Attribution and Indexical Belief

A very simple pragmatic rule governing the notions and ideas talked about in belief reports, is the rule of *self-attribution*. A self-attribution is a report of the form

I believe that *s*.   (25)

In ascribing a belief to oneself (in the present tense), one uses words in the content sentence that express one's alleged belief. The words one uses are attached to various notions and ideas, which thus become salient. A use of the name 'John', for example, is attached to a notion of a person, and a use of 'water' is attached to an idea of a kind of substance. So here is the rule: A use of an expression τ in the content sentence of a self-ascription ordinarily serves to provide the notion or idea attached to that use of τ.

Thus, when I say 'I believe that John is drinking water', my report is about the notion of John that is attached to my use of the name 'John' in the report. Similarly for my uses of 'water' and 'is drinking'.

This yields a natural solution to Richard's 1983 steamroller puzzle, which was described in chapter 1. A is looking at the phone booth across the street, containing B, to whom A coincidentally is talking on the phone. A says to B, "I believe that she is in danger." The use of 'she' refers directly to B and is attached to A's notion n_{vis}, which is linked to his perception of the scene across the street. So his report is true if he has a belief in the proposition that B is in danger, involving his notion n_{vis}. He has such a notion, so his report is true. If A were to say, "I believe that you are in danger," his use of 'you' also would refer directly to B, but would be attached to his notion n_{you} that is linked to his conversational attitudes. So his report would be true if he has a belief in the same proposition as before, involving this time his notion n_{you}. He has no such belief, so the report would be false.

The rule of self-attribution is not exceptionless; what universality it has comes from the difficulty in overriding the salience of the representations that are attached to the words uttered by the self-ascriber. Suppose I know you as a philosopher, and you now convince me that you have been leading a double life. Further, you convince me that I know you well in your other guise (though you will not tell me what it is), and that, on that way of thinking of you, I think you too simple to have done anything so clever as disguise yourself. I am now willing to assert, for instance, 'I falsely believe that you are not clever'. There is nothing very like Moore's Paradox here, of course, as there would be if I were to say that I falsely believe the proposition *in the way I now understand it*.

Geach (1972), Castaneda (1966, 1968), Perry (1977, 1979), and others have stressed that belief reports of a certain kind are very special. When I claim that Carl believes that he is being chased by a bear, the belief I attribute to Carl is not simply a belief that *Carl* is being chased by a bear. Carl could have *that* belief and not be worried (if he was not aware that he was Carl). There seems to be a mysterious, indexical, self-

referential element to what Carl must believe. Castaneda claims that
this suggests that the word 'he' that occurs in the belief report is not
the same word that occurs in the sentence I use to attribute to anyone
else a belief about Carl that 'he is being chased by a bear'.

But there is nothing mysterious here, and there is no reason to
postulate two different pronouns 'he'. What happens in these cases is
simply that the agent is claimed to have a belief about herself *via her
self-notion*. The puzzles about indexical belief reports really amount to
just that. There is no special indexical *object of belief*, but there is a
special kind of notion—the self-notion—that each of us has.

5.4.4   De Dicto Reports

Recall the plight of Quine's Tom:

Tom believes that Cicero denounced Catiline.   (26)

Tom believes that Tully denounced Catiline.   (27)

According to Quine, sentence (26) is true and (27) false. But, of course,
it is not sentences that are true or false; more properly, in the circumstances Quine envisions, a statement of (26) would be true, while one
of (27) would be false. If we try to imagine the natural sets of circumstances in which these reports would come out as Quine expects,
one important feature that they share is this: Tom has two notions of
Cicero, one of which, n_{Cicero}, he associates with ideas of being called
'Cicero' and having denounced Catiline, the other of which, n_{Tully}, he
associates with an idea of being called 'Tully', but not one of having denounced Catiline. It will be helpful to assume that n_{Cicero} is a *normal*
notion of Cicero—surely one must know that Cicero is called 'Cicero'
to have a normal notion of him (in most circles), though probably one
need not know that he is called 'Tully'.

These reports, then, seem to imply something about how Tom would
express his beliefs, and they do so by containing the very names that
Tom would use. One way of honoring this "*de dicto*" intuition would
be to hold that, for example, the report (27) *claims*, in part, that Tom
would use the name 'Tully' in expressing his belief (and it is easy to
capture this in the official semantics). But there is a more natural way
of honoring the *de dicto* intuition, one that does not treat these reports

as at all semantically different from the "notionally specific" sorts of belief reports we have considered so far.

My suggestion is that, in the circumstances Quine imagines, the statement of (26) is *about* n_{Cicero}, while the statement of (27) is *about* n_{Tully}. These notions are unarticulated constituents of the two reports. What happens in these *de dicto* reports is that the speaker raises a notion to salience by raising a *name* to salience. The speaker provides a notion as an unarticulated constituent of the report by using, in the report, the very name that Tom associates with that notion.[5] Since the notions these reports are about are pointed out by the names Tom associates with them, it is clear how these reports can convey, without containing, information about what names Tom would use to express the beliefs ascribed.

This claim, to be sure, requires some defense. Belief reports do not *always* work in this way—sometimes the words used by the speaker do not play this role in determining an unarticulated constituent. There are reports using the sentences (26) and (27) that do not convey information about how Tom would express his belief. What, we may ask, is special about Quine's case and other *de dicto* cases[6]—in which the words used in the content sentence are assumed to be ones the agent would use to express his belief?

The answer is straightforward. The speaker of a belief report presents herself as having information about a belief. When the name the agent would (allegedly) use is relevant and the speaker is assumed to know it, and the speaker uses no other means to make a specific notion salient, there is a presumption that the speaker is *using* that name in the report. The speaker exploits this presumption to make a specific notion

---

5. It is crucial not only that the name is used, but that an utterance of it is responsible (in analogy to responsibility for notions) for the correct role in the content proposition (in this case, the denouncer role). To see the reason for being this picky, consider the case of 'Tom believes that Cicero denounced Tully'.

6. Traditionally, though not universally, it has been belief reports that are classified as *de dicto*; thus, people have held that the content sentence is *read de dicto*, or that the belief predicate gets a *de dicto* reading. But it is easy to think of examples in which there are two names in the content sentence, such that one is used in a *de dicto* way while the other is not. So it would be more appropriate to call, not a report, but a use of a name (or other expression) in the content sentence, *de dicto*. Here, I adopt the practice of calling reports *de dicto*, when some expressions in it are used in a *de dicto* way.

salient, so that it winds up a constituent of the responsibility condition in the content of the report.

In order for Quine's case to work as an example of *de dicto* reporting, we need to assume that there is some suspicion of misrecognition among the participants in the dialogue. To see this, consider our intuitions about what would happen if there were not such a suspicion. Suppose the speaker were to utter (27) in more ordinary circumstances, in which we have no way of knowing, or reason to care, whether Tom knows, as we do, that Cicero is called 'Tully' (these would need to be circumstances in which it is not in the least unusual for the speaker and her audience to use the name 'Tully' for Cicero, say, because they, unlike Tom, are classicists). Then, since we have no reason to think otherwise, the report would be a normal belief report, about Tom's assumed normal (for nonclassicists) notion of Cicero, n_{Cicero}. There would be no allegation that Tom thinks of Cicero in a way associated with the name 'Tully'—although, because his notion is assumed to be normal, it would be assumed that he thinks of Cicero in a way associated with the name 'Cicero'! The *de dicto* case is not the normal one; in the normal case, utterances of (26) and (27) make the same claim.

The actual report of (27) manages to be about n_{Tully} instead of n_{Cicero} only because it is either common knowledge or "common suspicion" that Tom is confused about Cicero in the way we have assumed—not knowing that Cicero is Tully. One way (Quine's) to arouse this suspicion is for the speaker to assert both (26) and the denial of (27)—to contrast these reports. This would make it clear that Tom has two notions of Cicero, and the speaker's use of two different names for Cicero would lead the hearer to assume that those are the names Tom would use to express his belief. Another way for the speaker to set the stage for the *de dicto* reports would be to say 'Tom does not know that Cicero and Tully are the same man'.

Which uses of sentences like (27) are *de dicto* reports? Though we can say 'Tom believes, as he would put it, that...', in *de dicto* reports we do not. There is no tone of voice or syntactic clue to tip us off that a name used in the report is meant to point to a notion to which the agent attaches that name. Semanticists sometimes have claimed that there *is* a *de dicto* "reading" of a belief sentence, and left it at that, without explaining when and how that reading is understood to be the correct one by the hearer of the report. In my view, there is no distinct *de dicto* reading of belief sentences. Instead, *de dicto* reports are ones in which the speaker attempts to provide notions for his report to be about, by using—and being understood as using—the words that the agent would use to express the alleged belief. This view not only unifies the account of the semantics of *de dicto* reports with that of the other reports so far considered, but it also explains just why and when a report is *de dicto*, and how such a report conveys information about the words the agent would use to express his belief.

It is in *de dicto* reports that names behave like the 'Giorgione' in 'Giorgione was so-called because of his size'. The names 'Cicero' and 'Tully', in the *de dicto* reports, serve the *semantic* role of standing for Cicero. The content proposition in each case is

$$\langle\!\langle \, Denounced; \, Cicero, \, Catiline \, \rangle\!\rangle \, .$$

But the names play an additional, *pragmatic* role, in helping to determine which notion it is that is claimed to stand for Cicero in Tom's belief.

5.4.5   Notional Specificity

I have suggested that the mechanisms discussed so far provide specific representations rather than conditions on them, as constituents of the contents of belief reports. Why not conditions? Why not hold that what gets provided in the examples I have considered are not specific notions but conditions: say, the condition of being a normal notion of Jackson, the condition of being involved in Pierre's perception of the travel brochure, and the condition of being associated with the name 'Cicero'?

I find the suggestion that conditions are generally provided unattractive for a simple reason. If the proposition expressed by a given belief report involves a certain condition, then *someone* ought to be able to say which condition it is—either the speaker or the fully understanding listener or ourselves as theorists. But in none of the examples mentioned does any specific condition seem clearly to be *the* condition intended by the speaker, or *the* condition understood by the hearer, or *the* condition doing the communicative work—let alone all three.

For instance, the suggestion is that in reporting that Pierre believes that London is pretty, I require not that his belief involve a specific notion, but that it involve some notion meeting a certain condition.

But which condition? Being formed while viewing b (where b is the travel brochure)? Being formed while viewing the travel brochure that a mentioned at t (where a is the speaker who tells us Pierre's story)? Being associated with the name 'Londres'? It strikes me that a choice among these could only be arbitrary. (Notice too that on the different choices, the proposition expressed is taken to be *about* a travel brochure, or the speaker a, or the name 'Londres', which seems implausible in itself).

Given this, it seems to me that the only plausible condition-based options are (i) that the what is provided is a *cluster* of conditions, or (ii) that the report does not determinately express a single proposition, but hovers between a number of different claims, containing different conditions on notions. It may be that these possibilities can be worked out and defended—and I think something like the cluster of conditions may in any event be wanted for phenomena such as denials of statements that involve reference failure ('Santa will *not* come tonight; there is no such person'; I will return to such cases in chapter 6). But I do not find them at all plausible as treatments of the simple reports in question. The attraction of retreating to such sophisticated condition-based accounts owes largely, I think, to two sources. There are legitimate concerns about situations in which the speaker is mistaken about the existence of a notion she wishes to discuss; I will address this concern in chapter 6. But the heavier weight on our intuitions seems to be intuitive discomfort with the idea that we refer to specific representations in other agents' minds. We feel that we are not epistemically *close* enough for reference, so it must be merely description; no single description seems right, so it must be a loose cluster (this pattern is familiar from the debate about description theories of reference). But I think we *are* close enough for reference in these cases, and that this is precisely why we do not bother to make specific conditions salient—when you can refer, why merely describe? Retreating to clusters of descriptions here seems like buying into unnecessary difficulties mainly to humor a mistaken epistemology. It is clear that any account on the lines of (i) or (ii) can be plausible only if there is no way to make a more semantically specific account work. And I think the view that we standardly refer to representations can be made to work; the discussions of the last few sections begin to show how.

5.4.6 De Re Reports: Are There Any?

While there really seems to be a legitimate category of *de dicto* reports, the flip side of the *de re/de dicto* distinction is much more of a muddle. Of course, there are many reports that are not *de dicto*, and these form a legitimate class if the *de dicto* ones do. But I will hold that, on one natural construal of what '*de re*' means, lots of *de dicto* reports are also *de re*, and on a natural construal that excludes *de dicto* reports, it can be doubted whether there *are* many *de re* reports. The issue of whether there is a legitimate class of *de re* reports is not in itself of great importance, but a discussion of it will lead to useful further considerations about the notional specificity of ordinary belief reports.

The defining characteristic of a *de re* report is supposed to be that in it, the agent is claimed to be *related to a real individual*, rather than merely to a name or description. One way of construing this requirement is as meaning that we attribute to the agent a *singular* belief—our belief report is true only if the agent has the ascribed sort of belief involving a notion that is *of* an appropriate individual. This would exclude from the category of *de re* reports those in which descriptions are given narrow scope[7] (and in which no other singular terms occur), because such reports attribute only general beliefs. It would, however, include as *de re*, reports in which descriptions either are used with wide scope or are used referentially. These seem like good results for a criterion of *de re* reports.

But this criterion—ascribing singular beliefs—also admits any report with a *de dicto* use of a name as a *de re* report. Above, I suggested that such a *de dicto* report claims that an agent believes a singular proposition via a belief involving a certain notion (such that she would express that notion using the same name used by the speaker). If this is right, then on the assumed *de re* criterion there is no *de dicto/de re*

---

7. I will briefly explain the distinction of wide-scope vs. narrow scope vs. referential uses of descriptions (see Neale 1990 for more). In the sentence 'Joe said the man behind us is a spy', the description may be given either narrow or wide scope, and (I will suppose) may be used referentially. The three different readings of the descriptions yield three different claims: narrow—Joe said the following: the man behind us is a spy; wide—The man behind us is such that Joe said he is a spy; referential—Joe said that he [the man behind us] is a spy. The first two claims are about us and the property of being behind us, while only the third is about the man himself.

distinction; instead, there is a significant overlap between the two kinds of reports.

This result may prompt dissatisfaction with the proposed *de re* criterion. Any correct criterion, we may require, must exclude *de dicto* reports. Now, philosophers commonly have described *de re* reports as making no implications about *how* an object is thought of, but as claiming merely that the object *is* thought of. So we may devise a second criterion: *de re* reports are ones in which singular beliefs are ascribed, without any requirement about how the agent thinks of the individuals involved—the reports are *notionally uninformative*. Certainly, this criterion strictly excludes *de dicto* reports. But what does it allow?

The kinds of belief reports we have considered so far, including "normal reports" and reports of beliefs linked to actions and perception, all imply something about how the agent thinks about the individuals his belief is about, since (if I am right about them) particular notions are specified in these reports. At least some of these reports—especially those having to do with perception and action—are paradigmatic cases of what have been called *de re* belief reports, so already this second criterion cannot capture all of what has usually been meant by '*de re*'. But the questions remain: what have we been missing? What are the kinds of reports that make no requirements at all about how an agent thinks of a thing?

First of all, let me point out that it is consistent with the semantics given in (20) that a report not be *about* any particular notion, since I allow that not particular representations, but only conditions on notions, can be provided in belief reports. Further, it is consistent with the semantics that the responsibility clause be entirely empty—specifying and describing none of the agent's representations. If the responsibility condition for a report in which the agent is attributed a singular belief about a thing does not have a conjunct for the notion the agent attaches to that thing, then the report is notionally uninformative in the way required—conveying no information about how the agent thinks about the thing. So notionally uninformative reports are not excluded by my semantics.

But I want to argue that, even if notionally uninformative reports would be easy to describe semantically, because of pragmatic phenomena that go hand in hand with underarticulation it is very difficult to devise a natural example of a belief report that *clearly* is notionally uninformative.

One candidate for a notionally uninformative report would be a report in which a description is used referentially or with wide scope: 'Ralph believes that the man behind us is a spy'. Since the description in such a case is not attributed to the agent, it does not serve to convey the way in which the agent allegedly thinks about the thing. But we cannot assume that nothing *else* in the circumstances of the report conveys information about an alleged way of thinking about the thing. For instance, the report might be given in circumstances such that we are wondering why Ralph, standing across the room from us, is alternately staring at the man behind us, whom we know to be a spy, and consulting a German phrase book. In that case, it is plausible to take the report to be about the notion Ralph attaches perceptually to the man. And we also can invoke, with a referential use of a description, Ralph's *normal* notion of an individual: for example, watching Reagan on television, I say 'Ralph believes that the clown on the TV is a nice man'. Note that these examples can be set up so that the descriptions are replaced by pronouns ('he') or demonstratives ('that man'). Such referential expressions are for these purposes much like wide-scoped or referential descriptions—they do not themselves provide any information about how the agent thinks of a thing, but the reports containing them still might convey such information. (Of course, nothing important for my purposes turns on whether there really are referential uses of descriptions, or only variously scoped uses.)

Certainly, the fact that *some* belief reports in which referential descriptions, demonstratives, and pronouns are used convey information about how a thing is thought of does not show that they all do. There may still be notionally uninformative reports of these sorts. I have doubts about how widespread such reports are in ordinary conversation; indeed, I wonder whether there are any at all. I have not found an unassailable example of a singular belief report—about a single agent and a specific singular content proposition—in which there clearly is not any notion that the speaker is talking about, and that clearly would be true *no matter what* notion was involved in a belief of the agent's with the correct content.

My suspicions are in sharp contrast to the views of those who subscribe to the "naïve" semantics for belief reports discussed in chapter

1. These philosophers claim that, strictly speaking, belief reports do not truth-conditionally discriminate among notions—a report ascribing a singular belief about a thing to an agent is true if the agent has a belief with that content, involving any notion at all of the thing. What they think is true of all belief reports, I suspect, may be true of very few.

I have no knockdown argument to show that there are no ordinary notionally uninformative belief reports—and I am not convinced that there really are none (surely there are very artifical such cases)—but I have found it hard to find a clear example and hard even to imagine a case in which it would be useful to be able to make one, instead of an informative report. My doubts are based on a survey of likely candidates for this kind of report, and on certain pragmatic considerations that I will soon explain.

Consider the following scenario. Ann enters my office, points to a man (whom I do not know in any way) passing my window, and says,

John believes that he is tall.   (28)

I have no clue about how John thinks about the man; there is nothing that could count as a *normal* notion, since there is, as far as I know, no appropriate community to which John and I belong; I have seen nothing to indicate either that John has encountered the man in perception or that he has performed actions directed at the man; and there is no salient name or other expression that I may attribute to John's notion of the man. If there are ordinary notionally uninformative belief reports, this surely is one of them. Should we, then, take Ann as claiming merely that there is *some* notion John has of the man via which he believes that the man is tall?

It may seem natural to take this report as being notionally uninformative, as being *de re* according to our second criterion. It is not, however, inevitable. In fact, there are very good reasons for thinking that in this report, like others we have considered, the speaker is really talking *about* a specific notion of John's—the content of the report has that notion of the man as an unarticulated constituent.

In saying (28), Ann presents herself as having information about John's beliefs. That is, she presents herself as knowing what she is talking about. I want to suggest that because of the presumptions that she is informed and that she is presenting her claim perspicuously, I am justified in assuming (and I am expected to assume) that Ann is talking about a particular notion of John's for the man. And *that* is how a notion gets into the content of her report: I rightly take her as talking about the notion that..., well, *the one that she is talking about!* Ann may know that the notion she is talking about is one to which John attaches the name 'James', and that it is involved in John's beliefs that James is tall, that he is a student, and so on. But none of this knowledge is conveyed to me in her report. I have a thin grasp on the notion of John's that she is talking about, but it is a grasp nonetheless.

I assume that Ann is abiding by the rules of the game; she cannot be saying something for which she has no grounds. Now, the normal grounds for such a report is knowledge about one of John's notions of the man. This is because our information about others' beliefs comes nearly always from considerations about actions, perceptions, or normal attitudes. I cannot imagine an ordinary case in which a speaker knows that an agent has a belief in a certain proposition, without knowing something more about the notions and ideas involved in it. (Certainly, if there are notionally uninformative reports, *that* would be a way of acquiring this limited kind of information; but to rely on this possibility merely pushes the question backward: why should we think that the report the speaker heard was uninformative?)

One presupposes, where it matters, both that the speaker has normal grounds for her statement and that she is being as informative as is required for the purposes of the conversation. These kinds of presuppositions can be semantically relevant—they can constrain the proposition a speaker can cooperatively intend to express in a statement. It is conceivable that in uttering (28), Ann knows about two or more such notions of John's and knows only that John believes the man to be tall via *some* of them. For instance, someone familiar with all this theoretical talk about beliefs may simply have *told* her that John has several notions of the man and believes that proposition via some of them (not that this would count as an ordinary situation!). Even in such a bizarre case, if Ann were to say (28), without any caveats, she would give the misleading impression of having normal grounds for her statement. And this impression would lead me to infer that information about a specific notion grounds her statement. I thus am licensed by conversational rules to believe that there is a unique relevant, salient notion she is providing for her report to be about.

If there is no such notion, she fails to convey what she means. This would be somewhat like saying 'Bill is tall' in a room with two tall people named 'Bill', without any further indication of who one is talking about. The listener assumes that there is one Bill being discussed, and might ask, "Which one?" The speaker is not playing by the rules if she answers only 'one of them' or even 'both'. And she does not express any proposition at all unless she refers to one Bill or the other. The listener need not know anything helpful about *which* Bill she is talking about, but the assumption that she is talking about a particular individual gives the listener a thin grasp on the referent.

In any statement of a kind that is ordinarily specific, there is a presumption that there is something the speaker is talking about. Exploiting the presumption that this requirement is fulfilled, the speaker can *provide* an individual as part of the the content of her statement without conveying any information about the thing, other than (i) the fact that she is talking about it, and (ii) whatever she claims about it in the statement. The speaker raises the individual to salience and ultimately to propositional constituency by *referential bootstrapping*: she talks about *it* in virtue of talking about it. This is why I can convey knowledge to you about someone with whom you are not until now acquainted, simply by saying 'Charles Sullivan lives in Providence'.

So, if I am right that most ordinary belief reports are notionally specific, there are pragmatic reasons based on (i) ordinary grounds for making belief reports, and (ii) presumptions of informedness and informativeness, for thinking that uninformative reports are hard to come by. I will offer two additional kinds of support (none of it, admittedly, conclusive) for this view. First, I will argue that the bootstrapping account of how John's notion gets provided squares well with intuitions about how the dialogue about John might continue. Second, I will compare this sort of case to other cases, involving indefinite descriptions and proper names, in which a similar salience-raising phenomenon occurs, and point out a difference between the cases that makes a nonspecific, uninformative analysis of the belief report harder to justify.

I might respond to Ann with

Does John believe he is a good volleyball player?   (29)

My intuition about this question is that I would be asking whether John believes this proposition *via the specific notion Ann is talking about*. The correct answer to my question would be yes only if there is a single notion via which (if Ann is right) John believes that the man is tall and that he is a good volleyball player. Now, there are three ways for this to come about. If Ann's claim is simply that there is *some* notion via which John believes the man to be tall, I may be asking whether there is some *such* notion via which he believes the man also to be a good volleyball player. That is, I can be asking whether John has *some* notion of the man to which he ascribes both height and volleyball prowess. But this conflicts with natural intuitions about the case. Suppose that Ann is entirely familiar with one of John's notions of the man and knows that John does not believe the man to be a volleyball player via that notion. And suppose that unknown to Ann, John has a second, unconnected notion of the man that was formed when John saw the man playing volleyball, without recognizing him. In this case, I claim, Ann is correct in answering no to my question; John does *not* believe the man to be a good volleyball player, via the notion that Ann was talking about. This conflicts with the proposed content of my question.

The second way of assigning content to my question gets the truth conditions (or yes conditions) right: Ann is talking about a particular notion that John has of the man, and I ask whether John believes the man to be a good volleyball player, via *that notion*. In using (28), I am suggesting, Ann provides an object (John's notion) in the content of her statement without conveying much information about it, and the object thereby becomes legitimate subject matter for further discussion.

A third suggestion would be to paraphrase Ann's report not as

There is a notion via which John believes that the man is tall,   (30)

but instead as

There is a *certain* notion via which John believes that   (31)
    the man is tall.

In (30), the indefinite description 'a notion' is given an existential reading, as claiming simply that there is some, unspecified notion; it can be entirely appropriate for Ann to make this claim if she has no specific information about any notion of John's. In contrast, the indefinite description in (31) would be inappropriate unless Ann has a particular notion in mind.

Peter Strawson (1956) holds that 'a certain ϕ' does a *referential*

job—a speaker uses such a description to refer to the particular ϕ she has
in mind. Others have disagreed, holding instead that, while 'a certain ϕ'
is semantically equivalent to 'a ϕ' (which in their view is equivalent to
'some ϕ or other'), what is distinctive about it is simply that 'a certain
ϕ' can be non-misleadingly used only when the speaker has a particular
thing (which she believes to be a ϕ) in mind (for example, Kripke 1977;
Ludlow and Neale 1991). Thus a use of 'a certain ϕ' may not refer to any
particular individual, and may nonetheless make salient the individual
that the speaker has in mind.

On either the referential or the descriptive account, 'a certain ϕ'
raises an individual to salience. Subsequently, the speaker, as well as
other parties to the conversation, can *refer* to that individual, either
with 'the ϕ', or with a pronoun. So, given that it seems right (because
of how the conversation might proceed) to analyze Ann's report (28)
in the way suggested by (31), it would seem to be a strong possibility
that the report is notionally uninformative—that it is truth-conditionally
equivalent to (30). This is the third strategy.

However, there is a key feature of belief reports that is not shared
by uses of indefinite descriptions and that weighs against a nonspecific
analysis. Belief reports *are* ordinarily notionally specific, and, when they
are specific, considerations of salience are crucial to determining which
notions are talked about. The plausibility of the nonspecific analysis of
'a certain ϕ' turns on the unity this allows in the semantic treatment of
indefinite descriptions: we have semantic-unity reasons for adopting the
descriptive analysis, and we can explain anaphoric references to particular individuals (as in 'A certain student knocked on my door. *He* had
a paper for me') purely pragmatically, so there is no reason to think 'a
certain ϕ' is semantically any different from 'a ϕ'. This kind of reasoning
is unavailable in the case of belief reports. Belief reports are normally
specifically about notions that are relevant and salient; if we admit that
Ann's report makes a particular notion conversationally salient, then
surely the presumption is that her report is specifically about that notion.

Though I have no argument that *all* ordinary singular, positive belief reports are about specific notions, I take the analysis of the 'John
believes that he is tall' case to suggest that exceptions may be quite
rare. At the very least, it is not at all obvious that they are common.
The notional nonspecificity of other kinds of statements about beliefs,

including some denials, questions, general and plural reports, is beside the point. The evidence for the notional specificity of ordinary belief reports is like that for the direct reference (referential specificity) of ordinary uses of names. There are uses of names that may require different treatment (e.g., negative existentials), but these uses are best explained with reference to general semantic and pragmatic mechanisms interacting with the very mechanisms responsible for ordinary direct reference (more on this in chapter 6).

Let me summarize. We looked at two ways of construing the *de re* side of the *de dicto/de re* distinction, and only the second construal preserves a distinction. But according to the second criterion of a report being *de re*—namely, that it makes no implications about how the agent thinks about a thing—it is likely that there are few ordinary *de re* reports.

In arguing for this last point, I noted the phenomenon of referential bootstrapping—an important way in which an object can be provided as a constituent of a statement. When, according to semantic and pragmatic rules, it can be presumed that a speaker must be talking about *something* in her statement, she can do so without providing any further information about what she is talking about. This is what happens in statements in which a proper name is used to acquaint the hearer with the individual referred to. And this is what happens in belief reports in which the listener has, or is thought to have, no prior knowledge of, or any other handle on, a notion the speaker is talking about.

The bootstrapping phenomenon, under various names, has been widely recognized in contemporary semantics (for example, Stalnaker 1973; Karttunen 1974; Lewis 1979). In fact, it was noticed by Peirce. After presenting a criterion of prior acquaintance as a condition for understanding a statement about an object, and insisting—apparently as a corollary—that the statement ('the Sign') "cannot furnish acquaintance with or recognition of that Object," Peirce presents a terrific example in which just that phenomenon occurs:

Two men are standing on the seashore looking out to sea. One of them says to the other, "That vessel there carries no freight at all, but only passengers." Now, if the other, himself, sees no vessel, the first information he derives from the remark has for its Object the part of the sea that he does see, and informs him that a person with sharper eyes than his, or more trained in looking for such things, can see a vessel there; and then, that vessel having been thus introduced to his acquaintance, he is prepared to receive the information about it that it carries passengers exclusively. (1960, 2.231–2)

Peirce goes on to claim that the statement as a whole is strictly speaking not about the vessel, but only the objects, like the sea, with which the hearer already is acquainted. This claim, with which I disagree, is why Peirce can retain in spite of the example his principle that one must *already* be acquainted with what a sign represents in order to comprehend the information it conveys.

6 Other Reports

The account of singular belief reports in chapter 5 can be plausible only if there are also plausible, appropriately related treatments of related statements, including denials of belief reports, general reports (about no particular agent), embedded reports, and reports of other propositional attitudes. What counts as appropriately related depends on some very general questions concerning presupposition, denials, anaphora, and so on that I cannot begin to address adequately here. But I do want to show that the semantics I have given for singular belief reports suggests promising treatments of these other kinds of statement, on at least some reasonable approaches to these general semantic issues. As a component of the discussion of embedded reports, I will also consider a phenomenon that is of independent interest: beliefs reported with content sentences that involve reference failure.

6.1   Presuppositions and Denials

If singular belief reports typically involve tacit reference to representations in the minds of other agents, then there ought to be cases of tacit reference failure. But are there? In this section I will argue that there are indeed reports with failed references to representations and that intuitions about the truth values of the denials of these belief reports are just as we would predict from other cases of reference failure. While these claims do not depend on a particular theoretical account of reference failure and denial, I will introduce one such account to structure the discussion.[1]

I have argued that a typical singular belief report—ascribing a specific content proposition to a specific individual—is successful in making a claim only when the total circumstances of the report (including aspects of the report itself) manage to provide notions and ideas for the report to be about, through the mechanisms discussed in chapter 5. (I ignore for now those positive reports in which conditions on representations are provided, since such cases do not raise the issues about denials with which I will be concerned in this section.) When a speaker utters a belief sentence, if it is obvious that she presents herself as attempting

---

1. An intriguing account of these matters that is somewhat different from the one sketched here, but consistent with the account of singular belief reports in chapter 5, is explored in Braun, 1991.

to make a successful report of this kind, then her statement *presupposes* that there are unique notions and ideas provided by the circumstances. Since nearly all belief reports are expected to be successful, these kinds of presupposition are the rule, not the exception.

Say that a proposition p is a *pre-assertive* presupposition of a statement if it is mutually obvious to the speaker and her audience that the truth of p is needed for the statement to express a proposition. This is a sub-species of pragmatic presuppositions of an utterance, which are (roughly) those propositions the speaker obviously treats as uncontroversial in making the utterance.[2]

Consider referential presuppositions. When a speaker utters a typical positive sentence containing a proper name, expecting to make a successful statement, the utterance carries a presupposition that his use of the name refers uniquely to an individual. If it is obvious in context that for this to happen, the individual must meet a certain condition (have a certain property), then that condition is a *providing condition*; and there is a pre-assertive, referential presupposition to the effect that the condition is fulfilled. It is thus obvious in context that if a referential presupposition fails, then the statement is unsuccessful—it fails to make a claim, because there is nothing for the claim to be about. For example, take Stich's 1983 case of Mr. Binh's confusion: Binh has confused Thomas Jefferson with Solomon Feferman. When Binh says, "Jeferman is the eminent logician who wrote the *Declaration of Independence*," the presuppositions that his use of the name 'Jeferman' refers to someone, and that there is a unique individual he has heard of as 'Jeferman', fail, and so Binh does not express a proposition. The providing conditions of being the referent of that use of the name, and being the individual Binh has heard of as 'Jeferman' (among others), are not satisfied. Depending on what is obvious in context about the connections the speaker relies on for reference, there may be a large cluster of related providing conditions for an attempted reference. Because of how we have defined providing conditions, any two providing conditions for one attempted reference must be such that it is obvious in context that if there is a referent, both conditions are satisfied by it.

---

2. This notion of statement presupposition reflects a tradition from Frege (1952) and Strawson (1956) through Sellars (1954), Stalnaker (1973, 1974, 1978), Karttunen (1974), Karttunen and Peters (1979), and Soames (1982).

Similar considerations apply to cases in which a speaker unknowingly fails to provide unarticulated constituents for his statement to be about—there are presuppositions of tacit as well as of explicit reference. When a rider on the carousel at the North Pole says to her companion (on the other side of the carousel), "It is three o'clock," there are failed pre-assertive presuppositions that the speaker is providing a specific time zone for the statements to be about, and that the current situation is within a single time zone. If those presuppositions were correct, the speaker would be talking about a specific time zone. But unexpected circumstances have conspired to make her statement a failure—she expresses no proposition; there is nothing for her "claim" to be right or wrong about.

In chapter 5, I explored a handful of different kinds of pre-assertive presuppositions that can ground the provision of notions and ideas as unarticulated constituents of the claims made in belief reports. In most positive, singular belief reports, there are presuppositions that the speaker is talking about specific notions and ideas. Depending on what is obvious in context, there can also be presuppositions that the agent has a normal notion of a thing (or a normal idea of a property), that there is a notion of a thing linked to the agent's action or perception, that the agent has a notion or idea that would be expressed in a certain way, that the reporter has one of the agent's notions in mind, and so on. Each such presupposition is to the effect that the agent has a notion or idea meeting a certain providing condition. Such a presupposition fails when there is no notion or idea meeting that condition. When any of these presuppositions fails, tacit reference fails, and a gap results in the subject matter of the report; the speaker fails to express a proposition.

Whether this or another account of referential presupposition is correct, the semantics of chapter 5 entails that many belief reports have no content, and hence no truth values, unless specific notions and ideas are provided for them to be about. Alas, there are reasons to be uncomfortable with this result. The main one is that there seem to be belief reports, in which there is just this kind of presupposition failure (if I am right that this is what it is), that are simply false—and falsity is a truth value.

A representative example of this problem (first discussed in Crimmins and Perry 1989) is the following. You and I are walking along the

Mall in Washington, D.C., and we see a man to all appearances staring with great awe at the Washington Monument. I say,

That yokel believes it's the tallest thing in the world.   (1)

Suppose that the man is in fact blind, and is simply lost in thought. It is a referential presupposition of my statement that the man has a perceptual notion of the building; I attempt to claim that via *that* notion, he believes the monument to be the tallest thing in the world. Since my presupposition fails, I am talking about nothing, I fail to make a claim, and therefore my belief report is neither true nor false. Or so my account predicts.

But can that be right? Isn't my use of (1) just *false*? Don't I claim something quite specific about the man's beliefs, that turns out simply not to be true? Certainly, if you know of the man's blindness, you would be right to claim 'No he doesn't; and he's blind', and I would withdraw my statement immediately. Usually, we correctly deny something only when it is false.

Usually, granted, but not always. In general, it seems, we can truly deny a statement (at least) whenever the speaker does not say something true—this can happen when the statement is false, or when any of its pre-assertive presuppositions fail. If this is right, then we can reconcile the truth of your denial with the claim that my report (1) has no truth value.

Compare the other cases we have seen in which pre-assertive presuppositions fail. When Mr. Binh claims that 'Jeferman wrote the *Declaration*', if we understand his confusion, we can reply 'No. *Jefferson* wrote that', or 'Jeferman did *not* write the *Declaration*; there is no Jeferman'. This is similar to someone telling a child, in response to 'Santa lives up North', that 'Santa does *not* live up North; there is no Santa'. In cases of reference failure, no proposition is expressed. But we feel free to deny statements where this happens; and we have strong intuitions that our denials are true.

Consider also the polar carousel rider's claim, 'it is three o'clock'. What she says cannot be true or false, since there is no time zone for it to be about, as is presupposed in her statement. But knowing this, we can appropriately deny her statement: 'It is *not* three o'clock—or any other time for that matter, since you are spinning around the North Pole'. (A

clearer case might have the speaker "transported" unknowingly to the moon.) It seems that such a denial would be true as well as appropriate.

This seems enough to show that the cases of tacit reference failure and denials in belief reports are not importantly different from other cases of reference failure. These phenomena are to be expected. But since expecting a problem does not make it go away, it will be useful to sketch one suggestion for dealing with cases of reference failure and denials in general, and to show the application to belief reports.

In cases of reference failure, it seems, a statement can fail to express a proposition, while the denial of the very same statement is true. To make sense of this, we can adopt an account of the truth conditions of these denials that is very different from a truth-functional account of sentence negation. This is by no means an ad hoc move; it is common in semantics to hold that there are varieties of negative statements that can be true *because* of presupposition failure (see, for example, Horn 1989). I will focus here on the special case of pre-assertive presuppositions.

In denials, I suggest, what is normally a mere pre-assertive presupposition can crash the semantic party and become part of the proposition expressed. A denial can be true because of the falsity of what would be a presupposition of a use of the corresponding positive sentence. Spelling this out will provide a solution to the blind-man denial puzzle case, a solution that falls directly out of the account of singular belief reports given a semantic/pragmatic mechanism—of *raising providing conditions to constituency*—that we have independent reason to posit for denials involving other types of reference failure.

When the child says 'Santa will be coming tonight', he fails to express a proposition because nothing meets the providing conditions of the attempted reference, including that of being the subject of Christmas stories named 'Santa'. When the child's parent says 'Santa will *not* be coming tonight', the content of her claim is that there is nothing *meeting those conditions* that will be coming tonight. When we say 'It's *not* three o'clock', we claim that the cluster of providing conditions (those that would accompany a positive use of 'it's three o'clock' in the context) are not fulfilled. When a providing condition ends up in the proposition expressed, as here, that condition is *raised to constituency*. A device, in this case a proper name, that would normally require an *object* to fill a spot in the content proposition, can in this way supply instead a cluster of providing conditions. (From here on I will cease to distinguish between single providing conditions and clusters of them, and adopt the convenient pretense that there is just a single providing condition for an attempted reference, tacit or explicit. It might be that in general this role could be filled by a presupposition that a particular referential tradition—in some cases one created on the spot—is grounded in reference.)

Exploiting the phenomenon of raising to constituency in our semantics for denials yields a very flexible account, but this flexibility leads to a new problem. In the denial about Santa, what was our reason for choosing the providing conditions for just one propositional slot to raise to constituency? Why not raise the conditions providing the time (tonight) and the relation of coming as well? The problem is to explain, for an arbitrary denial, just which conditions are, and which are not, raised to constituency.

Two implausible ideas present themselves immediately: (i) all providing conditions are raised to constituency, and (ii) all and only the providing conditions that are not uniquely satisfied are raised to constituency. Consider the denial

Homer was *not* friends with Odysseus.   (2)

It seems to me that if a speaker believes it is uncontroversial that Homer existed but disbelieves that Odysseus existed, he would use (2) to attempt to express a truth *about Homer*; he would elucidate his claim by saying 'there was no such person as Odysseus'. Thus there would be an attempted reference to Homer, and so the first candidate principle is mistaken. Given the same speaker beliefs and intentions, if it happens that Odysseus, *but not Homer*, really existed, then the second candidate principle would take the proposition expressed to be the true claim that no person meeting the providing conditions associated with the use of 'Homer' was friends with Odysseus; and this is surely an incorrect result.

I propose that the proposition the speaker expresses is just the one he intends to express, where this of course depends crucially on his beliefs about whether Homer and Odysseus existed. It is consistent with his asserting (2) that the speaker maintain any combination of positions on these issues. That is, he might think there was a Homer but no Odysseus, no Homer and no Odysseus, an Odysseus but no Homer, or both a Homer and an Odysseus. Call the condition of being 'a Homer' (that is, the providing condition that would accompany an attempted reference using

Table 6.1
Expressed proposition, based on speaker's beliefs and the facts

The Facts:	Speaker's Beliefs:	
	$p_H \& p_O$	$p_H \& \neg p_O$
$p_H \& p_O$	$\neg \langle\!\langle \textit{Friends}; \textit{Homer}, \textit{Odysseus} \rangle\!\rangle$	$\neg \langle\!\langle \textit{Friends}; \textit{Homer}, \boxed{C_O} \rangle\!\rangle$
$p_H \& \neg p_O$	$\neg \langle\!\langle \textit{Friends}; \textit{Homer}, \underline{\quad} \rangle\!\rangle$	$\neg \langle\!\langle \textit{Friends}; \textit{Homer}, \boxed{C_O} \rangle\!\rangle$
$\neg p_H \& \neg p_O$	$\neg \langle\!\langle \textit{Friends}; \underline{\quad}, \underline{\quad} \rangle\!\rangle$	$\neg \langle\!\langle \textit{Friends}; \underline{\quad}, \boxed{C_O} \rangle\!\rangle$

'Homer' in the context), C_H; call the condition of being 'an Odysseus', C_O; and call the propositions that these conditions are satisfied uniquely, p_H and p_O. Then, some of the propositions determined by what the speaker would likely intend to express, depending on his beliefs and given the facts, might be charted as in table 6.1. (In the table, a box around a condition is a descriptionlike notation indicating that the containing proposition is to the effect that there is a unique entity meeting the condition such that...; the uppermost proposition in the right-hand column is that it is not the case that Homer was friends with the unique thing meeting C_O. I adopt this notation for suggestiveness, not brevity; it displays the idea that a providing condition is provided *in place of* an individual. The notation, like definite descriptions in natural language, leads to ambiguities of scope.)

The pattern here is that the speaker attempts to *provide* the objects satisfying the conditions he supposes to be satisfied, and to raise to constituency those he believes not to be satisfied. When the speaker's assumption that a providing condition is satisfied turns out to be false, a gap results—there is no (complete) proposition of the kind he intends to express. My proposal is that when the speaker is being cooperative, he expresses and conveys the proposition he intends to express (if there is such a proposition). In practice, this means that to fulfill the maxims of cooperation, the speaker must try to make it clear which proposition he means to express. He must, if what he means is not otherwise clear from context, provide explicit caveats to make it apparent which conditions he is raising to constituency. This, I think, is why we are uncomfortable with saying simply 'Santa will not be coming tonight', but more comfortable with saying that followed immediately by 'There is no such person'. The caveat does not simply explain the grounds for our denial, it in fact helps clarify which of several things we might be saying with that sentence. (It seems also to support this proposal that the 'such' in caveats like this must mean *something*—a providing condition is just the thing.)

Back to denials of the form '*A* does not believe that *s*'. In such statements, the speaker would normally be expected to provide as unarticulated constituents of his claim a number of notions and ideas; these would be provided in virtue of their satisfying providing conditions. If the speaker believes a providing condition not to be satisfied, he must make it clear that he intends to raise that condition to constituency in his denial. For example, when you say 'He does not believe that it's the tallest thing in the world. He's blind', you make it clear that you believe the condition, C_m, the property of being his current perceptual notion of the monument, is not satisfied. So your true denial is of the form:

$\neg \exists \tau \ [\ Believes(a, t, p, \tau) \ \&$

$\qquad Responsible(\boxed{C_m}, \tau, r_m) \ \& \ \cdots].$

This is the proposition that it is not the case that there is a notion meeting C_m such that the yokel at t has a belief in proposition p and in which that notion is responsible for filling the role r_m (the role the Monument plays in the proposition). A perspicuous paraphrase of your denial might be, 'He does not believe that it's the tallest thing in the world via *that* notion; there is no such notion'. So, although my report 'That yokel believes that it's the tallest thing in the world' does not succeed in expressing a proposition due to C_m's being unmet, that same fact makes your denial true.

Thus, the phenomenon of raising providing conditions to constituency in denials gives an explanation of the intuition that my claim about the blind man is false. Though what I say does not express a proposition, your natural *denial* of my statement is true.

Still, there may be a lingering discomfort: your denial of my statement is just that, a *denial*. It is in *disagreement* with my statement. My semantics, on the other hand, seems to miss the obvious fact of disagreement by taking your denial to be a negative statement about a proposition that I never in fact have expressed—the proposition that the man has a perceptual notion via which he believes the monument to be tall. I think this objection can be met. Your denial is in direct contradiction, not to a proposition I *express* (there isn't one), but to a proposition to which I am *committed* (I have acted in a way that obviously licenses your inference that I believe the proposition)—and not committed in the sense of having implicated or insinuated it, but committed *pre-assertively*.

If I make an unsuccessful statement, as long as it is mutually obvious in context how I am *trying* to say something, I am committed to various other propositions, in virtue of how I present myself to be expressing a claim. If I say 'Jeff is here', at location l I commit myself assertively to what I express:

$$\langle\!\langle \, At; Jeff, l \, \rangle\!\rangle \, .$$

But if it is obvious that the success of my attempt to provide Jeff as a constituent of that proposition turns on his satisfying a providing condition, say, of being the person called 'Jeff' whom you have just been talking about, I am committed also to the proposition that there is a unique individual meeting the condition (C_{Jeff}) of being someone named Jeff whom you have just been discussing. I am *pre-assertively* committed to this presupposition because my being able to express the kind of proposition I obviously intend to assert depends on its truth (and this fact is itself mutually obvious). So I am committed, in virtue of how I expect, and present myself as expecting, my claim to be determined, to this proposition:

$$\langle\!\langle \, At; \boxed{C_{Jeff}}, l \, \rangle\!\rangle \, . \tag{3}$$

Now, if you say 'Jeff is not here; there is no such person', the providing conditions that would attach in this context to an attempt by you to refer using 'Jeff' are, if not identical, obviously related to C_{Jeff}— your reference obviously would depend on the same crucial conditions as mine. So you have denied a proposition which in context is an obvious consequence of (3), and so to which I am also committed.

Similarly the proposition you deny when you claim that the yokel does not believe that the monument is the tallest thing in the world, is one to which I am committed pre-assertively. Even though I have asserted no proposition, you have correctly denied a proposition to which I am committed in virtue of my statement.

6.2   General Reports

Belief reports that are not about specific agents, but only about all or some agents of a certain kind, seem clearly to involve conditions on notions and ideas.

Barbara says,

The Egyptians believed that Tut was divine.   (4)

This is a *general* belief report, about all, or most, Egyptians of Tut's day. It would be crazy to maintain that the proposition Barbara expresses has as a constituent every Egyptian's notion of Tut, or any such notion, for that matter. That would be to construe her statement as a *singular* claim about all, most, or some Egyptians, when really it is a general claim about these people. Barbara's claim does not contain the notions and ideas of the Egyptians, but merely constrains them. Her claim is that nearly every Egyptian believed the proposition that Tut is divine, in a way involving her normal notion of Tut.

Having conditions provided in place of individuals in general statements is no peculiarity of belief reports. Take the statement

In the U.S., whenever a lunch bell sounds, it's noon.   (5)

The claim here is that in any location in the U.S., when the lunch bell sounds, it's noon *there*—in the time zone containing that location. The locution 'it's noon' usually requires a time zone to be talked about. But in a general claim of this sort, the unarticulated time zone is "quantified out"—there is an implicit quantifier over places, and an implicit condition on time zones, $C_t(z, l)$, of being the time zone containing a certain location. The proposition expressed is

$$\langle\!\langle\, All;\; [l : In(l, U.S.)],$$
$$[l :\, \langle\!\langle\, The;\; [z : C_t(z, l)],$$
$$[z : \forall t [\;\; Rings(LunchBell, l, t)$$
$$\rightarrow Time(Noon, t, z)]] \,\rangle\!\rangle\,]\,\rangle\!\rangle\,.$$

A similar treatment would be needed for 'On our trip around the world it rained every day'. In these cases, rather than tacit reference, there is tacit description.

A special case of a general report is one in which a claim is made about the unique agent satisfying a certain property—that is, where the agent is described with an attributive description. If the referential/attributive distinction is semantically real, then reports of this type may be less common than might be suspected. When the speaker has evidence about a particular agent's beliefs, she usually will refer directly to that agent (perhaps with a referential description), rather than offering merely a general characterization. And when the speaker lacks such particular evidence, there rarely is a reason to make a belief report.

But there certainly are cases in which the agent clearly is described in the required way:

The Olympic Games are awaited with great hope in Korea. The poorest farmer in the country believes that the Games will bring him greater prosperity.

Here, the claim is that, whoever is the poorest farmer in Korea, he believes, via his *normal* notion of the Olympics that are about to visit his country, the proposition that the Games will bring him prosperity.

Notice also that, in this case, the proposition that the described agent is claimed to believe is not specified, but instead is described as being the proposition that a certain man will be wealthier, where that man is the poorest farmer in Korea. The speaker's utterance of the content sentence 'the Games will bring him greater prosperity' does not express a proposition, but only a partial proposition—something that, given an individual, determines the proposition that that individual will be wealthier. It clearly is required for the truth of the report that in the belief the man thinks of himself via his self-notion and thinks of the Games in a normal way (for Koreans at the time).

So the claim expressed by the descriptive belief report is this (taking some liberties for readability):

$\langle\!\langle$ *The*; $[x : PoorestFarmer(x)]$,
$\qquad [x : \exists \tau \, [Believes(x, t, p, \tau) \, \&$
$\qquad\qquad \exists n_1, n_2(C_1(n_1) \, \& \, C_2(n_2)) \, \&$
$\qquad\qquad [b : Responsible(n_1, b, r_1) \, \& \, Responsible(n_2, b, r_2, t)]]) \, \rangle\!\rangle$.

where p is the proposition that x will be wealthier soon after t because of the Games, C_1 is the condition of being a self-notion, r_1 is the subject role in p, C_2 is the condition of being a normal notion of the Games, for Koreans at the time, r_2 is the role played by the Games in p, and t is the time of utterance.

One gross "liberty" I have taken is to assume that though we do not have a specific content proposition, we have specific roles (r_1 and r_2) in it. There are two reasonable ways of remedying this deficiency, which I will sketch but will not develop seriously here. First, we might supply a role-type rather than a role. The concept of a role's *pedigree* developed in chapter 4 would be useful in characterizing the appropriate concept of role-type. We then would require, in this example, that the farmer's self-notion be responsible for a role of a specified role-type. Second, we might extend the concept of representational responsibility in this way: a notion is responsible (in a belief) for an empty role in a partial proposition p if it is responsible (in the belief) for a corresponding role (with the same pedigree) in a completion of p (a proposition with the same structure as p, but with an entity filling the gap). In the example, then, we would require that the farmer's self-notion be responsible for the empty role in the partial proposition,

$$\langle\!\langle\ WealthierSoonBecause; \_, Games, t\,\rangle\!\rangle\,.$$

A famous case in which the content proposition in a belief report is not specified, but only described, is Russell's 1956a example of a man telling an acquaintance:

I thought your yacht was larger than it is.   (6)

Here the agent is specified, but the content proposition is merely described as involving a size, and being to the effect that the yacht is larger than that. That is,

$$\langle\!\langle\ The;\ [x : Size(x, yacht)]$$
$$[x : \exists\tau\ (\ Believes(a, t, \langle\!\langle\ Larger; yacht, x\,\rangle\!\rangle, \tau)\ \&\ \cdots\ )\ ]\ \rangle\!\rangle\,.$$

This proposition involves a specific agent, but a described propositional content.

Another important sort of case involves specific reference to more than one agent:

Ann and Tom believe that Max has fleas.   (7)

One might decide to treat such "plural" reports in the same way as general reports: as claiming that the agents have beliefs involving notions that meet a certain condition—or in a manner more like singular reports: as specifying the notions involved for each agent. It may be that some plural reports should be handled in each of these ways. In any case the decision should cohere with a general account of plural statements. I will not pursue the question further here.

6.3   Embedded Reports and Reference Failure

Consider statements of belief sentences whose content sentences are themselves belief sentences.

A believes that B believes that s.   (8)

A normal use of 'B believes that s' would express a proposition having among its constituents the constituents of the content of s, as well as various of B's notions and ideas. And so the semantics for singular belief reports applied directly to this example would take the utterance of the embedded belief sentence in (8) to express a complex proposition about those individuals, properties, relations, notions, and ideas. The larger report, then, would express the claim that A has a belief in this complex proposition, involving certain of A's notions and ideas. This seems right in many cases, as in the following report (in the obvious kinds of circumstances):

You believe that I believe that you're reading that book.   (9)

Or, less tongue-twistingly:

You think I believe you're reading that book.   (10)

The belief this report attributes to you can quite plausibly be taken to be about my notions of my hearer and the book. I attribute to you a belief about these notions—and in doing so I talk about your notions of these notions.

That it is important to have notions of notions around for work in embedded reports becomes clear when we consider that, like any individuals, notions can be misrecognized. Suppose Quine was wrong about Tom, and that really Tom has a single notion n_{CT} he attaches to the names 'Cicero' and 'Tully'. Then, Quine's statement of 'Tom believes that Cicero is not Tully', is after all false. But we can truly say,

Quine thinks Tom believes that Cicero is not Tully.   (11)

On my account, what goes on is the following. Quine has two ways of thinking about Tom's notion n_{CT}—that is, Quine has two notions of that notion, call them n_C and n_T. Keep in mind that these are notions, not of Cicero, but of Tom's notion n_{CT}, which itself is a notion of Cicero. Via n_C, Quine believes that n_{CT} is involved in a belief that Cicero was named 'Cicero'; via n_T, he believes that n_{CT} is involved in a belief that Cicero was called 'Tully'. The proposition that Cicero is not Tully is this (with two of its roles indicated):

$$p \ = \ \langle\!\langle\, Not; \ \langle\!\langle\, Identical; \underbrace{Cicero}_{r_1}, \underbrace{Cicero}_{r_2} \,\rangle\!\rangle \,\rangle\!\rangle \,.$$

Now, what we claim in (11) is that Quine believes this proposition (with two roles indicated):

$$\exists \tau \,[\ \ Believes(Tom, t, p, \tau) \ \&$$
$$Responsible(\underbrace{n_{CT}}_{r_3}, \tau, r_1) \ \& \ Responsible(\underbrace{n_{CT}}_{r_4}, \tau, r_2) \,].$$

That is, we attribute to Quine the belief that Tom has a belief that Cicero is not Cicero, with the notion n_{CT} responsible for the first occurrence of Cicero and the notion n_{CT} (the same notion) responsible for the second occurrence of Cicero. But of course we do not merely specify the proposition that Quine believes; we also say how he believes it. In particular, we specify that his belief is of a type τ such that

$$Responsible(n_C, \tau, r_3) \ \& \ Responsible(n_T, \tau, r_4).$$

So our report is indeed true. This is a direct application of the strategy used in chapter 5 for solving belief puzzles involving misrecognition of individuals to a case in which the individual in question is a notion, n_{CT}. The application of the account to the recalcitrant puzzles about embedded reports discussed by Mates (1950) and Church (1954) is equally straightforward.

Recall the example in which I mistakenly suppose a blind man to have a notion of the Washington Monument. You can remind me:

You believed that he believed that it was a tall monument.   (12)

Or, more manageably:

You thought he believed it was tall.   (13)

What you would be getting at is relatively clear: I assumed the man had a certain notion of the monument, and I thought he had a belief that the monument was tall, involving *that* notion. But of course *that* notion does not exist.

The key to explaining (13) is to note its relation to these:

Ann [on the moon] believes it's three o'clock.   (14)

Jerry believes that he saw Santa.   (15)

In each of these cases, the content sentence of the report does not express a proposition, owing to a failure of a providing condition to provide a propositional constituent. In the case of (14), the providing condition is the property of being the time zone where Ann is; in the case of (15), it is the property of being the Christmas hero called 'Santa'; and in the case of (13), it is the condition of being the man's perceptual notion of the monument. But, as in the case of denials, the speakers of these embedded belief reports need not be committed to the fulfillment of the providing conditions; that is, they need not *employ* the providing conditions to attempt to provide constituents of their claims.

Recall that we took partial propositions to be contents of statements in which providing conditions fail. In the same way, we can view the content of a belief in which a notion fails to be *of* any object, as a partial proposition—an entity like a proposition, but lacking an object at the argument role the empty notion is responsible for filling. If we allow partial propositions as contents of beliefs, then the application of the account of chapter 5 is direct. For example, the content of (14), where n_Z is Ann's empty notion purportedly *of* her local time zone, is that Ann has a belief (i) whose content is the partial proposition,

$$\langle\!\langle\ Time; t, Three, \underbrace{\quad}_{r_Z}\ \rangle\!\rangle\ ,$$

and (ii) in which the notion n_Z is responsible for filling r_Z.

According to your report (13), I had a belief whose content was this partial proposition (with its single empty role indicated):

$$p\ =\ \exists \tau\ [\ Believes(a, t, p_{WM}, \tau)\ \&$$
$$Responsible(\underbrace{\quad}_{r_n}, \tau, r_{WM})\ ],$$

where a is the blind man and r_{WM} is the role filled by the Washington Monument in the proposition p_{WM} (that the Monument is the tallest thing in the world).

In (13), you claim that I had a belief with the content p, such that my notion (call it n_n) purportedly *of* the man's perceptual notion of the monument is responsible for the empty role r_n. That is:

$$\exists \tau \ [\ Believes(Crimmins, t, p, \tau) \ \& $$
$$Responsible(n_n, \tau, r_n) \ ].$$

Like the report of Ann's belief about the time, this claim is true. The truth of these reports falls out of the direct application of the account of chapter 5 to cases in which properly partial propositions are reported to be the contents of beliefs.

6.4   Other Propositional Attitudes

It should be clear that the extension of the present account of belief reports to *some* other attitude reports, including reports of desire, intention, doubt, suspicion, and so on, is straightforward. Consider a report of

Tom intends to give Mary a copy of his paper.   (16)

Without much violence, this can be analyzed as claiming that Tom has an at-least-tacit intention with the content that he, at some time, gives Mary a copy of his paper.[3] We can easily imagine puzzle cases to show us that this cannot be *all* that the report claims—cases, for instance, in which Tom has two unconnected notions of Mary. The report specifies, in addition to the propositional content of Tom's alleged intention, the notions and ideas involved in it—just as in the case of belief reports. This move can, as far as I can see, equally well be made in all cases of reports of conceptual attitudes. And that is a good sign; the cases of substitution failure with 'believes that' do not seem importantly different from those with 'intends to', 'wants', 'doubts that', and so on.

---

3. No doubt, variations of the account of belief reports would be needed if we were to take the objects of other conceptual attitudes to be not propositions but some other entities involving individuals, properties, and relations as constituents.

But reports of these other conceptual attitudes are not the only kinds of statement for which we can concoct puzzles exactly like the belief puzzles. Reports of the following kinds are equally susceptible to such problems:

Caius said that Hesperus is an evening star.   (17)

Caius denied that Hesperus is an evening star.   (18)

Caius meant that Hesperus is an evening star.   (19)

The first of these, for example, in the obvious kinds of circumstance, is true if Caius said 'Hesperus is an evening star', but false if Caius said only 'Phosphorus is an evening star'. Can we explain this fact with the tools I have used in the analysis of belief reports? There are two ways we might try to do this.

First is a strategy common in the analysis of opacity in indirect quotation (statements involving the 'says that' construction). What the report of (17) claims, on this strategy, is that Caius made a statement with the content that Venus is an evening star, using the *name* 'Hesperus' for Venus. The strategy easily could be detailed along the general lines used above for belief reports, with the exception that, where notions and ideas are involved in belief reports, words (or uses of them) are involved in indirect quotation.

A better analysis of indirect quotation and the related constructions would proceed *exactly* along the lines used in the analysis of belief reports. On this second account, the use of (17) claims that Caius made a statement with the content that Venus is an evening star, involving a certain *notion* of that planet (namely, the notion to which he attaches the name 'Hesperus'). One way of filling out this account would be to analyze '*A* said that *S*' as '*A* assertively expressed her thought that *S*'. Thoughts, like beliefs, can be described by giving a content proposition and a responsibility clause assigning representations to roles in the proposition. I want to suggest that an account in terms of notions and ideas is not just open to us, but is in fact superior to an account in terms of the agent's words, precisely because notions are what explain the substitution puzzles, and words do not correspond to notions one to one.

The report of (17) is an example of *de dicto* indirect quotation: the words used by the reporter are assumed to be the same as those used in

the statement reported. The two analyses of indirect quotation account
for such examples equally well. If the *de dicto* phenomenon were the only
sort of case in which more than the content of a statement is specified
in indirect quotation, there would be nothing to choose between the two
analyses—except perhaps the relative simplicity of the first. But this is
not the actual situation. In fact, there are examples of indirect quotation
paralleling each of the different kinds of belief reports, in which notions
and ideas are provided in different ways.

Consider the typical statement of

Columbus said that he would one day land in India.   (20)

Here, it is claimed that Columbus asserted something, with the content
that he landed in India. Is it claimed in addition that he used the *name*
'India'? It may be that Columbus understood and used that name; I
don't know. But it may also be that he did not; he may have used a
closely related name, or an entirely unrelated name, or even a pronoun.
Surely, my ignorance about this doesn't affect my understanding of (20),
or even my knowing that it is true. Given this, it cannot be part of
the claim it makes that Columbus used the very name 'India'. This is
not a *de dicto* report of Columbus' statement, and there is no obvious
extension of the first account of indirect quotation to explain what it
claims. Nor is it a purely notionally unspecific report; it is clear that
the report would not be true unless Columbus had said such a thing in
a way appropriate to expressing his thought involving his normal notion
of India. This is a *normal* report, in analogy to those belief reports in
which normal notions and ideas are provided (see section 5.4.1). What is
claimed is that Columbus used an expression for India that was attached
to his *normal notion* of that place. In the context of (20), what would
count as a normal notion of India is clear: Columbus's notion must have
been involved in a belief that India is reachable over land to the East,
and in a host of other ordinary beliefs of the time about the exotic land.
The report is true just in case Columbus used a word that he attached
to a normal notion of India.

Consider now a statement in the same context of

Columbus said that America was India.   (21)

Again, it is claimed that Columbus used an expression attached to his
normal notion of India. But what about America? Assuming that

Columbus did not know about America until he landed here, it is likely that he had no name at all for America at the time of his landing. What (21) claims is that Columbus used an expression for America that was attached to the notion he formed upon arriving at the place.

Indirect quotation is subject to all of the subtleties we have found in belief reporting. The second account of indirect quotation, along the same lines as the account of belief reporting, gives a unified account of these circumstantial subtleties, unmatched by the first, simpler account shaped only for the *de dicto* case.

For a decisive counterexample to the word-based account that is explained easily by the notional account, consider Kripke's 1979 example of Peter, who has two notions of the man Paderewski. Peter has heard of this man twice, both times under the name 'Paderewski'; on one occasion the discussion concerned Paderewski's political achievements, on the other his musical talents (and, we can assume, the other discussants knew that Paderewski had both callings). But Peter thinks he has heard of two different men. Suppose in fact Peter once said 'Paderewski is a hard worker; it takes great effort to be a politician'. Suppose that we know of Peter's confusion, and that we are talking about Paderewski's music. If I say,

Peter said that Paderewski is a hard worker,   (22)

then, since you legitimately take me to be claiming that Peter was talking about 'the musician Paderewski', I speak falsely. In different contexts, I can make either of two different claims, one true and one false, with this sentence. To clarify which claim I mean to make, I need only to ensure that one or the other of Peter's notions is especially salient.

In this example, we can distinguish, using indirect quotation, between two different sorts of statements that Peter might have made, using exactly the same words. The names Peter attaches to his two notions are not merely spelled the same; he gets them both from informed members of his linguistic community in the perfectly normal way that suffices for learning to use the same name the others do. Thus a strategy of distinguishing carefully among words that are spelled alike (I believe that David Kaplan has advocated such an approach) will not save the day for a word-based approach—unless words are distinguished finely enough to make them nearly impossible to transmit. We distinguish more finely among statements than words allow. The notional account explains why, and handles this case easily.

There are cases, however, that suggest that an adequate account of indirect quotation may need to be more complex. Suppose that you and I each have only one notion of Cicero, and we know that Cicero is called both 'Cicero' and 'Tully'. Suppose I report, of my conversation with Tom, 'I said that Tully was an orator'. Here, I take it, using the name 'Tully' rather than 'Cicero' affects what I say, and yet I have only a single notion of Cicero. So the direct application of the semantics for belief reports will not work. While I am unsure how to treat such cases, I suspect the disanalogy from similar belief reports has to do with the relevance, in indirect quotation, of the *audience's* attitudes. So a promising option is to take into account the thoughts of the audience, at least in cases of this kind (I am not sure whether the sources of substitution failure in indirect quotation are as unified as in the case of belief reports). One way of doing this would be to hold that (at least sometimes) what is tacitly referred to is not a condition on the *speaker's* notion, but on the notion that someone would need to employ were he to *understand* the statement. Understanding a statement, as I suggested in chapter 3, involves more than merely representing its propositional content; understanding can involve representing the proposition's constituents in the right way—with representations meeting certain conditions. So it is plausible that when one reports what was said, one can ordinarily indicate what is needed to understand what was said. For example, when you say 'You said to Tom that Tully was an orator,' you may tacitly stipulate as a condition on understanding what I said, that one's notion of Cicero be a 'Tully' notion (that it be involved in a belief that Cicero is called 'Tully'). This seems a promising line to pursue, but I will leave its pursuit for another occasion. I hope the line works, since it seems it would be useful also in explaining the following statements, which do not directly attribute an assertion to any individual, but report on what is written in a certain place (and may have been written by several authors, corrected by an editor, and so on):

This article says that Hesperus is an evening star.   (23)

It says here that Hesperus is an evening star.   (24)

Cases to which the account of belief reporting surely cannot be extended include the following:

Smith brought it about that automobiles now use unleaded gas.   (25)

The black smoke means that the fuel mixture is not correct.   (26)

But of course it is not surprising that the account of belief reports does not apply to all constructions with "that" clauses. We use such clauses to talk about propositions, and our interest in propositions is not always accompanied by an interest in representations. I hope I have demonstrated the fruitfulness of holding that in many propositional constructions we talk not only about propositions, but also about representations.

7 Frege and Russell

Since my account of belief reports is reminiscent of Frege's, it is worthwhile to summarize just how the present analysis avoids some of the major problems often thought fatal to the Fregean program and saves some of its insights. Frege clearly recognized that in a belief report of the form

$$A \text{ believes that } \phi(b), \tag{1}$$

something is conveyed about a way of thinking about the individual that b stands for (the ordinary referent of b). A view about belief reports that Frege suggests in various places is this: a belief report is true just in case the agent has a belief in which he thinks about the individuals and properties mentioned in the content sentence, in the ways associated with the words that make up that sentence.

A difficulty that Frege saw but never conquered is that different agents can attach different ways of thinking about a thing to the same name. In particular, the speaker of the report (1) and the agent A might think about the thing the speaker calls b in a different ways. The problem is to choose which way of thinking makes it into what the speaker claims; the forced choice puts us in a dilemma. If, on the one hand, we choose the speaker's way of thinking about the referent of b, then it seems to be a requirement for a true report that the agent thinks about the individual in the same way (and surely this is an unreasonable requirement). If, on the other hand, we choose the agent's way of thinking, then it would seem in many cases almost magical that the speaker can attach to his word b *that* way of thinking, which he need neither share nor be able to express or describe in any detail; he might not know *how* the agent thinks about the individual. In addition, we can report the beliefs of an agent who is not even familiar with the names we use (in translation or otherwise). So how is it that in such cases we can refer to the agent's ways of thinking at all?

The Fregean line is quite closely allied to the one pursued here. In a belief report, I have suggested, the speaker claims that an agent believes a proposition *in a certain way*. So I must take the Fregean dilemma seriously. I am of course already happily committed to one of its horns: a belief report is about a way that the *agent* thinks about the individual mentioned in the embedded sentence. It is about a specific notion that the agent has of that individual.

Certainly, I am not *quite* in the same boat as the Fregean; I have
not claimed that the words the speaker uses in the embedded sentence
are attached to, stand for, or even always help to pick out the operative
ways of thinking. So I am not faced by the second problem attaching to
the chosen horn of the dilemma: it is not at all a worry that the agent
can be unfamiliar with the words the speaker uses. But my account
is confronted head-on by the other problem: how can the speaker talk
about a "way of thinking" with which he may be almost entirely unfamiliar? And, with respect to this epistemological problem, the differences
between my account and the Fregean's are crucial.

Notions, unlike Frege's senses, are not things that can be *understood*
or *grasped*. A notion is a *particular* that for the purposes of comparison with senses can helpfully be viewed as a mental "simple" that is in
the head of just one agent. Thus, the appearance of mystery that may
attach to a speaker's talking about a sense that he does not *grasp* does
not transfer to a speaker talking about a notion that is not *his*. Talking about another person's notion with which one is unfamiliar is no
more mysterious than talking about another's heart or knee, with which
one need not be terribly familiar in order to speak perfectly meaning-
fully. Notions have lots of features that we exploit to gain a referential
hold on them: they may be normal, attached by an agent to certain
words, involved in perception and actions, and so on. As I argued in
chapter 5, most belief reports are made in circumstances in which it is
perfectly obvious to us that the agent has a certain notion—despite our
not "grasping" it.

Also, whereas the Fregean takes a "thought" composed of "ways
of thinking" as the truth-conditional *thing* which the agent is claimed
to believe in a belief report, I distinguish the notions and ideas talked
about from the proposition that is thereby believed—thus separating
what is believed from how it is believed. This too makes it less bizarre
that the speaker can be relatively unfamiliar with the way of thinking
that he is talking about. For, in my view, the ways of thinking being
talked about do not do the work of determining which individuals the
belief is claimed to be about and which proposition the agent is claimed
to believe.

Russell at one point believed in singular propositions—propositions
about (or "containing") real individuals rather than just properties and
descriptions. And he held that belief was a "propositional attitude"—a

way of being related to a proposition. All this is retained in the account of this book. But Russell placed severe limits on which singular propositions we can believe, by requiring that we be directly acquainted with all its propositional constituents. I have abandoned this requirement, for the reasons given in section 3.3.

My analysis of belief retains the view that our beliefs relate us to singular propositions, in virtue of our ideas and notions relating us to properties and to real individuals. Belief reports express claims that agents are related to propositions: the speaker claims that the agent believes the proposition expressed by the utterance of the embedded sentence of the report.

The Russellian analysis of belief reports par excellence is the "naïve" analysis discussed in chapter 1. On the naïve account, a belief report claims *simply* that the agent believes the proposition expressed by the embedded sentence. The obvious criticism of this view is that it seems clearly to fail as a truth-conditional analysis of belief reporting: it makes predictions about substitutivity and so on that simply do not correspond to our intuitions about the truth values of reports. The way my account avoids this Russellian difficulty is simple: belief reports do more than claim that an agent believes a proposition. A belief report specifies just which proposition the agent allegedly believes and also just how she is claimed to believe it (that is, just which notions and ideas are parts of the alleged belief). The pragmatics of just *how* the agent is claimed to believe a proposition, in a given report, explain the observed failures of substitutivity.

The naïve theory of belief reports comports well with independently plausible semantic rules, in large part because it takes the uses of content sentences of belief reports to express just the singular propositions they normally would express (on these plausible semantic rules). My account retains this attractive Russellian feature. The departures from the naïve theory are not departures from the Russellian style of semantics in which that theory has evolved, but are the results of finding referential complexity in our idioms for talking about representation.

I hope that, amid all the details, the essentials of my project have become clear:

- a structured, "Russellian" notion of proposition

- a notion of representational responsibility

- an account of thought as involving particular representations such that it is plausible that we ordinarily think and talk about them

- tacit, pragmatically driven reference in belief reports to representations allegedly involved in the ascribed belief.

Some of the details may be useful, too, but mainly I hope that I have shown that these basics form a package compelling enough to qualify as a promising "new game in town."

References

Ackerman, F. 1987. "An Argument for a Modified Russellian Principle of Acquaintance." In J. Tomberlin (ed.), *Philosophical Perspectives, 1: Metaphysics*, 501–512. Atascadero, CA: Ridgeview.

Armstrong, D. 1973. *Belief, Truth and Knowledge*. London: Cambridge University Press.

Asher, N. 1986. "Belief in Discourse Representation Theory." *Journal of Philosophical Logic* 15:137–189.

Audi, R. 1982. "Believing and Affirming." *Mind* 91:115–120.

Barwise, J., and J. Etchemendy. 1987. *The Liar*. Oxford: Oxford University Press.

Barwise, J., and J. Perry. 1983. *Situations and Attitudes*. Cambridge: MIT Press.

Böer, S. E., and W. G. Lycan. 1985. *Knowing Who*. Cambridge: MIT Press.

Brachman, R., and H. Levesque (eds.). 1985. *Readings in Knowledge Representation*. Los Altos, CA: Morgan and Kaufmann.

Braun, D. 1991. "Empty Names." Unpublished draft.

Cartwright, R. 1971. "Identity and Substitutivity." In M. K. Munitz (ed.), *Identity and Individuation*, 119–133. New York: New York University Press.

Castaneda, H.-N. 1966. " 'He': A Study in the Logic of Self-Consciousness." *Ratio* 8:130–157.

Castaneda, H.-N. 1968. "On the Logic of Attributions of Self-Knowledge to Others." *Journal of Philosophy* 65:439–456.

Church, A. 1954. "Intensional Isomorphism and Identity of Belief." *Philosophical Topics* 5:65–73.

Crimmins, M. 1989a. "Having Ideas and Having the Concept." *Mind and Language* 4:280–294.

Crimmins, M. 1989b. *Talk About Beliefs*. Ph.D. thesis, Stanford University.

Crimmins, M. 1992a. "Context in the Attitudes." *Linguistics and Philosophy*. Forthcoming.

Crimmins, M. 1992b. "States of Affairs Without Parameters." Unpublished draft.

Crimmins, M. 1992c. "Tacitness and Virtual Beliefs." *Mind and Language*. Forthcoming.

Crimmins, M., and J. Perry. 1989. "The Prince and the Phone Booth: Reporting Puzzling Beliefs." *Journal of Philosophy* 86:685–711.

Dennett, D. C. 1987a. "Styles of Mental Representation." In *The Intentional Stance*, 213–225. Cambridge: MIT Press.

Dennett, D. C. 1987b. "Three Kinds of Intentional Psychology." In *The Intentional Stance*, 43–68. Cambridge: MIT Press.

Dummett, M. 1973. *Frege: Philosophy of Language*. New York: Harper and Row.

Evans, G. 1973. "The Causal Theory of Names." *Proceedings of the Aristotelian Society Supplementary Volume* 47:187–208.

Evans, G. 1982. *The Varieties of Reference*. Oxford: Oxford University Press.

Field, H. 1978. "Mental Representation." *Erkenntnis* 13:9–61.

Forbes, G. 1990. "The Indispensibility of *Sinn*." *Philosophical Review* 99:535–564.

Frege, G. 1952. *Translations from the Philosophical Writings*. Oxford: Oxford University Press. Translated by P. Geach and M. Black.

Geach, P. 1957. *Mental Acts*. London: Routledge and Kegan Paul.

Geach, P. 1972. "On Beliefs about Oneself." In *Logic Matters*, 128–129. Berkeley: University of California Press.

Goldman, A. 1976. "Discrimination and Perceptual Knowledge." *Journal of Philosophy* 64:771–799.

Goldman, A. 1986. *Epistemology and Cognition*. Cambridge: Harvard University Press.

Hintikka, J. 1962. *Knowledge and Belief*. Ithaca, NY: Cornell University Press.

Horn, L. R. 1989. *A Natural History of Negation*. Chicago: University of Chicago Press.

Jackendoff, R. 1983. *Semantics and Cognition*. Cambridge: MIT Press.

Kamp, H. 1988. "Comments on Stalnaker." In R. Grimm and D. Merrill (eds.), *Contents of Thought*, 156–181. Tuscon: University of Arizona Press.

Kamp, H. 1990. "Prolegomena to a Structural Theory of Belief and Other Attitudes." In C. A. Anderson and J. Owens (eds.), *Propositional Attitudes*, 27–90. Stanford, CA: CSLI.

Kaplan, D. 1969. "Quantifying In." *Synthese* 19:178–214.

Kaplan, D. 1978. "Dthat." In P. Cole (ed.), *Syntax and Semantics 9: Pragmatics*, 221–243. New York: Academic Press.

Kaplan, D. 1989. "Demonstratives." In J. Almog, J. Perry, and H. Wettstein (eds.), *Themes From Kaplan.* New York: Oxford University Press.

Karttunen, L. 1974. "Presuppositions and Linguistic Context." *Theoretical Linguistics* 1:181–194.

Karttunen, L., and S. Peters. 1979. "Conventional Implicature." In C.-K. Oh and D. Dinneen (eds.), *Syntax and Semantics 11: Presupposition*, 1–56. New York: Academic Press.

Kripke, S. A. 1977. "Speaker's Reference and Semantic Reference." In P. French, T. Uehling, and H. Wettstein (eds.), *Contemporary Perspectives in the Philosophy of Language.* Minneapolis: University of Minnesota Press.

Kripke, S. A. 1979. "A Puzzle About Belief." In A. Margalit (ed.), *Meaning and Use*, 239–283. Dordrecht: Reidel.

Lewis, D. K. 1979. "Scorekeeping in a Language Game." *Journal of Philosophical Logic* 8:339–359.

Loar, B. 1972. "Reference and Propositional Attitudes." *Philosophical Review* 81:43–62.

Ludlow, P., and S. Neale. 1991. "Indefinite Descriptions: In Defense of Russell." *Linguistics and Philosophy* 14:171–202.

Lycan, W. 1986. "Tacit Belief." In R. Bogdan (ed.), *Belief: Form, Content and Function*, 61–82. Oxford: Oxford University Press.

Mates, B. 1950. "Synonymity." *University of California Publications in Philosophy* 25:201–226.

Peirce, C. S. 1960. *Collected Papers.* Cambridge: Harvard University Press.

Perry, J. 1977. "Frege on Demonstratives." *Philosophical Review* 86:474–497.

Perry, J. 1979. "The Problem of the Essential Indexical." *Nous* 13:3–21.

Perry, J. 1980a. "Belief and Acceptance." In P. French, T. Uehling, and H. Wettstein (eds.), *Midwest Studies in Philosophy*, Vol. 5, 533–542. Minneapolis: University of Minnesota Press.

Perry, J. 1980b. "A Problem About Continued Belief." *Pacific Philosophical Quarterly* 61:317–332.

Perry, J. 1986. "Thought Without Representation." *Proceedings of the Aristotelian Society Supplementary Volume* 60:263–283.

Putnam, H. 1988. *Representation and Reality.* Cambridge: MIT Press.

Quillian, R. 1967. "Word Concepts: A Theory and Simulation of Some Basic Semantic Capabilities." *Behavioral Science* 12:410–430.

Quine, W. V. 1951. *Mathematical Logic.* Cambridge: Harvard University Press. Second edition.

Quine, W. V. 1953. "Reference and Modality." In *From a Logical Point of View.* Cambridge: Harvard University Press.

Quine, W. V. 1960. *Word and Object.* Cambridge: MIT Press.

Quine, W. V. 1966a. "Quantifiers and Propositional Attitudes." In *The Ways of Paradox and Other Essays.* New York: Random House.

Quine, W. V. 1966b. "Variables Explained Away." In *Selected Logic Papers*, 227–235. New York: Random House.

Richard, M. 1983. "Direct Reference and Ascriptions of Belief." *Journal of Philosophical Logic* 12:425–452.

Richard, M. 1987. "Attitude Ascriptions, Semantic Theory, and Pragmatic Evidence." *Proceedings of the Aristotelian Society* 87:243–262.

Richard, M. 1990. *Propositional Attitudes: An Essay on Thoughts and How We Ascribe Them.* Cambridge: Cambridge University Press.

Russell, B. 1956a. "On Denoting." In R. Marsh (ed.), *Logic and Knowledge*, 39–56. London: Unwin Hyman.

Russell, B. 1956b. "On the Nature of Acquaintance." In R. Marsh (ed.), *Logic and Knowledge*, 125–174. London: Unwin Hyman.

Russell, B. 1959. "Knowledge by Acquaintance and Knowledge by Description." In *The Problems of Philosophy*. Oxford: Oxford University Press.

Salmon, N. 1986. *Frege's Puzzle*. Cambridge: MIT Press.

Schiffer, S. 1987. *The Remnants of Meaning*. Cambridge: MIT Press.

Searle, J. 1969. *Speech Acts*. London: Cambridge University Press.

Sellars, W. 1954. "Presupposing." *Philosophical Review* 63:197–215.

Soames, S. 1982. "How Presuppositions Are Inherited: A Solution to the Projection Problem." *Linguistic Inquiry* 13:483–545.

Soames, S. 1985. "Lost Innocence." *Linguistics and Philosophy* 8:59–71.

Soames, S. 1987a. "Direct Reference, Propositional Attitudes and Semantic Content." *Philosophical Topics* 15:44–87.

Soames, S. 1987b. "Substitutivity." In J. Thomson (ed.), *Essays in Honor of Richard Cartwright*. Cambridge: MIT Press.

Soames, S. 1989. "Semantics and Semantic Competence." In J. E. Tomberlin (ed.), *Philosophical Perspectives 3: Philosophy of Mind and Action Theory*, 575–596. Atascadero, CA: Ridgeview.

Stalnaker, R. 1973. "Presuppositions." *Journal of Philosophical Logic* 2:447–457.

Stalnaker, R. 1974. "Pragmatic Presuppositions." In M. K. Munitz and P. K. Unger (eds.), *Semantics and Philosophy*. New York: New York University Press.

Stalnaker, R. 1978. "Assertion." In P. Cole (ed.), *Syntax and Semantics 9: Pragmatics*, 315–332. New York: Academic Press.

Stalnaker, R. 1984. *Inquiry*. Cambridge: MIT Press.

Sterelny, K. 1990. *The Representational Theory of Mind*. Oxford: Blackwell.

Stich, S. 1978. "Belief and Subdoxastic States." *Philosophy of Science* 45:499–518.

Stich, S. 1982. "On the Ascription of Content." In A. Woodfield (ed.),

Thought and Object. New York: Oxford University Press.

Stich, S. 1983. *From Folk Psychology to Cognitive Science: The Case Against Belief.* Cambridge: MIT Press.

Strawson, P. 1956. "On Referring." In A. Flew (ed.), *Essays in Conceptual Analysis.* London: Macmillan.

Index